THE COLT ARMORY

A History of Colt's Manufacturing Company, Inc.

The Colt Armory

A History of Colt's Manufacturing Company, Inc.

by

Ellsworth S. Grant

MOWBRAY PUBLISHING • P.O. BOX 460 • LINCOLN, RHODE ISLAND 02865
WITH THE GRACIOUS COOPERATION OF COLT'S MANUFACTURING COMPANY, INC.

LIBRARY OF CONGRESS
CATALOG CARD NO.: 95-076812
Grant, Elsworth S.
The Colt Armory
Lincoln, R.I. : Andrew Mowbray Incorporated — Publishers
pp. 232

ISBN: 0-917218-69-8

Printed in the United States of America

1 2 3 4 5 6 7 8 9 10

PREFACE

The year 1994 will long be remembered as a watershed year in the history of Colt's Manufacturing Company, Inc. In the typical condensation of historical perspective, 1994 will probably be anointed the **YEAR COLT EXITED CHAPTER 11**. However, the issues are considerably more complex and meaningful than the *"sound bite"* above.

The period 1992-94 was a time of renewal for Colt. It was a time of radical change — manufacturing processes, market insights, internal communications, labor relations, facilities utilization and financial restructuring — all aspects of a modern day business were touched. The date 28 September 1994 was the culmination of legal and financial proceedings that recognized the rejuvenation of Colt.

It is proper that a history of Colt be commissioned at this time. Few can appreciate the meaning of the changes at Colt without the historical background contained herein. A scholar once said *"we must learn from our mistakes, or be doomed to repeat them."* I would add we must learn from our successes, or fail to achieve more. Much of the effort described in the chapter entitled **Resurrection** is mirror-image effort that Sam Colt started so many years ago.

Ellsworth Grant is one of the foremost scholars of both Sam Colt the man and Colt the company. I am proud that he has chosen to devote his talent to the history of Colt. The hundreds of men and women who worked so hard over the last thirty months to preserve the legacy of Sam Colt appreciate the attention, time, talent, and factual integrity that Mr. Grant brings to this work.

Ronald C. Whitaker, President & CEO
Colt's Manufacturing Co., Inc.

A model of the colt rampant that once graced the famous Colt dome in Hartford. (Courtesy of E. Irving Blomstrann)

TABLE OF CONTENTS

LIST OF ILLUSTRATIONS

Photos of the new factory in West Hartford – Courtesy of Colt Manufacturing Co.

Oval of the Connecticut River and the Colt Armory painted about 1857 by an unknown artist. (Courtesy Wadsworth Atheneum)

INTRODUCTION

Motorists passing through Hartford, Connecticut cannot help but notice it — the famous Colt dome, high atop the old Colt Armory. While Colt's Manufacturing Company, Inc. no longer resides under its protective shadow and the Rampant Colt statue no longer rears proudly at its pinnacle, the dome remains a fascinating icon of one of the boldest ventures ever launched on our shores.

The rags-to-riches story of Samuel Colt is a particularly American tale. From the fertile mind and dogged persistence of this one man came a startling innovation that revolutionized the firearms industry world-wide. Gunmakers from the earliest times had dreamed of achieving truc multiple-fire, the ability to discharge repeated shots from a single weapon without the need to reload. While numerous solutions were offered over the generations, many of them quite ingenious, each suffered from one or more important flaws; they were all either dangerous, hard to load, allowed only two or three shots in a row, or were too large to be carried about with ease. Colt's solution, while in many ways similar to some previous attempts, solved all of these problems...with the added advantage that the entire firing cycle could be completed with a single hand. And while early models were not immediately accepted by a skeptical public, later improved types made Colt rich beyond all imaginings and changed Hartford (the new home of his burgeoning empire) forever.

It is particularly apt that Hartford was the stage for this brave industrial drama. The Connecticut Valley was the unquestioned cradle of our nation's growing arms trade. In this region, American artisans had struggled, since well before the Revolution, to manufacture arms comparable to those crafted in Europe. While their earliest efforts were often crude or even shamefully defective, this situation quickly changed as the Valley became a teeming laboratory for startling improvements in design and productivity. But it took Samuel Colt, an outsider with little knowledge of manufacturing techniques, to give the Valley its first true industrial giant — and a company, bearing his name, that would dominate the world pistol trade in a way never-before imagined and would introduce, even after the great man's death, guns that would become emblematic of entire periods in history. Colt. The very word itself came to embody the concept of an American pistol.

While the pistol constituted the heart-beat that made Colt tick, the firm additionally offered a complete line of firearms, civil and military. The Model 1861 Special Musket — felt by many collectors to have been made just a tad better than similar arms offered by competitors — was a Civil War favorite of many states. Other military types, including trapdoor, falling block and the very rare Colt-Franklin bolt action, followed. Hunters could choose from lever and slide action systems…and there was a popular series of double-barrel shotguns.

In league with the innovative spirit of the industrial giant, Colt did not hesitate, during the latter years of the 19th century, to diversify, giving the firm an almost unlimited number of new markets to explore. Printing presses (some still in service today), sewing machines, adding machines, typesetting equipment, electrical fixtures and even the lowly plastic button joined the wares offered by Colt. The list also included willow furniture, steam engines and electric vehicles — all in testimony of the versatility and aggressive salesmanship of Colt.

A reputation for exceptional quality, a skilled and loyal workforce, a world-wide clientele, repeated government contracts for military sidearms... Colt had it all. And for a period extending well over 100 years. Every time Colt seemed to show vulnerability, the right combination of designers and managers would happily result in more legendary firearms, guns that didn't just dominate the market but define it.

The 1980s and early 1990s, however, brought the company its first truly desperate days. Expiring patents, unhappy workers, lost contracts, corporate reorganizations and a general shift in the market away from domestically produced handguns, all seemed to assault the company at once. The eventual, tragic result was bankruptcy. Enthusiasts of Colt products, both antique and modern, were deeply saddened by these events. And Connecticut residents, who had seen so many manufacturing jobs leave the state, were especially worried that the loss of Colt, which was operating under Chapter 11, would mean economic disaster. However, like all good stories, this one has a happy ending.

Today, Colt's Manufacturing Company, Inc. has stable new ownership and an energetic, problem-solving President/CEO. The company has a positive outlook and seems eager to reclaim its glorious heritage. The venerable Colt Armory in Hartford, however, will not be a part of this promising future. The last of the gunmaking operations moved to West Hartford in May of 1994. And with the approach of the 150th Anniversary of Colt's operations in Hartford in 1997, this seems an especially opportune time to re-examine all the events of the past that have made Colt's so worth saving.

With this book, noted historian Ellsworth Grant tells the whole story of Colt's firearms empire, right up to the present time. The genius of the inventor himself, the further developments in technology, labor difficulties, marketing triumphs, wars and natural disasters are all covered in a style that is remarkably lively and entertaining. The Colt Armory was not in any sense a dull or boring place over the years; Grant captures all of that excitement and then conveys it to the reader.

The author also takes time to examine the phenomenal impact Colt's factory and family had on Hartford's social life — a subject almost entirely neglected until the publication of this work. He carefully shows how the company developed a culture and style all its own. He details the personalities behind the famous guns and untangles the intricate web of corporate maneuvering behind some of the most exciting events in Colt history. No one with a love of history will want to miss this unique and intriguing story.

The Publisher

ACKNOWLEDGMENTS

Nearly everybody has heard of the Colt gun — protector of Texas Rangers, frontiersmen, prospectors, Indians, outlaws, policemen, and soldiers in every conflict as far back as the Mexican War. Many also know that the Colt Armory is located in Hartford, Connecticut, and generations of residents and visitors have gazed wonderingly at the bright blue, onion-shaped Colt dome. And certainly there have been published many outstanding books on Colt firearms.

Why then this volume? Simply that a history of Colt's itself has never been compiled from its beginning in 1847 until 1995 — a span of 148 years. Few are familiar with the human side of Colonel Sam Colt and his family, the company's prominent role in the munitions industry, its impact on the growth of Hartford and even on our nation's history, its precipitous decline during World War II, and its recovery twenty years later. For sixty years, from 1885 until 1945, the Armory functioned as the nucleus of the manufacturing economy that Hartford used to be; their symbiotic relationship was a microcosm of the bygone era of urban industry in America that is worthy of study by all those interested in industrial history.

I call this a social industrial history because it focuses as much as possible on the personalities involved. Since most corporations are woefully derelict about retaining information of historical value, the industrial historian must perforce be an indefatigable detective, assembling snips of information wherever he can find them — newspaper files, magazine articles, personal interviews, etc. I was fortunate to have access to as many resources as exist in the Hartford area. Let me list a few: I am especially indebted to R.L. Wilson of Hadlyme, Connecticut — the leading authority on Colt lore — for reading my first draft and making numerous suggestions and corrections. For the first edition, President Ed Warner and Vice-Presidents Dave Davis and Rob Roy of Colt's were most cooperative; Marty Huber gave me an extensive tour of the Firearms Division. The staffs of both the Connecticut Historical Society and the Connecticut State Library facilitated my research no end, the latter cheerfully meeting my frequent demands on the extensive Colt Collection. At the Hartford Public Library, Martha D. Nolan was most helpful, as was David White, director of the Museum of Connecticut History and in charge of the Colt Gun Collection at the State Library. I consulted numerous individuals with close connections to the Armory, its officers, and the Colt family. Colt Industries gave me permission to examine the Secretary's Record Book of Colt's Patent Fire Arms Manufacturing Company 1885-1936. In updating this second edition, I had the generous cooperation of President Ron Whitaker.

I am also grateful to the American Heritage Publishing Company for permission to reprint as part of Chapter I my article "Gunmaker to the World" which appeared in the June, 1968 issue of *American Heritage* (Vol. XIX, No. 4).

Terry Harlow deserves mention for his excellent photography. The photographs have been carefully selected and come mainly from the archives of the Connecticut State Library and the files of the Connecticut Historical Society with the assistance of, respectively, Ann Barry and Melancthon Jacobus.

ELLSWORTH S. GRANT
West Hartford, Connecticut
April, 1995

Samuel Colt (Courtesy Wadsworth Atheneum, Hartford)

CHAPTER I

THE FIRST TYCOON*

The funeral of Samuel Colt, America's first great munitions maker, was spectacular — certainly the most spectacular ever seen in Hartford, Connecticut. It was like the last act of a grand opera, with threnodial music played by Colt's own band of immigrant German craftsmen, supported by a silent chorus of bereaved townsfolk. Crepe bands on their left arms, Colt's 1,500 workmen filed in pairs past the metallic casket in the parlor of Armsmear, his ducal mansion; then followed his guard — Company A, 12th Regiment, Connecticut Volunteers — and the Putnam Phalanx in their brilliant Continental uniforms.

A half mile away, the Armory stood quiet — its hundreds of machines idle, the revolvers and rifles on its test range silent. Atop the long dike protecting Colt's South Meadows development drooped the gray willows that furnished the raw material for his furniture factory. Beneath the dike, a few skaters skimmed over the frozen Connecticut River. To the south, the complex of company houses was empty for the moment, as was the village specially built for his Potsdam willow workers.

On Armsmear's spacious grounds, snow covered the deer park, the artificial lake, the statuary, the orchard, the cornfields and meadows, the fabulous greenhouses. At the stable, Mike Tracy, the Irish coachman, stood by Shamrock, the master's aged, favorite horse, and scanned the long line of sleighs and the thousands of bareheaded onlookers jamming Wethersfield Avenue. After the simple Episcopal service, the workers formed two lines, through which the Phalanx solemnly marched — drums muffled, colors draped, and arms reversed. Behind them, eight pallbearers bore the coffin to the private graveyard near the lake.

Thus, on January 14, 1862, Colonel Samuel Colt was laid to rest, at the age of only forty-seven. At the time, he was America's best-known and wealthiest inventor, a man who had dreamed an ambitious dream and had made it come true. Sam Colt had raced through a life rich in controversy and calamity and had left behind a public monument and a private mystery. The monument, locally, was the Colt Armory; in the world beyond, it was the Colt gun that was to pacify the western and southern frontiers and contribute much to their folklores. The mystery concerned his family, whose entanglements included lawsuits, murder, suicide, and possibly bigamy and bastardy. His had indeed been a full life.

On that January afternoon, a kaleidoscope of colorful memories must have crowded the minds of the family and intimates who were present. The foremost mourner was the deceased's calm and composed young widow, Elizabeth, holding by the hand their three-year-old son Caldwell, the only one of five children to survive infancy. Elizabeth was to become Hartford's *grande dame,* and her elaborate memorials would ennoble Colt's deeds at the same time that they would help conceal the shadows of his past. Her mother, her sister Hetty, and her brothers Richard and John Jarvis, both Colt officials, sat behind her. Richard, then the dependable head of Colt's willow-furniture factory, would in a few years become the Armory's third president. Only the year before, the Colonel had sent John to England to buy surplus

* Originally published as "Gunmaker to the World" (AMERICAN HERITAGE, June 1968) © 1968 by American Heritage Publishing Co., Inc. Used by permission of the publisher.

guns and equipment. Colt had been extremely fond of both these men, in contrast to his tempestuous relationships with his own three brothers. Near the Jarvises sat Lydia Sigourney, Hartford's aging, prolific "sweet poetess," who had been Colt's friend from his youth and who looked upon Mrs. Colt as "one of the noblest characters, having borne, like true gold, the test of both prosperity and adversity."

Four of the pallbearers had played major roles in Colt's fortunes. They were Thomas H. Seymour, a former governor of Connecticut; Henry C. Deming, mayor of Hartford; Elisha K. Root, mechanical genius and head superintendent of the Armory; and Horace Lord, whom Colt had lured away from the gun factory of Eli Whitney, Jr., to become Root's right-hand man.

And in the background, obscured by the Jarvises and the Colt cousins, was a handsome young man named Samuel Caldwell Colt. In the eyes of the world, he was the Colonel's favorite nephew and the son of the convicted murderer John Colt, but according to local gossip he was really the bastard son of the Colonel himself by a German mistress.

Hartford was stunned by Colt's early death. True, he had suffered for some time from gout and rheumatic fever; he had indulged fully in the pleasures of life; he had labored from dawn to dusk to the point of exhaustion; then, at Christmas, he had caught a cold and become delirious. Perhaps pneumonia had set in. Whatever the cause of the Colonel's death, the general reaction was, as one lady put it, that "the main spring is broken, and the works must run down."

Sam Colt had made his mark in Hartford — and in the world — in less than fourteen years, beginning with his return to his native city to achieve his life's ambition of having his own gun factory. In the two decades before that, he had been a failure at school and in business, but not as an inventor, pitchman and promoter of himself and his wares.

To many, his brash nature and new-fangled ideas made him seem an outsider — a wild frontiersman rather than a sensible Yankee. Yet Sam's maternal grandfather, John Caldwell, had founded the first bank in Hartford, and his own father was a merchant speculator who had made and lost a fortune in the West Indies trade. Widowed when Sam was only seven — the year the boy took apart his first pistol — Christopher Colt had had to place his children in foster homes. At ten, Sam went to work in his father's silk mill at Ware, Massachusetts, and later spent less than two years at a private school at Amherst. Sam became interested in chemistry and electricity, and fashioned a crude underwater mine filled with gunpowder and detonated from shore by an electric current carried through a wire covered with tarred rope. On July 4, 1829, he distributed a handbill proclaiming that "Sam'l Colt will blow a raft sky-high on Ware Pond." The youngster's experiment worked too well: the explosion was so great that water doused the villagers' holiday best. Angrily they ran after the boy, who was shielded by a young machinist whose name was Elisha Root.

Yearning for high adventure, Colt in 1830 persuaded his father to let him go to sea. It was arranged for him to work his passage on the brig *Corvo,* bound for London and Calcutta. "The last time I saw Sam," a friend wrote to Sam's father, "he was in tarpaulin [hat], checked shirt, checked trousers, on the fore topsail yard, loosing the topsail... He is a manly fellow."

During this, his sixteenth year, Sam conceived, by observing the action of the ship's wheel, or possibly the windlass, a practical way for making a multi-shot pistol. Probably from a discarded tackle block, he whittled the first model of a rotating cylinder designed to hold six balls and their charges. The idea was to enable the pawl attached to the hammer of a percussion gun to move as the gun was cocked, thus turning the cylinder mechanically. Colt thus became the inventor of what would be the definitive part of the first successful revolver. Although he later claimed he had not been aware of the existence of ancient examples of repeating firearms until his second visit to London in 1835, it is likely that he had inspected them in the Tower of London in 1831, when the *Corvo* docked in the Thames. Moreover, he may have seen the repeating flintlock with a rotating chambered breech invented by Elisha Collier of Boston in 1813 and patented in England in 1818. But since Collier's gun was cumbersome and the cylinder had to be rotated by hand, Colt cannot be said to have copied its design.

Colt returned to Boston in 1831 with a model of his projected revolver. With money from his father he had two prototypes fabricated, but the first failed to fire and the second exploded. Out of funds, Sam had to scrimp to make his living and to continue the development of his revolver, which he was certain would make him a fortune. At Ware, his exposure to chemistry had introduced him to nitrous oxide, or laughing gas. Sam now set himself up as the "celebrated Dr. Coult of New York, London and Calcutta" and for three years toured Canada and the United States as "a practical chemist," giving demonstrations for

Statue of Sam whittling his first revolver — a detail of memorial in Colt Park, Hartford. (Courtesy E. Irving Blomstrann)

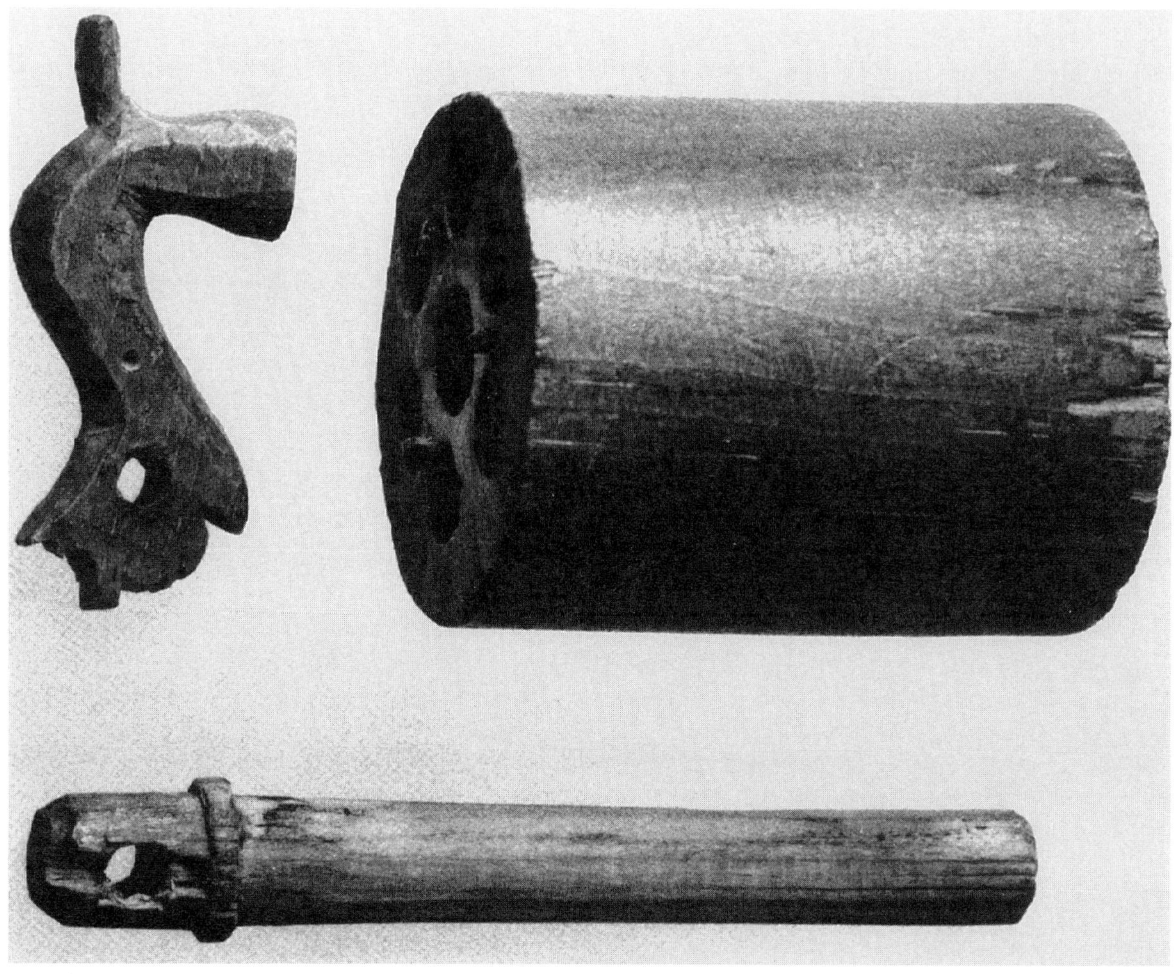

Original wooden model of revolver Colt carved on the *Corvo* in 1831. (Courtesy Wadsworth Atheneum)

which he charged twenty-five cents admission. Those who inhaled the gas became intoxicated for a few minutes; they would perform ludicrous feats, to the delight of the audience.

In the meantime, Colt had hired John Pearson of Baltimore to make improved models of his revolver, but he was at his wit's end trying to keep himself and the constantly grumbling Pearson going. Borrowing a thousand dollars from his father, Colt went to Europe and obtained patents in England and France. In 1836, aided by the U.S. commissioner of patents (a Hartford native named Henry Ellsworth), Colt received U.S. Patent No. 138, on the strength of which he persuaded a conservative cousin, Dudley Selden, and several other New Yorkers to invest some $200,000 to incorporate the Patent Arms Manufacturing Company of Paterson, New Jersey. Sam got an option to buy a third of the shares (though he was never able to pay for one of them), a yearly salary of $1,000, and a sizable expense account, of which he took full advantage to promote a five-shot revolver in Washington military and congressional circles. (The five-shooter was more practical to produce than a six-shot model based on Colt's original design.) At the time, the Army Ordnance Department, facing boldly backward, was satisfied with its single-shot breech-loading musket and flintlock pistol. A West Point competition rejected Colt's percussion-type arm as too complicated. Meanwhile, Cousin Dudley was growing impatient with Sam's lavish dinner parties, lack of sales, and mounting debts. At one point, he chastised Colt for his liquor bill: "I have no belief in undertaking to raise the character of your gun by old Madeira."

The clouds began to break in December of 1837 when Colonel William S. Harney, struggling to subdue the Seminole Indians in the Florida Everglades, ordered one hundred guns, stating, "I am...*confident* that they are the only things that will finish the *infernal war.*" Still, Colt failed to

Colt first manufactured guns in this plant in Patterson, New Jersey, 1836-1842.

win over the stubborn head of Ordnance, Colonel George Bomford, until the summer of 1840, when another trial proved his gun's superiority and forced Bomford to give in slightly: Colt got an order for one hundred carbines at forty dollars apiece. It was a Pyrrhic victory, though, because sales were otherwise too meager to sustain the little company, and in September of 1842 its doors closed for good.

Colt wound up in debt and in controversy with his employers, whom he suspected of fiscal skullduggery. Disgusted with bureaucrats, he determined to be his own boss thereafter. To a member of the family he confided in his half-educated but colorful way:

To be a clerk or an office holder under the pay and patronage of Government, is to stagnate ambition & I hope by hevins I would rather be captain of a canal bote than have the biggest office in the gift of the Government...however inferior in wealth I may be to the many who surround me I would not exchange for there treasures the satisfaction I have in knowing I have done what has never before been accomplished by man... Life is a thing to be enjoyed...it is the only certainty.

During this period, Sam Colt was also involved in a trying and frustrating family tragedy. His erratic but usually mild older brother, John, who was struggling to earn a living by writing a textbook on bookkeeping, had rented a small office in New York City. Then, in September of 1841, he killed his irascible printer, Samuel Adams, after the two had fought over the accuracy of the printer's bill — their versions differed by less than twenty dollars. John (in self-defense, he claimed) struck Adams with a hatchet, then stuffed the body into a packing case and had it delivered to a packet bound for New Orleans. A heat wave was his undoing; discovery of the decomposing corpse led to his arrest. Sam went to John's defense, engaging Cousin Dudley and Robert Emmet as attorneys and scrounging about for funds. The trial was the newspaper sensation of the year, for it had all the elements of melodrama: a crime of passion, a voluble defendant with friends of influence and means, an aroused populace, a lovely black-eyed blonde, and a bizarre climax.

The girl in the story was Caroline Henshaw, an unschooled young woman who gave birth to a son just before the trial opened in January of 1842. She told the court that she had met John Colt in

Philadelphia in 1840, but did not live with him until she came to New York the following January. He taught her to read and write, but eschewed marriage, he said, because of his poverty. Another version had it that Caroline was of German birth, and that it was Sam, not John, who met her first. On his trip to Europe in 1835, the story went, Sam met Caroline in Scotland and brought her back to America as his wife. According to this account, Sam was so preoccupied with his inventions and was away so much that John had, out of pity, made Caroline his common-law wife. Furthermore, because of their social differences, Sam was only too glad to be rid of a partner who might impede his career, which he always placed above personal ties.

In any event, John Colt was convicted of murdering Sam Adams and was sentenced to be hanged on November 18, 1842.

As dawn broke that day, Sam Colt was the first to see John. At about eleven o'clock, Dr. Henry Anthon, rector of St. Mark's Church, visited the prisoner, who had decided, after conferring with his brother, to make Caroline his lawful wife. John handed the minister five hundred dollars to be used for Caroline's welfare; he had received the money from Sam — a sizable gift from a man whose factory had failed the month before. A little before noon, Caroline, worn and nervous but smartly dressed in a claret-colored coat and carrying a muff, arrived with Sam. She and John were married by Dr. Anthon. For nearly an hour, she remained alone with John in his cell. Then she departed with Sam, and John was left undisturbed.

At five minutes to four, the sheriff and Dr. Anthon entered the cell to escort John to the scaffold. But the prisoner lay dead on his bed, a knife with a broken handle buried in his heart. The New York *Herald* speculated that Colt's relatives knew of his intention to commit suicide and that they might have smuggled the knife into his cell. The allegation was never proved — or disproved.

Colt secretly arranged for Caroline and her young son to go to Germany. He told his brother James that she "speaks and understands German and can best be cared for in the German countries... [I have] made all the necessary arrangements and will somehow provide the needful." At his insistence, she changed her name to Miss Julia Leicester, but the boy grew up as Samuel Caldwell Colt.

Caroline and her son remained abroad, supported by Sam. Eventually, she became attracted to a young Prussian officer, Baron Friedrich Von Oppen, whose father questioned her background and suspected that money, not love, was Caroline's motive. But Colt used all his influence to insure a quiet marriage and afterward did everything possible to make the couple and fifteen-year-old Samuel happy.

Apparently the boy did not like book learning any better than Sam himself, so Colt brought him back to America and placed him in a private school. He loaned Caroline $1,000 to enable her husband, who had been disinherited, to enter business. The money was soon dissipated, and Caroline feared debtor's prison. Sam came to the rescue again, making the Baron his agent in Belgium. But Von Oppen and Caroline drifted apart, and she was lonely without her child. She appealed to Sam to bring her back to America — and there the curtain drops: the beautiful, tormented Caroline Henshaw Colt Von Oppen vanished from Samuel Colt's life just as he reached the pinnacle of success. She never appeared again, except in a portrait that hung beside one of John Colt at Armsmear, and in the persistent stories (Hartford residents have never let them die) about her true relationship to Samuel Colt.

Even before the demise of the Paterson company in 1842, Colt had been working on two other inventions. In the late thirties, he began developing a waterproof cartridge out of tin foil, and he also returned to his experiments with underwater batteries. About the latter, he wrote to President John Tyler in 1841:

Discoveries since Fulton's time combined with an invention original with myself, enable me to effect instant destruction of either Ships or Steamers on their entering a harbour.

The Navy granted him $6,000 for a test. Using copper wire insulated with layers of waxed and tarred twine, he made four successful demonstrations, one of which blew up a sixty-ton schooner on the Potomac before a host of congressmen. But neither the military nor Congress took to the idea, which John Quincy Adams branded an "unChristian contraption," and Colt's Submarine Battery Company never surfaced.

The waterproof cartridges had a better reception, including an endorsement by Winfield Scott, General in Chief of the Army. In 1845, Congress spent one quarter of its $200,000 state militia appropriation on Colt's ammunition.

Meanwhile, Colt had become acquainted with Professor Samuel F.B. Morse and his electro-magnetic telegraph. The two inventors hit it off from the start. If Colt's cable could carry an electrical impulse under water to trigger an explosive charge, then it probably could carry telegraphic messages across lakes and rivers. Colt supplied Morse with batteries and wire and won a contract for laying forty miles of wire from Washington to Baltimore. In May of 1846, the same month in which war was declared on Mexico, the New York and Offing Magnetic Telegraph Association was incorporated by Colt and a new set of investors, with the rights to construct a telegraph line from New York City to Long Island and New Jersey. But again the operation was mismanaged, partly because of Colt's negligence, and at thirty-two he once more found himself as "poor as a church-mouse." Desperate, he sought — in vain — a captaincy in a new rifle regiment.

Although Colt was not destined to fight in the Mexican War, his guns were. For the five-shot Paterson pistol, having won acceptance against the Seminoles in Florida, had gained further renown in the hands of the Texas Rangers in the early forties. (The six-shot Colt .45, or "Peacemaker," the gun that supposedly won the West, did not appear until the early 1870s.) In the summer of 1844, for instance, Captain John C. Hays and fifteen rangers engaged some eighty Comanches in open combat along the Pedernales River and with Colt guns killed or wounded half of them. Altogether, 2,700 Paterson guns, mostly .34 and .36 caliber, were made for the frontiersmen in pocket, belt, and holster sizes. At the close of 1846, without money or machines but still possessed of his patent rights, Colt approached Ranger Captain Samuel H. Walker about buying "improved" arms for his men, who had been mustered into the United States Army. A veteran Indian fighter, Walker needed little encouragement. He wrote Colt:

Without your pistols we would not have had the confidence to have undertaken such daring adventures... With improvements I think they can be rendered the most perfect weapon in the World for light mounted troops... The people throughout Texas are anxious to procure your pistols.

That was certainly the case with General Zachary Taylor, commanding troops in Texas in the autumn of 1846. Taylor wanted one thousand Colts within three months, but Colt lacked even a model with which to start manufacturing again. That did not overly distress Colt, because Captain Walker wanted a simpler yet heavier gun — .44 caliber — that would fire six shots. So Colt designed the so-called Walker gun.

Armed with a $25,000 government order, Sam persuaded Eli Whitney, Jr., the Connecticut contractor for Army muskets, to make the thousand revolvers. They were ready six months later. A pair of guns for Walker, who had hounded Colt for delivery, arrived in Mexico only four days before he was killed in action. To General Sam Houston, who had praised the guns' superiority, Colt wrote:

I am truly pleased to lern...that your influance unasked for by a poor devil of an inventor has from your own sense of right been employed to du away the prejudice heretofore existing among men who have the power to promote or crush at pleasure all improvements in Fire arms for military purposes.

His appetite whetted, Colt obtained an order for another thousand guns. He borrowed about $5,000 from his banker cousin Elisha Colt and other Hartford businessmen, leased a factory on Pearl Street and hired scores of hands. Thus, in the summer of 1847, Colt started his own factory, promising to turn out five thousand guns a year. To a friend in Illinois he wrote a letter that reveals much of the basic Colt:

I am working on my own hook and have sole control and management of my business and intend to keep it as long as I live without being subject to the whims of a pack of dam fools and knaves styling themselves a board of directors ... my arms sustain a high reputation among men of brains in Mexico and ... now is the time to make money out of them.

Alert to the new methods being used in New England's machine-tool industry, Colt quickly adapted the system of interchangeable parts to the mass production of guns. Though two other Connecticut gunmakers, Simeon North and Whitney, had been the first to standardize parts, Colt perfected the technique to the point where eighty per cent of his gunmaking was done by machine alone.

Vital to his success was his able staff, especially Elisha Root, whom he had first met at Ware and whom he had now lured away from the Collins Axe Company by offering him the unheard-of-salary of $5,000 a year. As Colt's head superintendent, Root designed and constructed the incomparable Colt armory and installed its equipment.

Root's quiet, firm, perfectionist leadership made Colt's a training center for a succession of gifted mechanics, some of whom went on to apply his modern methods in their own companies. Charles E. Billings and Christopher M. Spencer

Eli Whitney's armory in Whitneyville, Connecticut, about the time of the Civil War.

started a company (now defunct) for making a variety of hand tools; Spencer invented the Spencer rifle, used in the Civil War, as well as the first screw-making machine. Other Armory graduates included Francis A. Pratt and Amos Whitney, who together founded a machine-tool company that today is part of Colt Industries.

While Root managed the factory, Colt functioned as president and salesman extraordinary. Far more than his competitors, he appreciated the necessity of creating demand through aggressive promotion. He paid military officers and others to act as his agents in the West and the South and as his lobbyists in Congress, while Colt himself solicited patronage from state governors. Until the approach of the Civil War, however, government sales were scanty compared to the thousands of revolvers shipped to California during the Gold Rush, or to foreign heads of state. From 1849 on, Colt traveled abroad extensively, wangling introductions to government officials and making them gifts of beautifully engraved weapons.

In May of 1851, Colt exhibited five hundred of his machine-made guns and served free brandy at London's Crystal Palace Exposition. He even read a paper, "Rotating Chambered Breech Firearms," to the Institute of Civil Engineers. Two years later he became the first American manufacturer to open a branch abroad, choosing a location on the Thames for supplying the English government with what he termed "the best peesmakers" in the world. So backward did he find England's mechanical competence, however, that he was forced to send over both journeymen and machines. Colt was ultimately unable to convince the English of the superiority of machine labor, and the London factory was sold in 1857, but not before it and the main plant in Hartford had between them supplied more than 30,000 pistols for use in the Crimean War.*

* While in England in 1851, Colt visited the armory in Warwick Castle to inspect an 18th century flintlock from India that revolved. He presented the Earl with a Colt Navy revolver #2885 with "Address Sam. Colt New York City" engraved on top of the barrel.

The Colt Arms Manufacturing Company. *(Courtesy R.L. Wilson)*

Colt had been successful in obtaining a seven-year extension of his basic American patent and in crushing attempts at infringement. He had become a millionaire in less than a decade. As a loyal Democrat, he had finally won his long-sought commission, becoming a colonel and aide-de-camp to his good friend Governor Thomas Seymour.

By the end of 1850, Colt had produced some 3,000 Dragoon pistols, first in a small factory on Pearl Street and then on Grove Lane in the center of Hartford. Larger and more permanent quarters were now a necessity. Ever since returning to his birthplace, Colt had dreamed of building the largest private armory anywhere in the world. In 1851, he began buying up property in the South Meadows that fronted on the Connecticut River. As lowland, it was swampy, prone to spring flooding, and considered of little value. Eventually he acquired 250 acres at a cost of $60,000 and reclaimed them by building a dike nearly two miles long and planting French osiers on top to prevent erosion. The project — Hartford's first redevelopment — took two years and $125,000 more of his money.

Behind the dike rose the Armory, of Portland brownstone. Both were finished in August, 1855. By 1857, Colt was turning out nearly 150 finished guns a day at a price of $24 each. He paid good wages but insisted on maximum effort in return. Said one factory notice evidently written by himself: "Every man employed in or about my armoury whether by piece wirk or by days wirk is expected to wirk ten hours during the runing of the engine, & no one who does not chearfully concent to du this need expect to be employed by me." Tardiness he looked upon as a cardinal sin. Any laggard not inside within a minute of the clanging of the steam gong at seven o'clock in the morning found himself locked out until noon.

On top of the Armory, the Colonel raised an elaborate, onion-shaped blue dome, supported by columns and crowned by a golden sphere on which perched a rampant colt holding a broken spear. The colt itself was made of bronze and cast in the Armory. All over New England it was customary to adorn factories with cupolas and weathervanes, but Colt's dome was such an eccentric, ostentatious landmark that it gave rise to endless speculation and rumor about its origin. One story had the dome shipped to Hartford as the gift of a

Colt's London factory at Pimlico near Vauxhall Bridge 1853-57.

Turkish sultan grateful for guns he received during the Crimean War. Another, closer to the truth, said Colt was inspired by the Byzantine churches he saw in Russia to imitate their architecture. The real reason seems to be, simply, showmanship. Colt wanted the Armory seen and admired by everyone. What better way to shake up the stagnant traditions which he felt stultified the city and at the same time to attract the attention and wonderment of steamboat passengers on the Connecticut River!

Now well on the way to fame and fortune, Sam Colt had remained a rather bibulous bachelor, a well-fleshed six-footer whose light hazel eyes were beginning to gather under them more than a few wrinkles. At the peak of his career, he had everything but a wife and home, and these he acquired with his usual despatch and pomp. Four years earlier, he had met the two daughters of the Reverend William Jarvis of Middletown, downriver from Hartford. He chose as his bride the gracious and gentle Elizabeth, who at thirty was twelve years younger than he. The extravagance of their wedding, on June 5, 1856, rocked Hartford's staid society. The steamboat *Washington Irving,* which Colt chartered for the occasion, carried him and his friends to the wedding in Middletown. They boarded in front of the flag-bedecked Armory; there was an immense crowd of spectators and Colt mechanics fired a rifle salute from the cupola. Two days later, the Colonel and his bride sailed on the *Baltic* for a six-month trip to Europe. On their return, Sam began to build his palatial Armsmear on the western edge of his property.

By the end of 1858, the Colonel, his lady, and young Caldwell were comfortably ensconced in Armsmear. The family saw little of Colt, however, as the North and South raced toward cataclysm, Colt was busy making enormous profits by filling the demands of both sides for what he sardonically called "my latest work on 'Moral Reform.'" He seriously considered building a branch armory in either Virginia or Georgia. The Armory's earnings averaged $237,000 annually until the outbreak of the Civil War, when they soared to over a million. His last shipment of five hundred guns to the South left for Richmond three days after Fort Sumter, packed in boxes marked "hardware."

Colt regarded slavery not as a moral wrong but as an inefficient economic system. He abhorred abolitionists, denounced John Brown as a traitor,

THE COLT DOME

When it opened in August of 1855 the Hartford *Times* praised the Colt Armory as "the greatest individual enterprise ever attempted in this country." Constructed in the shape of a large H of Portland brownstone, it was 500 feet long, steam-heated and gas-lighted. But its most visible feature, dominating the skyline of Hartford, was the elaborate, onion-shaped blue dome, supported by columns and crowned by a golden sphere on which perched a rampant colt holding a broken spear. In the eyes of a conservative citizenry, the dome was as flamboyant as the character of Samuel Colt himself.

All over New England it was customary to adorn factories with cupolas and weathervanes, but Colt's dome was such an eccentric, ostentatious landmark that it gave rise to endless speculation and rumor about its origin. One story claimed it was the gift of a Turkish sultan grateful for guns received: during the Crimean War. Another, closer to the truth, said Colt was inspired by the Byzantine churches he saw in Russia on his honeymoon. The real reason seems to be, simply, showmanship Colt wanted the Armory to be seen and admired by everyone. What better way to shake up the stagnant traditions which he felt stultified the city and at the same time attract the attention and awe of steamboat passengers on the Connecticut River!

According to Anstress Paine who has researched the Colt dome more deeply than anyone else, it is a unique appendage. It does not duplicate a particular national style. Nothing quite like it is to be found in India, Pakistan or Russia. It bears no resemblance to the church-like towers of New England mills that were designed to hold bells, pulley-lifts or stairs. In her view the Colt dome belongs to the tradition of "entrepreneurial capitalism." *The closest comparison is Iranistan, the dome-festooned mansion built in the same year as the Armory by the Bridgeport showman-industrialist, P.T. Barnum. In an unusual way, the Colt dome dramatized the product being made underneath — the patented Colt revolver — and enhanced his personal image, his desire to be an American na-bob. It synthesized everything he liked best: stars, noble columns, heraldic devices.

Elizabeth Colt understood this. Two years after his death, in February 1864, when 1,500 men were working two ten-hour shifts to keep General Grant's soldiers supplied with muskets and revolvers, the original Armory building was destroyed by fire. Thousands hurried to the scene as the flames rolled up into the sky and mixed with clouds of black smoke. A tiny, round figure stood in front of the spellbound onlookers. It was Mrs. Colt, accompanied by her father. At nine o'clock, the Colt dome teetered. With its glittering stars on a blue background, it looked like a huge balloon suspended in the air. Mrs. Colt burst into tears, its collapse seeming to her like a replay of her husband's funeral. It was one of the worst calamities ever to befall a Hartford industry, a thousand lathes and millers on the ground in ruin, 900 men thrown out of work when they were most needed.

Undaunted, Mrs. Colt ordered the rebuilding of the Armory exactly as her husband left it, no matter how much the cost. Under General William B. Franklin, the new general manager, the work was completed in early 1867. The new dome arose in 1872. As for its decoration of stars, Mrs. Colt wrote that Sam had a special affection for the American flag, and the spacing of the 36 stars was similar to

Continued on next page

the flag of that era. The rotunda is a form long associated with sacred places, such as the one supporting the Capitol dome in Washington. The most personal symbol, of course, is the "Rampant Colt," rearing up on a golden orb while holding an arrow in its jaws and another across its front legs. It represents the wondrous horse of ancient times that charged into battle even after losing its rider. As Henry Barnard, Colt's biographer, said: "Here we see the colt rampant...triumphant over the world."

The inventor had adopted the rampant colt as his trademark and family crest. Its earliest form appeared during the Paterson era of manufacturing in 1834-35, and around 1875 the colt medallion was applied to every revolver.

As the years passed and the skyline of the city changed, the Colt dome continued to be a major landmark, as familiar and revered as the Travelers Tower or the Soldiers & Sailors Memorial Arch. When in 1954 Colt's directors announced their decision to abandon the Armory and move its operations to Windsor Locks, there was consternation, not so much over the loss of jobs as over the possibility of losing the "Moorish dome." The Hartford Courant editorialized: "An incongruous cupola that annually commands the attention of the occupants of 18,500,000 cars crossing the Charter Oak Bridge...it stands today as a symbol of the founder's rugged individuality, a by-product of his desire to be different, and direct prospective customers to him and his revolvers."

But the old armory and the blue dome remained in place despite the sale of the company in 1955 to the PennTexas conglomerate, exactly 100 years after its incorporation by Sam Colt. Deterioration of both had by this time set in. The out-of-state real estate syndicate that eventually acquired the property paid little attention. A wealthy gun antiquarian undertook to restore the outside of the dome and replacing the gold-leafed stars. They were fabricated from aluminum in the Armory and installed in September 1976. The spirits of Elizabeth and Samuel Colt must have been pleased by this generosity, but today they are certain to be distressed by the loss and sale of the original Colt Rampant.

* *"The Gun & The Dome," article with footnotes, 1984*

and opposed the election of Lincoln for fear the Union would be destroyed — and a lucrative market thereby lost. Like many other Connecticut manufacturers, he believed that an upset of the *status quo* would be ruinous to the free trade on which the state's prosperity depended. Thus, he took a conservative stand on slavery and supported the Democrats because they stressed Union and the Constitution. But at the same time, he shrewdly prepared the Armory for a five-year conflict and for the arming of a million men; the prevailing sentiment in Hartford was that a civil war, if it broke out, could not last two months. During a vacation in Cuba in early 1861, Colt wrote Root and Lord, exhorting them to "run the Armory night & day with a double set of hands... Make hay while the sun shines."

During the 1860 state elections, Colt's political convictions and their manifestations caused a stir in the press, the *Courant* leading the attack and the Hartford *Times* waging a vigorous defense. Colt was known to have used dubious methods in previous campaigns, including having ballot boxes watched to make sure his workers supported Democratic candidates. This time, the hostile press accused him of discharging, outright, "66 men, of whom 56 are Republicans... Many of these were contractors and among his oldest and ablest workmen." Asserting that their dismissals amounted to "proscription for political opinion," the discharged Republican workers resolved that "the oppression of free labor by capital, and the attempt to coerce and control the votes of free men, is an outrage upon the rights of the laboring classes." Colt quickly issued a flat denial:

In no case have I ever hired an operative or discharged one for his political or religious opinions. I hire them for ten hours labor...and for that I pay them punctually every month.

This advertising broadside of the 1850s shows engraving that identified as well as decorated Colt revolvers.
(Courtesy Connecticut State Library)

Yet, a few months earlier he had suggested to a politician friend that he pen a resolution urging "us [manufacturers] all to discharge from our imploymen every Black Republican...until the question of slavery is for ever set to rest & the rights of the South secured permanently to them."

Now Colt's immense business responsibilities were beginning to wear down his seemingly inexhaustible energies. Bothered by frequent attacks

Photograph of Colonel Colt by Brady.

of inflammatory rheumatism and distressed by the death of an infant daughter, he drove himself as if he knew his days were numbered. Smoking Cuban cigars, Colt ruled his domain from a roll-top desk at the Armory, often writing his own letters in his left-handed scrawl.

Shortly before he died, he handed the family reins to his brother-in-law, Richard Jarvis, with the admonition that "you and your family must do for me now as I have no one else to call upon. You are the pendulum that must keep the works in motion." Two of his own brothers were dead, and the other, James, a hot-tempered ne'er-do-well and petty politician, had proved a miserable failure as Colt's manager in the short-lived London plant and later as an official of the Armory. The entire estate, which Mrs. Colt and their son Caldwell controlled, was valued at $15,000,000 — an enormous sum in those days — giving Elizabeth an income of $200,000 a year for life.

Other than Elizabeth and Caldwell, Colt's major beneficiary was Master Samuel Caldwell Colt, "son of my late brother John Caldwell Colt," whom even Mrs. Colt regarded favorably. For a short time this handsome, retiring man worked at the Armory; he became a director but eventually took up gentleman farming. He was always loyal to the memory of Colonel Colt, who his descen-

SAM COLT'S INVENTORY

His was certainly the largest estate left by a Connecticut resident up to that time. The total appraisal came to $3.2 million, equal to over $15 million today. His library contained 550 volumes, mostly American and English biographies, histories and novels — Cooper, Irving, Dickens, Hawthorne, and so on. Even more impressive were the contents of his greenhouse: 157 fig, peach and plum trees, 650 rose plants, 600 tomato plants, 350 grapevine slips, 250 pineapple plants, 800 pots of lettuce, and 4,000 strawberries.

In his stable were 14 carriages and sleighs, including one Russian droshky, seven horses, and two ponies. His wine cellars had a value equal to all his furniture and silverware:

AT ARMSMEAR

100 gallons of whiskey
24 gallons of madeira
90 gallons of brandy in demijohns
119 dozen port wine
78 dozen old sherry
5,400 cigars at 25¢ each

AT THE ARMORY

215 gallons of gin
149 dozen champagne
119 dozen Scotch whiskey
59 dozen Jamaica rum
58 dozen old pale brandy
26 dozen 25-year-old brandy

Nearly a quarter of the estate was in land. The 29 parcels he owned in the South Meadows included 24 houses and outhouses, a tobacco warehouse, a pistol lot, gas works, the willow factory with nine cottages, and two farms. Across the Connecticut River in East Hartford, on a tract of 89 acres, he raised cattle and chickens and had a brickyard.

Some of the miscellaneous items are interesting: a new scow boat, photographic equipment, a great deal of lumber, and in his office at the Armory 16 red woolen shirts, five views of Hartford, and a picture of Christ weeping over Jerusalem — which he left to E.K. Root. His 9,996 shares of Colt stock, appraised at $2 million, made up the bulk of his vast estate, which was not completely settled until 1894, the year of Caldwell Colt's death.

dants believe was his true father.

Colonel Samuel Colt had adopted as his motto *Vincit qui patitur,* "He conquers who suffers." But a better-fitting key to his character is found in a remark he once wrote to his half-brother William: "'It is better to be at the head of a louse than at the tail of a lyon!'... If I cant be first I wont be second in anything."

Colt's ambition was to be first and best, and his means were money and power, both of which he had in full measure. His patriotism, while stronger than that of the average munitions maker, was ever subordinate to his desire to see maintained a commercially favorable *status quo* between North and South. Colt was not above using bribery and was unashamed of profiteering; he seldom reflected on the moral implications of dealing in weapons of death and destruction.

In fairness, Colt was not alone in his evident amorality: the turbulence of the age had thrown out of focus more than a few of the old values for more than a few of his countrymen. Especially to Connecticut Yankees, who had made their state an arsenal for the nation since colonial days, gunmaking could be no sin. What did bother the diluted Puritan conscience of Colt's time was that a Hartford aristocrat flouted the tenets of the Congregational Church to which he was born — by a bizarre career, a love of high living, and an overbearing pride and flamboyance.

It can scarcely be denied that Sam Colt was one of America's first tycoons, a Yankee peddler who became a dazzling entrepreneur. The success of his many mechanical inventions and refinements was due less to their intrinsic merits — which were considerable — than to his showmanship in telling the world about them. He achieved his goals despite continual adversity for nearly three fourths of his short life. Proud, stubborn, and farsighted, he was a man apart; he was impatient with the old ways, preferring, as he said, to be "paddling his own canoe."

CHAPTER II

THE ARMORY

After the Colonel's unexpected death in January, 1862, before reaching his fiftieth birthday and only seven years after opening his Armory, Elisha K. Root, the quiet and brilliant superintendent responsible for setting up Colt's unique production line, took over as president. Mrs. Colt had inherited the largest fortune ever made in Connecticut, together with her only son and her husband's "nephew." As it turned out, neither son nor nephew would follow in the Colonel's footsteps, and by the turn of the century the Colt empire would pass into other hands.

Aerial view of Armory and South Meadows. Note Colt's dock, and Charter Oak Hall at the corner of the Charter Oak and Hyshope Avenues. Armsmear is at the top right. The greenhouse lies north of the mansion, while Potsdam Village is shown in the middle left off Hendrixon Avenue.

For almost a hundred years after its completion, the Armory changed little inside or out. Colonel Colt, if alive, could have walked through the various departments and felt right at home. As late as 1940, the methods were similar; some of the original machines continued in use, modified or improved but not basically changed. Root, recognized as the greatest mechanical engineer of his time, originated many of the machine tools that were essential to making guns in quantity, among them a shaving machine that now bears the label of Taylor & Fenn, the drop hammer, machines for boring and rifling gun barrels and making cartridges, and the hand screw machine. Moreover, Root and Colt had startled the manufacturing world by spending even more on dies, jigs, fixtures, and gauges than they did on machinery. No wonder the Armory attracted so many inventive machinists, many of whom made important contributions to the development of mass production in other industries like automobiles and aircraft.

When Mark Twain first visited Hartford in 1868, his tour of the Armory opened his eyes to Connecticut's industrial genius:

It comprises a great range of tall brick buildings, and on every floor is a dense wilderness of strange iron machines that stretches away into the remote distance and confusing perspectives — a tangled forest of rods, bars, pulleys, wheels, and all the imaginable and unimaginable forms of mechanism. There are machines to cut all the various parts of a pistol, roughly from the original steel; machines to rifle them; machines that shave them down neatly to a proper size, as deftly as one would shave a candle in a lathe. One can stumble over a bar of iron as he goes in at one end of the establishment, and find it transformed into a burnished, symmetrical, deadly 'navy' as he passes out at the other ... It must have required more brains to invent all those things than would serve to stock fifty Senates like ours...

Twain, of course, was in love with machines of all kinds. He said "an inventor is a poet — a true poet — and nothing in any degree less than a high order of poet." Yet, technology and its gadgetry proved his undoing; he poured $180,000 into the development of the unworkable Paige typesetter, an investment that finally led to his bankruptcy. The original model of this machine, containing 18,000 parts, was built and assembled by Pratt & Whitney Machine Tool in Hartford.

In *A Connecticut Yankee in King Arthur's Court,* published in 1889, Twain contrasted the dismal feudal life in 6th century England with that of "modern Christendom and modern civilization." It was a savage satire, in which chivalry becomes dishonorable, romance ridiculous, and justice inhuman. Significantly, the hero is Colt's head superintendent:

I am an American. I was born and reared in Hartford, in the State of Connecticut — anyway, just over the river in the country. So I am A Yankee of the Yankees — and practical; yes, and nearly barren of sentiment, I suppose — or poetry, in other words. My father was a blacksmith, my uncle was a horse doctor, and I was both, along at first. Then I went over to the great arms factory and learned my real trade; learned all there was to it; learned to make everything: guns, revolvers, cannon, boilers, engines, all sorts of labor-saving machinery. Why, I could make anything a body wanted — anything in the world, it didn't make any difference what; and if there wasn't any quick newfangled way to make a thing, I could invent one — and do it as easy as rolling off a log. I became head superintendent; had a couple of thousand men under me.

In those days, the largest manufacturers relied on a system known as inside contracting for efficient management. It wasn't enough to specialize the worker or his machine. To take fullest advantage of the principles of mass production, the manager also had to be specialized. The proprietor alone could not oversee everything as his plant expanded, and frequently, as in Colonel Colt's case, he lacked the technical know-how. On the other hand, the master armorer or tool builder liked to think of himself as an independent craftsman rather than an employee. Through the contract system, the owner could devote himself to financing and selling, leaving all responsibility for labor and production to his contractors.

Not Eli Whitney, but a Middletown sword maker named Nathan Starr, was probably the first to use inside contractors. As early as 1798, having received a government contract, Starr signed agreements with different people in his plant to supply him with forgings, scabbards, and the like. The system worked this way: the contractor or department manager recruited his own help, while the company furnished floor space, materials, machines, tools, and power. Although the company paid the wages of his employees and guaranteed him a minimum salary at a foreman's rate, the contractor was responsible for production and quality. For the day's output that passed inspection

Elisha K. Root

he received a credit; for wages paid, waste, or supplies used, a debit; the balance was his profit. Since every contractor needed apprentices, the system provided an opportunity for young boys to become craftsmen under a master's eye. As the real boss, the contractor-foreman played an important role in the factory and in the community.

Colt's alone had some thirty contractors who accounted for most of the Armory's total employment. Besides machining and filing, they managed the forging, rifling, polishing, and cartridge making operations. One of the earliest was Alexander Thuer, an English gunmaker whom Sam Colt lured to Hartford even before the Armory was finished. After the Civil War, Thuer handled the contract for both the hammer and hammerless shotguns. He lived across the river in Hockanum and got to work by rowboat or the Colt ferry, and sometimes in the depth of winter by walking across the ice. His brother John was a gun assembler, paid according to the number of guns he completed each day. To break up the long ten hour shift, John and his fellow workmen kept a pot of tea handy, which they heated on one of the gas jets. Contracting at Colt's and other armories flourished for half a century, gradually disappearing by the time of World War I, as the principles of scientific management introduced by Frederick Taylor took hold.

Although Colt and Root utilized as fully as possible the principles of interchangeability pioneered by Eli Whitney, no Colt revolver was always uniform with any other since each one required a certain amount of hand-fitting and hand-filing during final assembly. Sam Colt himself, as might be expected, boasted early on that "the separate parts travel independently through the manufactory [and are] assembled from promiscuous heaps and formed into firearms, requiring only the polishing and fitting demanded for ornament." A typical Colt exaggeration, as a Delaware museum curator and gun collector discovered recently.

In the journal *Technology and Culture,* Robert A. Howard of the Hagley Museum in Wilmington reported that after examining old records and revolvers, he found that the famed handguns of the West and the Civil War were made "of very similar parts but they were not interchangeable." He chose 1860 as the test year, by which time Colt had produced more than 300,000 revolvers. The critical part of a revolver lies in the loaded chamber, which must be in perfect alignment with the barrel during firing; the detent that locks the chamber must engage during the discharge and no longer, or the chamber will not rotate to the next round. In Colt's time the standard practice was to pick out from the supply of parts to be mated the two that fitted best together. Such precision was not involved in the production of muskets and muzzle-loading rifles, the parts of which were readily interchangeable. Even today, as Colt's admits, "all the guns require...varying degrees of hand fitting." The parts are filed, polished, and matched up at the work bench; the trigger mechanism is adjusted; and finally, each revolver is tested and adjusted some more before shipment. No gun manufacturer of precision guns has ever been able to achieve total interchangeability.

Within two years of the passing of the country's first manufacturing tycoon, a catastrophe almost put an end to the Armory. It happened in February of 1864 while running full blast, with over 1,500 men working two ten-hour shifts to keep General Grant's men in blue supplied with muskets and revolvers. Three years earlier, at a cost of a million dollars, the Colonel had built and equipped a brick duplicate of his original H-shaped factory, making Colt's the nation's largest producer of munitions whether owned privately or by the government.

Shortly after eight o'clock one Friday morning, the deep tones of the Colt steam gong sounded the alarm. Smoke was discovered emanating from the wing of the main brownstone building over the polishing room. The fire seemed centered in the attic near the main driving pulley for the machines. Men carried a hose to the location, but there was no water. In minutes, all the upper stories were aflame. The top floor, laden with wooden patterns, collapsed. The workmen below who, according to plant custom, were locked into their departments grew panicky until released. The fire now raced along faster than they could run, intensifying as it consumed the oil-soaked floors of yellow pine. A few escaped by the windows with their hair ablaze. With a terrible fury, flames shot through the aisles and doors amid the crash of falling timbers.

Like a tempestuous sea of fire, the flames rolled up into the sky and mixed with clouds of black smoke that hung over the city like a pall. Thousands hurried to the scene. The volunteer fire companies arrived with their newly-acquired steamers and laid out seven hundred feet of hoses from the river to the blazing building. Again and again they burst. Soon a tiny, round figure stood in front of the spellbound onlookers. It was Mrs. Colt herself, accompanied by her father, a retired minister. At nine o'clock the beautiful Colt dome teetered. With its glittering stars on a blue background, it

A lithographic view of the Armory fire in 1864.

Charred remains of the original Armory building after the conflagration.

Power house and steam engine were also destroyed...

looked like a huge balloon suspended in the air. As it fell, Mrs. Colt burst into tears, its collapse seeming to her like a replay of her husband's funeral.

Within half an hour, the entire front of the Armory was a mass of rolling, surging billows of flame, their roar mingled with the shouts of firemen, the crashing of woodwork, and the ceaseless wail of the steam gong. A drunk, wearing a fireman's hat and carrying a trumpet, climbed the office roof and pointed a rifle at the crowd. There was some pistol stealing, and one contingent of firemen found a hoard of liquor in the office cellar, disabling them for the rest of the day. An explosion of powder forced the mob back to escape the intense heat.

Using an old hand pumper, the Stillman Hose Company, assisted by a bucket brigade of workmen from Colt's and other factories, saved the adjacent new wing of the Armory, the brick walls of which made it more fire resistant. Thus, production of U.S. Contract rifled muskets and regular muskets continued without interruption. However, the office and one half of the Armory — the oldest part containing most of Root's machinery and a quantity of finished revolvers — were destroyed, as well as all the drawings and models. The giant steam engines and boilers were also silenced. Fortunately, only one man perished — a cabinetmaker named E.K. Fox, father of six children, who was helping to remove equipment when the roof fell on him and a coworker, Barney Rooney. The latter was knocked down but crawled to safety. Another employee, Amasa Colburn, was struck by a falling timber and badly burned.

It was one of the worst calamities ever to befall a Hartford industry. Nine hundred men thrown out of work just when their labor was most needed! A few pails of water in the attic might have held the fire in check. A thousand lathes and millers laid in ruin on the ground, surrounded by crumbled masonry and twisted iron. Altogether, the damage exceeded $1,250,000. During his lifetime, Colonel Colt had disdained buying insurance, believing his works were fireproof. His successor, having a different outlook, had recently covered part of the buildings and their contents, so that Colt's was able to recover about a third of the total loss.

On Sunday, the Rev. Bernard Peters preached a

...even the office was gutted. (Courtesy Colt Collection)

sermon based on verses from Job — "yet man is born into trouble, as the sparks fly upward." As the embers cooled, crowds continued to gather all weekend to see the devastation. The press called for a paid fire department with each steamer drawn by two horses instead of by human volunteers. Lydia Sigourney, Hartford's sweet poetess, penned a suitable condolence, as she did for every bereavement. Prescott & Gage, a local photographer, offered the public pictures of the ruins, while the city speculated on the cause of the conflagration. Some blamed it on friction from the pulley in the attic. President Root disproved this theory, pointing out that the gearing for the pulley was encased in heavy iron boxes. Others laid it to the combustible pistol stocks stored in the attic drying room, or to cotton waste left by a careless handyman after oiling the pulley. Mrs. Colt and several Colt contractors suspected sabotage, the work possibly of Jefferson Davis's secret agents. The real answer was never determined.

What would happen to the Armory? Elizabeth Colt did not hesitate a day. She ordered it rebuilt exactly as her husband left it, no matter how much the cost. The city officials also acted quickly, establishing a paid fire service in October. But the rebuilding of the Armory took several years. The end of the War had removed any sense of urgency. Nothing was started until a retired major general joined Colt's as vice-president and general manager in November, 1865, a few months after President Root's death. Mrs. Colt's brother, Richard Jarvis, now headed the company. The new executive, William B. Franklin, had been trained as an engineer, graduating from West Point in the same class as General Grant.

Franklin wasted no time in carrying out the widow's wishes. On November 20th, he wrote in his diary: "Examined roof of the New Armory building with reference to rebuilding the burnt part. Found New Armory had settled a great deal. Resolved to pile the foundations for the columns. Talked with Mr. Lord about increasing production of pistols."

By February of the following year, he had designed the new structure, estimated its cost at $130,000, and obtained approval from the directors. It was decided to make it four stories and as

1869 view of the armory from the west side. (Courtesy R.L. Wilson)

fireproof as possible. Meanwhile, as a safety measure, Horace Lord, the superintendent, was instructed to set up a fire brigade in each story of the existing buildings and to place the hoses on reels. In April, the foundations were laid and the work finished in early 1867, including a new dome.

As president, Richard Jarvis gingerly held the reins passed on by the Colonel and Root, comfortable only in the knowledge that he had under him a competent engineer to operate the Armory. No one could imagine a personality more unlike his brother-in-law. A quiet, retiring bachelor in his mid-thirties, Richard preferred studying history and literature to making guns. Educated at Trinity College and Columbia Law School, he had spent some time in the southwest overseeing Colt's land speculations and silver-mining venture — all of which ended in failure. The Colonel then brought him back to Hartford to manage the willow ware factory. Living at Armsmear with his sister, he now sat in the Colonel's chair primarily to serve her interests by holding the Armory together rather than expanding it. Maintaining a steady ten percent dividend was his major goal, and to spur on General Franklin he persuaded his sister to sell him forty-eight shares of Colt stock. As long as the dividends kept coming and he was left free to pursue his scholarly interests, he contentedly continued as president for thirty-six years.

With great executive ability and a super-abundance of common sense, General Franklin ran the works until he reached the age of sixty-five. When the state finally decided to build a new capitol, he was appointed head of the building commission, and for eight years, from 1872 to 1880, directed its construction within the amount appropriated by the Legislature. After his retirement from Colt's in 1888, he accepted an executive position with the Hartford Steam Boiler Inspection & Insurance Company but remained a director of the Armory until 1901.

With Franklin gone and President Jarvis in poor health, Mrs. Colt had to decide what to do next. The business had lost some momentum; her dividends might be in jeopardy. Somehow she wanted to keep the Colt identity with the Armory; she desperately needed a manager of Franklin's caliber. It was time, she felt, to give her son "Collie" more responsibility. Although he had been a director since 1880, at the age of thirty he was still dissipating his life away, chasing women and racing his schooner. Besides, in Hartford anyone who didn't work was regarded as peculiar. Yet, she knew he could not be depended upon to assume control.

To fill this void she turned to John Henry Hall of Portland, Connecticut, whose family had been friends of the Jarvises for a long time. In some ways, Hall was an odd choice; he had no engineering training but had made his mark as an energetic businessman. As a young man, he worked for a New York tea and coffee importer and then returned to Portland to become president of the family business, Shaler & Hall, which quarried brownstone. Mrs. Colt liked him because he was a devout Episcopalian. Others thought he had a mean, penny-pinching spirit. He accepted the position of general manager, while Caldwell Colt was named vice-president.

Although Richard Jarvis remained president in name, he surrendered most of his responsibilities to Hall. For his part, "Collie" had no desire to get involved and continued to be absent from town most of the time. Upon Hall fell the entire responsibility for directing the company's affairs, and to his credit he strengthened its finances. Mrs. Colt's income was assured once more. After Caldwell's sudden death in 1894, Hall was elevated to vice-president and treasurer. He served on the city's water board, one term as state senator, and as senior warden of Mrs. Colt's church. But neither his civic nor his religious pursuits endeared him to Hartford. Oh, for the good old days of Sam Colt, flamboyant and abrasive as he might have been! The stars on his dome glittered less brightly.

Richard W.H. Jarvis — 1865-1901.

* * *

Colt's was by no means the only successful gunmaker in Connecticut. Just as Colonel Colt finished buying the low-lying land in the southern part of Hartford for his new Armory, Robbins & Lawrence — a Vermont firm — was tooling up for the Sharps rapid-firing, breech-loading rifle. On pasture land behind the Little River, the company built a new plant, the first of several in the western section of the city that would later accommodate a number of illustrious manufacturers like Pope, Pratt & Whitney, Hartford Machine Screw, and Underwood. Thousands of Sharps guns, far superior to the old muzzle loaders, were used by buffalo hunters, settlers, anti-slavery fighters like John Brown, and Union troops. The famous preacher Henry Ward Beecher claimed there was more "moral power" in a Sharps rifle than in a hundred Bibles, prompting the nickname "Beecher's Bibles" for the cases shipped from Hartford. In 1860, the employment at Colt's and Sharps accounted for more than two-thirds of those working on firearms in the state. The Sharps factory remained in the city until 1875, when it moved to Bridgeport.

A former Colt machinist invented a revolutionary seven-shot rifle that matched the Sharps gun in popularity. A native of Manchester, Christopher Spencer began his career with the Cheney silk mills as a lad of fourteen. To round off his technical training, he spent a year or so in the Colt Armory and returned to the Cheneys in 1857. Always fascinated with firearms, he conceived the idea of a repeating rifle with the magazine in the stock. Encouraged by Frank Cheney, he devoted two years of his spare time to its development and obtained a patent in 1860. The Cheney brothers offered him $5,000 for the rights and a royalty of one dollar for each gun made. As Spencer recalled in his old age:

The inventor Christopher Spencer at age eighty-five. (Courtesy Richard W. Forbes)

Mr. Charles Cheney was quick to see the advantage of a repeating gun in the hands of Northern troops, and prevailed upon me to put my patent into his hands for one month, furnishing the money to pay for a model... Procuring from the Sharps Rifle Company the barrel, lock and such parts as we could utilize, I engaged an expert gunmaker in Worcester to make the parts needed, and together we completed the rifle within two weeks.

Mr. Cheney was an intimate friend of the Hon. Gideon Welles from Glastonbury, the Secretary of the Navy, and he readily secured an order for a trial at the Navy Yard in Washington. One thousand rounds were fired without cleaning the gun, and without mishap. The result was an order for a thousand rifles. With this as a nucleus, a company was organized for their manufacture and a factory secured in Boston where sewing machines were being made.

But this location proved unsatisfactory, and the operations were soon moved to the Chickering Pianoforte factory, where the Cheneys spent half a million dollars tooling up. Although the War Department contracted for ten thousand more to arm volunteers from Connecticut, Massachusetts, and Michigan, it was President Lincoln himself who insured the success of the Spencer rifle. As the inventor recalled:

On the 18th of August, 1863, I arrived at the White House with the rifle in hand, and was immediately ushered into the executive room. I found the President alone. With brief introduction, I took the rifle from its case and presented it to him. Looking it over carefully, and handling it as one familiar with firearms, he requested me to take it apart to show the "Inwardness of the thing." It was soon dissected, and laid on the table before him. After a careful examination and his emphatic approval, I was asked if I had any engagement for the following day. When I replied that I was at his command, he requested that I "Come over tomorrow at 2 o'clock and we will go out and see the thing shoot."

Arriving at the appointed time, I found all in readiness to proceed to the shooting place, which was about where now stands the Washington Monument. Accompanying us was his son Robert, and one of the officers of the Navy Department who carried the target and rifle, with the ammunition. Arriving at a point opposite the War Department, the President requested Robert to go over and ask Mr. Stanton [Secretary of War] to come and see this new gun fired. Robert soon returned and reported Mr. Stanton too busy to attend. "Well," says the President, in his humorous way, "they do pretty much as they have a mind to over there."

While we were waiting for Robert, Mr. Lincoln discovered that one of the pockets in his black alpaca coat was torn open. Taking a pin from his waistcoat, he proceeded to mend it, remarking, "That don't look quite right for the Chief Magistrate of this Mighty Republic, Ha! Ha! Ha!"

Arriving at the shooting ground, Mr. Lincoln looking down the field said, "It seems to me, I discover the carcass of a colored gentleman down yonder," and ordered the target placed to avoid accidents. The target was a board about six inches wide, and three feet long, with a black spot near each end. The rifle contained seven cartridges. Mr. Lincoln's first shot was low, but the next hit the bull's eye, and the other five were close around it. "Now," says he, "we will let the inventor try it." Being almost in daily practice, I naturally beat the President a little. "Well," says he, "you are younger than I am, have a better eye, and a steadier nerve." The end of the board which the President shot at was cut off by the Navy official and handed to me when we parted on the steps of the White House.

General Ripley was the "fossilized" incumbent of the Ordnance Department, and characterized any innovations as "New Fangled Jim Cracks." Notwithstanding this opposition, we soon received orders for all the rifles we could make, and the Burnside Rifle Co. of Providence, received an order for 30,000 Spencer Rifles, which they made and paid the Spencer Rifle Co. three dollars royalty upon each rifle.

The factory reached the production of one hundred and fifty rifles per day, and about two hundred thousand were furnished to the Government. Thus it was manifest that the Cheney brothers' patriotism and business acumen exerted an influence and power which did much to shorten the contest between the North and South.

When the war was ended, motives of patriotism were no longer an incentive to continue the making of weapons of warfare and the return to the peaceful industry of silk manufacturing was hailed with delight. The entire rifle plant was sold to the Winchester Arms Co., who utilized the machinery for their works, and squelched the Spencer rifles which had been a formidable competitor.

After the War, Spencer left Manchester, and with Charles Billings, another graduate of Colt's, formed a company to manufacture drop forgings and sewing machine shuttles. Here he had his most far-reaching brainstorm — an automatic turret screw machine. Spencer joined forces with George Fairfield, then associated with the Weed Sewing Machine Company, to found the Hartford Machine Screw Company in 1876. However, de-

Charles E. Billings in uniform of Colt band. (Courtesy Honiss Oyster House)

spite these successes he never lost his interest in guns. He continued to work on improving his original repeater, organizing, before his venture with Billings, the Roper Repeating Arms Company, which promptly lost $80,000. Undaunted, Spencer tried again, patenting in 1882 a gun which would fire eighty-six shots in two minutes, more than double his original model. The following year he went abroad and obtained orders from various governments, but the Spencer Arms Company was known mainly for its pump-action shotguns. Living to the ripe old age of ninety, Christopher Spencer was certainly the most durable, if not the most prolific and brilliant, Connecticut inventor in the 19th century.

Meanwhile in New Haven there had appeared a new corporation called the Volcanic Repeating Arms, which bought out the patents of Smith & Wesson for pistols and carbines. One of the investors was Oliver F. Winchester, a successful shirt manufacturer, who in a short time acquired complete control to save it from bankruptcy. He formed a new firm, the New Haven Arms Company, in 1857. During the Civil War, its operations were profitable but limited; the War Department, reluctant to substitute a repeating rifle for the standard muzzle-loaders or the newer breech-loading style, refused Winchester a large contract. By 1866, Winchester had sold out his shirt interests and renamed his firearms business.

Within a decade, the name Winchester became synonymous with "repeating rifle." By 1880, the best-known gunmakers in the United States were, besides Colt's and Winchester, Smith & Wesson of Springfield, which concentrated on revolvers; E. Remington & Sons of Ilion, New York; Marlin Firearms of New Haven; and Eli Whitney's old armory in Hamden — the granddaddy of them all. The latter, although active during the Civil War, now found itself out of step. Its single-shot and repeating rifles could not compete with Winchester's. For only $65,000, Winchester bought out the assets of the Whitney Arms Company in 1887 and withdrew the Whitney line from the market.

The following year, Winchester joined with Marcellus Hartley of the Union Metallic Cartridge Company in Bridgeport to purchase Remington. An energetic New Yorker, Hartley had made a fortune from his sporting goods partnership, the largest in America. President Lincoln made him a brigadier general and sent him abroad to purchase arms for the Union forces, in much the same manner as Silas Deane of Wethersfield had done for General Washington during the Revolution. In 1867, Hartley purchased two small New England cartridge companies to supply ammunition to the growing market for breech-loading rifles.

Remington, with its extensive line of firearms, had ended the War with an operation that employed nearly a thousand workers. Subsequently, it sold a million arms to foreign governments and branched out into typewriters, sewing machines, and agricultural machinery. But its financial position steadily deteriorated until it went into receivership. Winchester and Hartley paid $200,000 for the business. Hartley was elected president, acquired Winchester's half interest in 1896, and ran Remington and three other companies until his death in 1902 at the age of seventy-five.

During the 1890s, the Savage Repeating Arms Company of Utica, New York entered the munitions business with a line of high-powered, small caliber rifles. The Parker Brothers in Meriden were making shotguns, while Colt's dropped out of the rifle business in 1903. Winchester, however, remained the leading producer of firearms until the advent of World War I.

One individual in particular contributed significantly to the fortunes of Colt's, Remington, and Winchester. He was the son of a Mormon gunmaker, one of twenty-two children born in Ogden, Utah to Jonathan Browning and his three wives. At the age of twenty-eight, in 1883, John Moses Browning sold his first patent for a single-shot rifle to Winchester. For nearly two decades, this prolific inventor did business exclusively with the New Haven armory, selling them some forty-one of his inventions. At the same time, he took out a number of patents on pistols, including the first automatic model, which was purchased by Colt's and a Belgian munitions maker. For Winchester, he designed the first successful repeating shotgun. Once a year he traveled from Ogden to New Haven with a new model or improvements on those in production.

As time went on, Browning and his brothers turned their entire attention to automatic firearms. Earlier their idea for a machine gun had been rejected by Winchester, and now inventor and manufacturer parted company over Browning's semiautomatic shotgun. Winchester refused to negotiate a royalty agreement, preferring to acquire the patent outright. Browning immediately went to Remington. Marketed in 1905, the Remington-made Browning gun proved extremely popular. The contract paid the inventor more than a million dollars in the first ten years, and in addition he was hired to superintend its production in Ilion. Neither Winchester nor any other competitor ever overtook Remington's lead in shotguns for sportsmen.

At the height of the Civil War, Colt's annual production had reached 100,000 revolvers and nearly 50,000 muskets. Its output for the entire war period totaled 378,000 revolvers and 114,000 muskets. During peacetime, however, the demand for munitions declined sharply, and Colt's leased portions of its factory space to other manufacturers, such as Asa Cook who made wood-screw machinery for the New Britain hardware industry. Around 600 men were retained in the main building for producing — besides guns — Baxter steam engines, sewing machines, and printing presses. Before their deaths, Root and Colt had perfected a

5-shot pocket pistol which sold well until 1872. This was replaced by the .45 caliber Single-Action model which was among the first to use metallic ammunition instead of powder and ball. It rapidly won the favor of cowboy and frontiersman, giving rise to the axiom that "Abraham Lincoln made all men free, but Colt made all men equal." In the untamed West, the Colt gun became a legend as the pioneer trek into the wilderness of America resumed after the Civil War. The great caravans that pushed across the Alleghenies and the Mississippi relied on Colt six-shooters to protect them against Indians and outlaws. General Custer's men all carried Colt revolvers; pony express riders fought off attacking desperadoes with them; and Wild Bill Hickok dispensed "Colt Justice" in the Black Hills of Dakota.

Equally deadly were Colt's versions of the Deringer single-shot pistol. Only four inches long, they used a .41 caliber metal cartridge. Because they could be so easily concealed, they were a kind of secret weapon. In western mining camps, gamblers kept them up their sleeves, held there by rubber bands; in case of trouble, they could get the drop on an adversary who had to reach for the gun on his hip.

In 1867, Colt's brought out the first machine gun — the Gatling, a multi-barrel monster turned by a crank that spewed out 200 shots or more a minute. It was the invention of Dr. R.J Gatling, an Indianapolis physician, and first fired at Confederate troops in 1862. After improving the design, Gatling moved to Hartford and led a cloistered life. During his visit to the Armory, Mark Twain saw it in action and wrote this description:

It is a cluster of six to ten savage tubes that carry great conical pellets of lead, with unerring accuracy, a distance of two and one-half miles. It feeds itself with cartridges, and you work it with a crank like a hand organ, and you can fire it faster than four men can count. When fired rapidly, the reports blend together like a watchman's rattle... I like it very much, and went on grinding it as long as they could afford cartridges for the amusement — which was not very long.

Although Colt's found it expensive to promote, the Gatling was the most popular semiautomatic weapon abroad. General Pedro Villar of Colombia expressed his delight with his four Gatlings when he paid a call in 1893. But already a much better gas-operated and air-cooled machine gun was about to be marketed, thanks to the genius of John Moses Browning. Early in 1891, John and his brother Matt had made their first visit to the Colt Armory after writing to see if the company would be interested in their "new Automatic Machine Gun." General Manager John Hall welcomed them. "We smoked up the factory with those .45/70s and waked echoes clear back to the Colonel himself," Browning exclaimed later. The Colt officials could not believe their eyes when 200 rounds were fired without a hitch. It was the beginning of a cordial and profitable association with the inventor that lasted until his death.

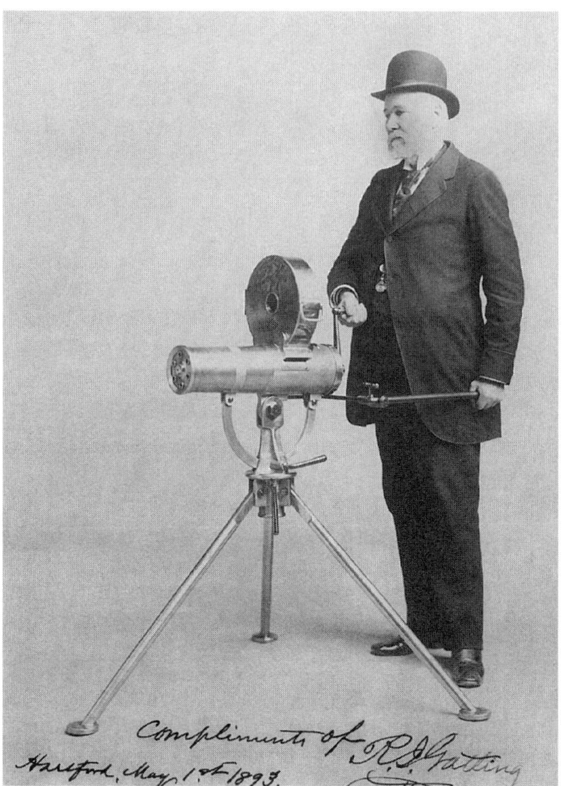

Dr. R.J. Gatling and his machine gun in 1893.

Soon the machine gun that became known as the Colt 1895 "Peacemaker" was demonstrated to Navy representatives. After three minutes of continuous fire and 1,800 rounds the barrel turned bright red. That night they all celebrated at the Heublein Hotel, and John drank his first glass of champagne. Hall offered Browning a generous royalty contract and suggested he go ahead and make the improved model he already had in mind. "One of these days," the general manager said, "the Army will wake up, and in the meantime there's all of South America." The inventor declined to sign a contract but assured Hall he would have first crack at making the new machine gun. This became the first automatic weapon to be purchased by the United States, the first fifty of

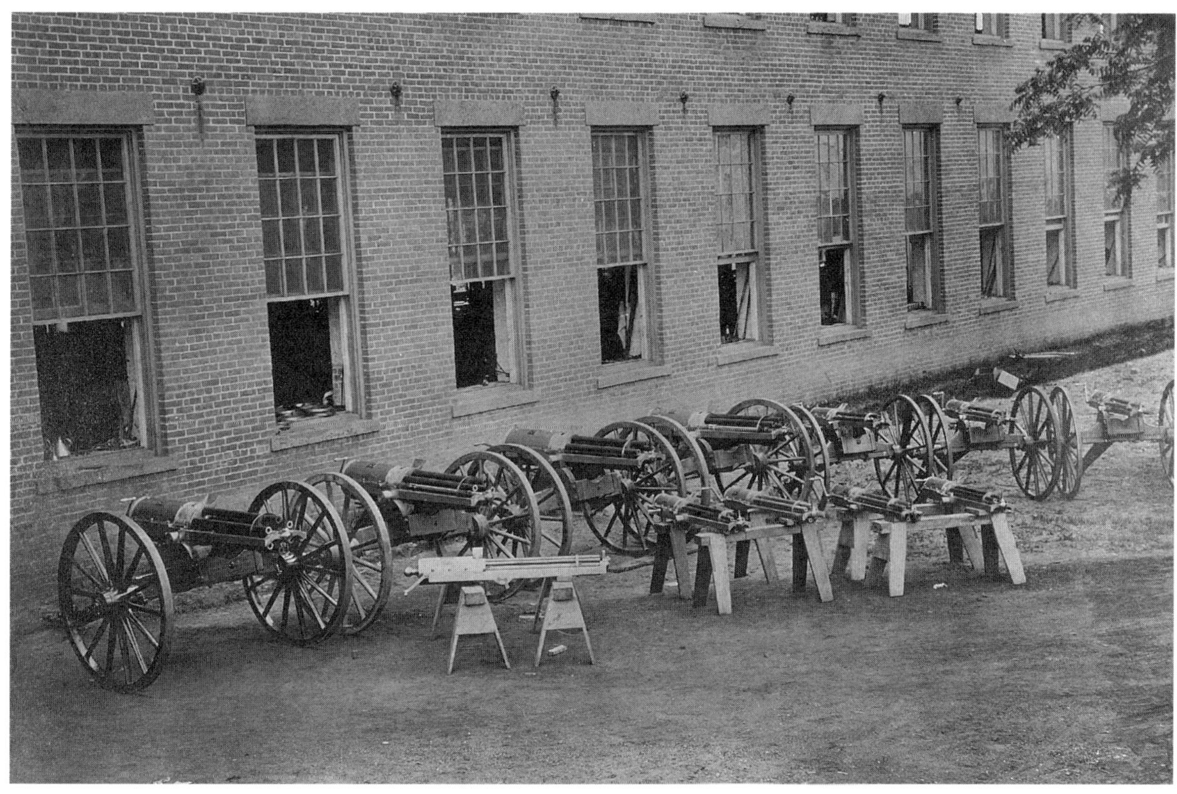

Model 1865-66 Gatling Machine Guns outside Colt's.

Two Colt employees, C. Goodrich and S. Goodell, fire an early Gatling model in 1879.

John Browning shows off a model of the first Colt machine gun which he designed in 1891.

which were delivered to the Navy in 1897. It saw action in the Spanish-American War and, in the hands of marines, saved the foreign legations in Peking during the Boxer Rebellion. The army, still as obtuse as it was during Colonel Colt's day, clung to the hand-cranked Gatling for another decade. In 1900, Browning started work on a water-cooled version which fathered all of the famous Brownings to follow.

In 1895, Browning test fired his first automatic pistol at Colt's, a .38 cal. recoil-operated gun. Upon his signing a royalty agreement the next year, every automatic pistol produced by Colt was based on his designs. In the Armory, he found a soul-mate in the person of Fred Moore, a young man in the model room. The two worked closely together on all of Browning's ideas. At John's tactful suggestion, Moore was advanced to the head of the machine gun division and then to production manager of the entire factory. The dignified inventor became a respected figure as he walked back and forth through the shop, swinging a pair of cheap iron spectacles, usually in company with Fred Moore. Browning loved to munch peanuts and always had a sack or two in his pockets. If something wasn't working right, he would eat them furiously, one after another.

The Brownings, however pleasant their relationship with the Armory, saw to it that they received their just due. Following John Hall's death, they filed a claim against his estate and the company for $115,000 in unpaid royalties, interest, and expenses incurred which, apparently, Hall had promised to pay. In February, 1903, the directors met with the brothers in Hartford. After some hard Yankee bargaining, as a result of which President Grover and his fellow directors had to raise their offer from $40,000 to $54,000, the difference was resolved. In exchange for giving Colt's all benefits on the new automatic pistol and automatic machine gun patents, the Brownings also received a royalty of $45 per gun.

As the century came to a close, near the midpoint of America's industrial dominance, Con-

1898 - Machining parts for the Gatling gun. Interior view of Colt's factory.

Hartford police department patrol wagon armed with model 1893 "Bulldog Police Gatling."

The entire work force lined up in front of the Armory and office in 1876.

necticut stood eleventh highest in manufacturing, though in population it was only twenty-ninth. It had nearly 177,000 wage earners, and its broad range of manufactures totaled over $350,000,000 annually. On the basis of production per capita the state ranked second, with Rhode Island at the top. In eleven major classifications such as munitions, brass, clocks, cutlery, hats, and hardware — Connecticut led the entire country. It made three-quarters of all the guns and ammunition. In June, 1901, Hartford acquired a new and promising industry when Underwood Typewriter leased the American Bicycle Company factory and hired 350 employees. Assessing Connecticut's position in the manufacturing world, William A. Countryman, formerly a member of the city council and now statistician for the U.S. Census Bureau, credited its superiority "to the ingenuity of its inhabitants; after that to industry and frugality."

Colt's, too, was at its mid-point, financially fat, technically smug, its gun-making skills never stronger, its reputation untarnished, yet its management already old and tired and the Colt family on the verge of giving up control of the great Armory.

CHAPTER III

THAT DEMON, STEAM!

In its early industrial history, Connecticut's most abundant natural resource was water. The Connecticut River served as a highway for maritime trade along the eastern coast, to the West Indies, and as far as China. Other rivers and streams provided the water power for operating the local gristmills, sawmills, and fulling mills. In fact, the availability of water determined the location of most mills and shops, as well as the villages founded around them, until well into the 19th century. America's first great engineer, Oliver Evans, developed the high pressure steam engine which enabled industry to convert from water to steam power; its first use in Connecticut was in a Middletown woolen mill in 1811. Without steam the Colt Armory could never have run at all, but it was always regarded with a great respect and even fear. For steam could be a demon.

By 1850, as Sam Colt started to plan his Armory, steam power had become as common as the horse and buggy, pushing sidewheelers up and down the Connecticut River, moving trains on the spreading network of tracks, and running machines. In Hartford shops, thirty engines of various sizes panted and heaved. In many eyes, however, stationary as it might seem, a steam engine was an occult force that spewed forth a hot white breath, a monster that on occasion men were helpless to control. Few understood how steam worked. Explosions occurred with alarming regularity — in the entire country once or twice a week. Thousands had lost their lives. But these were all considered "acts of God" caused by "mysterious agencies," static electricity or a combination of gases.

Colt's engine was the biggest of all — 250 horsepower. Built by Woodruff & Beach in Hartford, it had a three-foot cylinder and seven-foot stroke, with a flywheel thirty feet in diameter. Two large boilers supplied the steam. A leather belt over a hundred feet long carried the power to the attic and thence to the 1,400 machines by means of an intricate network of overhead shafts and smaller belts. To start up in the morning, the engineer had to light his fire two hours before the seven o'clock gong. The buildings themselves were steam-heated through pipes running along the walls. Gas burners supplied light. The same engine also operated a cam pump that raised water from the Connecticut River to a reservoir supplying both the Armory and its surrounding dwellings. Later, another engine — almost twice as powerful — was installed.

A few blocks from Colt's, near the waterfront, stood the Fales & Gray Car Works, builders of railroad cars. In the blacksmith shop, iron was annealed in white-hot furnaces and hammered into various shapes by sooty smiths and their helpers, called strikers. Next to the shop, separated by an eight-inch thick wall of brick, were the boiler room and steam engine, only one fifth as powerful as Colt's.

Its operator was John McCune, an easy-going but temperamental young man under thirty who had been firing boilers for nine years. He was generally regarded as competent, no better and no worse than his counterparts in other manufacturing establishments. He had received no professional training — in fact, like other stationary engineers his education was minimal, and he had learned his trade on the job.

For quite a while, the blacksmiths had been uneasy about the old boiler and their proximity to it. Its two flues could barely get up enough steam to

East Armory steam engine installed by General Franklin.

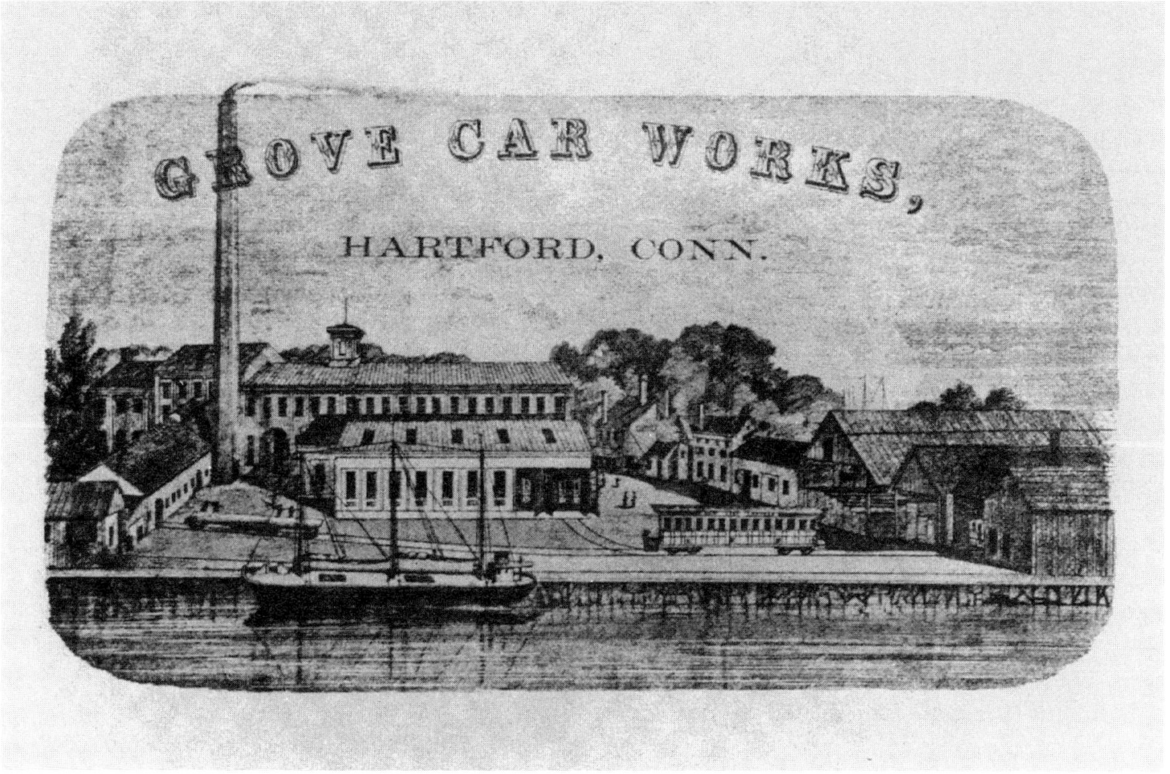

Fales & Gray shop near the armory, later known as Grove Car Works.

keep the machines operating. The boss was doubtless on McCune's neck every day for more pressure. But the boiler leaked, and the only way McCune could do his job was to cheat. He hung lead weights on the safety valve. If Fales or Gray noticed, they never said a word. But the blacksmiths were not blind.

Some of the workers also suspected that McCune drank too much. Downing a beer or two during the dinner hour at the Front Street saloon was no crime, and on Saturday night a man might be expected to take a few too many and stagger home. But if an engineer returned from dinner drunk, he might forget to keep the water level up in the boiler. McCune was headstrong and surly if crossed, and there were rumors of trouble within his family. Not that he beat his wife, but his neighbors couldn't help overhearing the verbal warfare that rattled the walls of his Pearl Street home.

These concerns about the boiler and McCune were passed off as jokes. They never reached management's ears. No one dared to complain or squeal. So their shared fear remained silent, that a leaky boiler, over-pressured and perhaps neglected now and then, could send them all into the next world without time enough for even a "Hail, Mary."

Six months before, McCune had quit his job. He told his boss the boiler was no good; he was overworked and needed a second fireman to help load in the coal. His replacement was a failure. The company recalled McCune, giving him a raise from $1.50 to $1.75 a day, another helper, and a special favor. Unlike the rest of the work force, he could collect his wages every Saturday night. Furthermore, the company promised to order a new boiler, with five flues, from Woodruff & Beach, the best boiler and engine makers in Hartford and suppliers to factories all over Connecticut.

The new boiler had been in operation about a month when it happened. Thursday, March 2, 1854, was an unseasonably warm day. As if ending a winter of hibernation, people emerged from their houses and tenements to enjoy the sun. After a leisurely dinner, William Skinner, a local printer, strolled past the blacksmith shop, delaying, as long as possible, his return to work. A friend rapped on the window and invited him inside, though it was against company rules to admit visitors. It was fifteen minutes before two o'clock. The engine was pounding away as usual, the wheels overhead turning smoothly, and the anvils ringing with rhythmic hammer blows. After chatting a few minutes, Skinner headed for the door through the boiler room. He stopped to talk with the engineer, whom he knew slightly. As he departed through the door, a tremendous explosion shook the factory, breaking timbers, mangling machinery and men, knocking down walls for a hundred feet, and collapsing the roof. The blacksmith shop and the boiler room were completely demolished. Nine men were killed at once; twelve more died later. Fifty were seriously injured.

McCune's body was hurled through the boiler room door and landed, minus one arm, next to William Skinner. Skinner was flattened, his left arm broken, his neck scalded, and his head cut. Two men were blown through the windows. A falling timber crushed Samuel Parsons at his lathe, but he was pulled out alive. Alex Nodine was sitting on the toilet on the second floor. The force of the explosion lifted him ten feet into the air, and as the floor under him gave way, he fell to the floor below, with only his head gashed.

Within minutes, a crowd gathered at the scene of destruction. Hysterical wives and their children searched for their husbands. Some soon realized they were widows and orphans. So great was the excitement that the South District School was dismissed for the afternoon. Before dark, the injured and dead were removed and a coroner's jury of twelve leading business and professional men summoned. It was the worst calamity in Hartford's history.

At ten o'clock the next morning the jury, after inspecting the site and the remains of the boiler, convened for the investigation. For six days they heard testimony under oath from the workers, managers, the boiler manufacturer, consultants, and others. The first witness was Patrick Munhall, the 25-year-old fireman. A minute or two before the explosion he had told McCune either he had too much steam on, or the water was low, and then went into the cellar for more coal, thus saving his life:

"Around two p.m. I asked McCune 'Is there water in the boiler?' and he replied, 'I'm just taking water on from the pump.' I warned him the gauge was up to 82, and he ought to take down the damper. McCune said not to worry, everything was all right. I don't know if he did anything about the water or the damper."

A high pressure steam boiler of this kind had a rated safe operating limit of about 50-60 pounds of pressure per square inch. Munhall and others confirmed that it was customary to push it up to 80 pounds or higher, otherwise all the machines couldn't be kept running. At 88 pounds per square inch, the pressure on the entire boiler would equal 4,320,000 pounds.

Daniel Duffy was the next witness. He had

looked after the boiler while the engineer went out for dinner at noontime. Under questioning, he admitted that he knew McCune drank, but he had never seen him drunk. The foreman of the machine shop, Gordon Grant, opened up another line of investigation: "Sometimes I thought McCune was careless in letting the water get low, and I used to speak to him about it. He'd say the new boiler made steam very fast, but he wasn't concerned at all. No, the water pump was not out of order. It's my business to repair it."

Grant said in his opinion McCune was always sober at work, although he knew he drank outside. "But he wasn't much of an engineer. Sometimes he'd have the steam up as high as 95, and sometimes he'd allow the water in the flues to drop below the lowest gauge cock." George Stone, a machinist, agreed with Grant that the engineer was occasionally sloppy, yet he considered him as good as other engineers he knew.

Seth King testified that shortly after the dinner hour he had seen McCune talking with the visitor Skinner. According to him, Skinner and McCune conversed for about fifteen minutes near the door of the boiler room. When he finished, the jurors looked at each other, eyebrows raised.

The jury then called Thomas J. Fales, 38, the proprietor. Fales had been at dinner when the disaster occurred. He reviewed McCune's employment record over the preceding five years. "After two or three years here he became slovenly in the care of the engine. I reproved him, and he did better. He liked the new boiler and often said 'see how easy I can now get up steam enough.'"

Question: "Wasn't it dangerous to operate the boiler at 80 pounds pressure or higher?"

Fales: "No, sir, that boiler would be safe at 150. It was made of the best iron and had extra thick plates."

Question: "Did you have any reason to believe McCune was careless?"

Fales: "Well, as I have said, he was sometimes sloppy — he didn't keep the room clean. But I always thought him a reliable worker...never heard any complaint about his being careless. Of course, if he was talking to Skinner, it was wrong. We don't allow that sort of thing."

Question: "Did you ride him about keeping the pressure up?"

Fales: "He had orders to produce sufficient power, but I warned him against doing anything rash or unsafe."

Question: "Did you suspect McCune ever drank too much?"

Fales: "No, sir. I never heard that said about him. Once I had to bawl him out...I think it was last summer...for leaving his engine to get a glass of beer. But nobody ever mentioned to me that he was intemperate or careless."

From George Balmer, McCune's father-in-law, the jury tried to find out more about the engineer's personal life, without success. All that Balmer would admit was that many husbands and fathers were more agreeable at home than John McCune. Dr. David Crary, the family physician, knew of McCune's drinking habits and had urged him to leave the stuff alone. "But I never could get him to promise he would stop."

John Cook, a 50-year old mason, was full of bitterness: "I told somebody this boiler'd blow up in six weeks. John had been used to attending a boiler with two flues, and this one had five, and he would get a little careless, and the water would get down before he was aware of it. 'Watch out,' I said. All he said was, 'I can manage.'"

The jury by now had a pretty good lead on the cause of the explosion, but they still wanted to interview two witnesses, Charles Gardner and William Skinner, who had been so badly injured they were unable to attend the hearing. They also wanted to determine the safety of the boiler itself. They called Samuel Woodruff, president of Woodruff & Beach, builders of engines for Colt's, the Hartford Water Works, and the U.S. Navy.

Woodruff insisted the boiler had been especially built for the heavy demands that would be put on it. "We never turned out a better boiler than that one. It was fully able to sustain a pressure of 88 pounds. If it had plenty of water, it would have borne a pressure of 150 pounds without bursting." Woodruff, however, was critical of the engineer and the trade in general. McCune never should have left his boiler and engine even for a minute. Furthermore, there ought to be a board to examine operating engineers and license them, and boilers should be regularly inspected, just like steamboat boilers.

Edward Reed, superintendent of the Hartford Railroad Company, called up as a consultant, conceded he had no reservations about the boiler being well made. "There is evidence, however," he chose his words carefully, "that the boiler was out of water. I examined the flues, and inside they were blue. Now, blueness denotes that they had been subjected to a red heat. In my opinion the accident was caused by a lack of water in the boiler, and steam was generated faster than it could escape. The boiler would not be unsafe even at 88 pounds if it were full of water."

The last expert to testify was Samuel Ward, a

After the Fales & Gray explosion in 1854.

steamboat inspector. He took issue with Woodruff and Reed on the question of the boiler's safety limits. In his opinion, 80-90 pounds of pressure were too much. Then he roundly condemned those who called themselves boiler engineers. "Seven-eighths of these damn engineers are incompetent. They can only build a fire and start an engine. To show their daring, they attach extra weights to the safety valves. They know nothing about the dangers. What they do is criminal!"

To complete the testimony, depositions were taken from Gardner and Skinner. Gardner was only twenty years old, a striker in the blacksmith shop, who had his leg broken and his body burned. His account made quite an impression on the jury: "Two or three minutes before the explosion I saw McCune start the pump. He usually ran it every fifteen minutes or so, but sometimes he'd forget. I've seen the safety valve blow off steam a half dozen times. I've seen him away from the boiler so long the fireman had to go and start the pump. That very morning I told him, 'if that thing blows up, it'll kill me and a lot more.' He said he didn't like five flues, they worked his water off too fast, and he was always tired out at the end of the day. 'God,' he said, 'I'll have a blowup if I'm not more careful, I guess.'"

William Skinner did his best to counteract the previous testimony so damaging to McCune's reputation: "When I reached the boiler room, the engineer urged me to sit down. Daniel Camp came up. 'Come, Bill,' he said, 'can't you afford to give us a glass of beer, John and I?' But McCune declined: 'No, gentlemen, I can't leave my engine, you must excuse me.' Camp then headed for the blacksmith shop, and McCune returned to his boiler. We were only together for five...no more than eight...minutes."

But it was to no avail. Otis Long, a blacksmith, described how the water pump had suddenly stopped after McCune's last start-up. "I was just picking up an iron, my striker had struck two blows, and as I turned to the fire I was blown down. Just before the blowup I heard a funny noise. The pump started up all right, then it hissed and stopped. The noise seemed to come from the pump's steam cylinder. I know that the pump had not run a half hour before dinner and during the hour after dinner."

Finally, the jury produced a surprise witness, a painter named John Proffitt, who lived next door to McCune.

Question: "Did you accompany John McCune home to dinner on the day of the explosion?"

Proffitt: "I did."

Question: "Did both of you stop on the way?"

Proffitt: "Yes, we did."

Question: "Where?"

Proffitt: "At the saloon. We had a few drinks."

Question: "What did you drink?"

Proffitt: "Well, I had an ale or two. John drank ale or brandy, or maybe both, I forget."

The hearing ended on that note. The jury promptly concluded that the explosion was due to the carelessness and inattention of John McCune, to an abnormally high steam pressure, and to the sudden injection of cold water, which collapsed the red-hot flues. They also chided the company for not locating the boiler room in a separate building away from the employees.

They were not content merely to establish blame. They suggested several ways to prevent a recurrence of this and similar tragedies. There should be regulations preventing unqualified persons from being hired as operating engineers. There should be regular safety inspections by the city or state. Employers should pay heed to worker safety and isolate boiler rooms. And there should be standards set for steam pressure.

Hartford was in no mood to write *finis* to the case after the jury adjourned. For the relief of those injured or bereaved, a collection was taken up in the city. The men at Rogers Brothers gave $153.00. Amos Whitney, then a foreman at Phoenix Iron Works, raised $113.00 in his shop, and Wyatt's Dramatic Lyceum collected $150.00 from its patrons. Altogether, $8,100 was contributed.

The city council was moved to appoint a committee to study steam boiler safety, but like most committees it produced no concrete results. Ten years would pass before the state legislature enacted a boiler inspection law. A more immediate result came from a public meeting to discuss the lack of medical facilities. Well-to-do citizens were outraged that those injured in the explosion could be cared for only in nearby homes or in overcrowded doctors' offices. Before the end of May, Hartford's first public hospital was chartered.

The clergy had their say, too. From the pulpits of at least two churches, they made a moral issue of the disaster. The Hartford *Courant* printed the sermons, and in response to a heavy demand made reprints and sold them for two cents apiece.

Thomas Clark, rector of Christ Church, had as inspiration for his text: "There is but a step between me and death." *I Samuel, XX,* 3. In his view, mechanical power in the rapidly changing world around him was a mighty, mysterious force whose strength seemed to increase as it reached toward the spiritual, unknown realm. The import of his sermon eluded most of his parishioners. Did he mean that only God understood and had mastery of steam power? But his conclusion, that suffering was in some way essential to our permanent good, made them feel better for having attended the service.

Frederic Hinckley, pastor of the Church of the Saviour, delivered a down-to-earth inflammatory discourse entitled "Where is Abel thy Brother?" *Genesis, IV, 9.* Abel, of course, was dead, and the culprit was not only the imprudent engineer but a pernicious attitude common to the captains of industry. The men who died, he told his aroused audience, were "sacrificed to the reckless spirit of enterprise of this mid-century; uselessly, murderously destroyed that more physical power might be obtained, more speed secured, more work performed, and greater material results produced... Life is thus turned into a race between power and speed on the one hand, and human safety and human existence on the other."

The Fales & Gray management naturally interpreted this diatribe as an accusation of their personal guilt, and Mr. Fales wasted no time in issuing a flat denial that he pushed or drove his work force beyond the proper limits of safety. Then he neatly turned the tables against the Reverend Mr. Hinckley.

In a letter to the local paper Fales wrote:

Hardly three months ago one of your servants was burned to death upon your very hearthstone... Such accidents are much more frequent in this community than steam boiler explosions. Very few of those who go to church have to do in any way with the management of steam engines and boilers, while there is scarcely a congregation in this state which does not contain a score of people who nightly use burning fluids or camphene, without comprehending the principles, as utterly ignorant as was your unfortunate servant.

Suppose some clergyman of this city charged the guilt of this woman's awful death upon you? Sacrificed *perhaps he would have said, uselessly, murderously destroyed that a cheaper light might be obtained for the use of a single family. The immediate cause of this deplorable accident, he might have continued, was the carelessness of the girl herself. But in this, as in most other instances, that cause did not stand alone. And, then, in tones of solemn severity he might have accused you before the public of culpable neglect, of sinful carelessness, in permitting her to use this dangerous stuff.*

Subsequently, Edward Reed, who had testified at the hearing, and a number of younger businessmen formed the Polytechnic Club to discuss "matters of science in relation to everyday life." It was natural that steam power would be their favorite topic. They wondered how boiler explosions could best be prevented and logically concluded that an inspection and insurance company, modeled after a similar experiment in England, was both a desirable and feasible solution. Nothing happened, however, until after the Civil War, by which time Hartford, with more than a dozen fire, life, and marine insurance companies flourishing, already had the reputation of being the Insurance City. In 1866, the Hartford Steam Boiler Inspection & Insurance Company was organized, and among the first directors were Charles M. Beach, who had served as a juror, and the president of Colt's, Richard Jarvis.

The coming of electricity thirty years later caused nowhere near the amount of concern and resistance that steam power aroused. Because of electricity's obvious suitability for public consumption, the question of who would supply it involved a good deal of political jockeying for control. By 1880, the streets of Hartford were well-lighted by more than a thousand gas jets that bathed downtown in a yellow glow. The Hartford Gas Company had been founded in 1849. Several local businessmen were evincing a keen interest in the new science of electricity, especially as it might apply to industry. Two of them were Austin C. Dunham,* son of the founder of the Willimantic Linen Company (which made cotton thread), and Morgan G. Bulkeley, who as a Hartford alderman had launched what would be a wide-ranging career. In 1878, they experimented with a simple six-lamp arc system in one of Willimantic Linen's buildings.

It was a success, inspiring Alderman Bulkeley the following year** to stage a spectacular demonstration of outdoor illumination on the occasion of Battle Flag Day, an annual event that featured a mammoth parade. That night, 30,000 people gathered in Bushnell Park and gaped in amazement at the giant arc lights strung around the Capitol and the searchlight with changing colors which played over the throng. Power was supplied from a small Baxter engine borrowed from Colt's. During this period, the Armory was not only making steam engines but also Universal printing presses and punches for train conductors.

The event helped to elect Bulkeley mayor in 1880. At the same time, fully conscious of the future of this new, silent source of power, he laid the groundwork for creating a public utility to supply it. Despite opposition from the Gas Company and two other petitioners, the Hartford Electric Light Company was granted a charter by the state legislature in 1881. Austin Dunham became president. At first the city's common council was hostile to the electrification of street lights, condemning poles as ugly and overhead wires as hazardous. The Gas Company, to protect its investment in municipal lighting, used its political clout to delay a decision as long as possible. In 1884, a contract was finally approved, and within four years the last gas lamp had been replaced, making Hartford the first city to have electric street lighting. In 1886, Colt's had begun to switch to electrical power, buying its first generator from a local concern backed by a group of manufacturers including Colt's, Billings & Spencer, and Pratt & Whitney.

* Austin Dunham was one of five Hartford businessmen who endorsed a note in the amount of $3,000 to start Sam Colt's first factory in Hartford 1847-48.

** Thomas Edison invented the incandescent lamp in 1879.

Mrs. Colt (Courtesy Connecticut Historical Society)

CHAPTER IV

THE COLONEL'S WIDOW

Upon their release from the hardships of the Civil War, the people of Hartford plunged into a frenzied period of money-making and business expansion. The city enjoyed the highest per capita wealth in America. The well-to-do pursued culture, philanthropy, sports, and other ways of using their newly-acquired leisure. These changes amounted to a sharp break with the simple rigorous, pastoral life of earlier times, a leavening of the old Puritan shibboleths, if you will, but not to such an extent that the right people disavowed the illusive dictates of false modesty, female sensibilities, and stilted as well as double standards. At the very top of the social pyramid stood the tiny aristocratic figure of Mrs. Colt, still in her thirties. Her immense fortune gave her undisputed title to society's crown. With an annual tax-free income of $200,000, she could set the tone for the city's residential and religious life. And set it she did with great dignity, a determined widow whose hands glittered with diamonds, but whose heart beat with compassion and rectitude.

These were the days when the city's liberal arts college atop the hill near the Little River moved to another location in order to make way for the new state capitol; when hangings at the jail were still public spectacles; when four-wheel phaetons, dog carts, and family victorias rolled up and down the unpaved streets; when, for seven cents a ride, one-horse cars transported school children and old ladies in white lace caps along Farmington and Asylum Avenues; and when Gold Street downtown, next to the old burying ground, was an insidious miniature Sodom, infested with gambling dens, saloons, pawn and lottery shops, and bawdy houses. There were only two places of entertainment nice people could attend: Allyn Hall, which featured children's plays, glass blowers, and curiosities like General and Mrs. Tom Thumb; later, the Roberts Opera House, where Edwin Booth, Henry Irving, and Ellen Terry trod the boards.

At the bottom of the pyramid struggled more than six thousand Irish immigrants. Pitifully poor and ignorant when the first 400 came in the 1820's, they had little to offer except strong backs and willing hands. Before the War, their picks and shovels built the state's canals and railroads. Gradually, they filtered into the factories, although for a long time many employers hung out signs reading "No Irish Need Apply." They, and those who followed them off the steamboats at the Hartford docks, found lodgings in the shabby brick and wood tenements owned for the most part by prominent Yankee families along Front and Market Streets near the river. As time went on, they would become landlords and, in turn, rent to later newcomers like the Italians and the Polish.

On Saturday nights, Irish laborers vented their frustrations in boisterous drinking bouts that often ended in brawls. They were the most frequent guests of the county jail. Their women folk held the family together; many served as domestics in the finest homes of the city. As soon as the Irish became acclimated, they threw themselves into politics. Cornelius O'Neill became city auditor, and James O'Leary was elected to the council. The saloon and firehouse were the gathering places for the faithful, all of them fanatic Democrats, and the ward leader was the political priest. Once in the party, they could look forward to sharing the local patronage from city hall as firemen or policemen, or by going into construction work.

With a keener eye for the dollar than the convivial sons of Erin, thrifty and home-loving German Jews were already entrenched on Front Street, in jig time advancing from pushcart to store as butchers, grocers, tailors, watch repairers, and dry goods merchants. Some ventured into tobacco growing and the fur trade. As early as 1850, they numbered about 200 and soon had a synagogue on Main Street. Believing firmly that they must look out for each other, the Jews founded their own charitable organizations. The men supported Ararat Lodge on Front Street, while the Jewish women formed the Deborah Society for the purpose of visiting and nursing the sick, washing and dressing the dead, and comforting the mourners. As soon as a *minyan* or quorum could be formed, they worshipped together in private homes. In 1860, two Jews served on the city council. Their businesses were located on the East Side, but they preferred to live in the South End away from the more numerous Irish.

Black families had been natives of Hartford long before the Irish or German Jews came. Good Republicans, they worshipped at Center Church until they founded their own churches before the Civil War. Now, at least a thousand blacks were scattered around the city. Mostly servants and coachmen, they held other jobs like barbers, farmers, carpenters, and saloonkeepers. But although they had a fixed place in Hartford society, blacks were being pushed aside for jobs by the Irish and fell behind in the competition for self-betterment. The well-to-do who had moved "higher up" to Washington Street, Lord's Hill, and further west tried to ameliorate the condition of the poor, motivated by the combination of a watered-down Puritan conscience, a sense of *noblesse oblige,* and boredom at home. The Union for Home Work on Market Street, headed by Mrs. Colt for many years, looked after needy women and children and did its best to improve sanitation in the tenements. Here, wives of leading citizens also organized the Friendly Visitors, each member of which was responsible for caring for two or three indigent families. There was also the Flower Mission, which gathered every Saturday to assemble bouquets for hospital patients.

When not playing lady bountiful, mothers took their youngsters to Riley's Dancing Academy on Saturday afternoons to learn the quadrille, polka, waltz, and even the highland fling. Tennis, both indoor and outdoor, came into vogue. As important as the game itself, was the proper costume — long skirts, a flannel waist with collars and cuffs, and a tam-o'-shanter for the ladies; white flannel trousers and blazers for the gentlemen. Parties, with due regard for the proprieties, began at eight and ended promptly at eleven. On summer moonlit nights, it was considered the "in" thing to charter a boat, take along a picnic supper, and cruise down the Connecticut River to Middletown and back. In winter, there was the excitement of racing sleighs on Washington Street or skating on the river. New Year's Day meant open house from morning to night, the young blades dashing from door to door and partaking liberally of the punch and goodies spread out in each home.

Across the Connecticut River stretched the covered toll bridge which was usually jammed with pedestrians and horse-drawn vehicles. On one occasion a lady, bringing vegetables to market and fearful of being late, was arrested for driving her wagon too fast. Mortified, she took her problem to a prominent lawyer who told her to appear in court the next morning. When her case was called, he rose and said: "Your Honor, I contend there is no case against my client." "Why not?" asked the judge. "The law distinctly reads, 'no man shall drive a horse across the bridge faster than a walk.' " "The lawyer's response brought a dismissal: "I still claim there is no case. She is a woman and she was driving a mare." The rickety, smelly old bridge was regarded as a blot on the landscape, and to the joy of many it burned in 1895. Thirteen years later, a fine stone bridge named after Governor Bulkeley replaced it.

The river itself provided a delicacy for Hartford tables. Every morning during the spring months, a fresh catch of shad was sold on the docks. Members of the legislature who frequented the numerous taverns looked forward to shad dinners broiled over a wood fire. There was still considerable river traffic, over a thousand vessels a year tying up at the docks, half of them barges laden with coal, lumber, stone, and sand.

At the western end of the city, where the horse cars terminated their run, a unique intellectual colony flourished. This was Nook Farm, a wooded estate of over a hundred acres. Here gathered a lively group of writers and activists the prolific editor Charles Dudley Warner; America's first great woman novelist, Harriet Beecher Stowe; Senator Francis Gillette, whose son William created the stage version of Sherlock Holmes; the controversial suffragette Isabella Hooker, wife of a distinguished attorney; and, most illustrious of all, the irrepressible storyteller Mark Twain. It was a stimulating, closely-knit neighborhood. Each member's home was always open to the others. Mark Twain and his wife Livy often entered Mrs. Stowe's house by the kitchen door. Once, the great

Horse-powered omnibus on Farmington Avenue. (E. Irving Blomstrann)

author appeared without a tie or collar. Reprimanded by his wife for his unbecoming attire when he returned home, he decided to right matters by sending over, via his butler, a black tie and a collar. The aging Mrs. Stowe, not without wit herself, sent back this note: "Dear Mr. Clemens. You have discovered a principle…that a man can call by installments!"

Mark Twain's impression of his first visit to Hartford in 1868 had, on the whole, been favorable, although to his disgust he observed that nobody smoked on the streets and cigar stores were few and far between:

I think this is the best built and the handsomest town I have ever seen. They call New England the land of steady habits, and I can see the evidence about me that it was not named amiss... They have the broadest, straightest streets...that ever led a sinner to destruction, and the dwelling houses are the amplest in size...and have the most capacious ornamental grounds about them. This is the centre of Connecticut wealth.

In his report to the San Francisco newspaper for which he wrote, this free spirit from the untamed west was somewhat flabbergasted that Puritanism had not completely expired:

The Blue-Law spirit is not entirely dead in Connecticut yet. The law prohibiting the harboring of sinful playing cards in dwelling houses was annulled only something over a year ago. Up to that time, conscientious people...would no more think of keeping an entire pack of cards in their dwellings than they would have thought of driving for pleasure in these beautiful streets on the blessed Sabbath. Therefore, they never entered into a friendly game of 'draw' or 'old sledge'... without first taking a couple of cards from the pack and destroying them.

The morality of this locality is something marvelous. I have only heard one man swear and seen only one man drunk in the ten days I have been here. And the same man that did the swearing was the man that contained the drunk... Young ladies walk these streets alone as late as ten o'clock at night and are not insulted... Ladies of the highest respectability go freely to lectures and concerts at night in this city of 40,000 souls, without other escort than members of their own sex.

His long dark-brown hair falling in masses around his neck, his rolling gait like a sailor's, Twain became Hartford's most conspicuous figure on the street after he settled there. In winter he wore, instead of an overcoat, a sealskin jacket with the fur outside. Notoriously amusing to his neighbors and friends, nonetheless few appreciated his exalted literary reputation. As a schoolboy William Lyon Phelps was fascinated to hear him read from his new novel *Tom Sawyer.* Phelps said "he was the greatest master of the art of public reading then living, though he did not know it."

Phelps frequently saw Mark Twain standing on the balcony outside his billiard room, a cue in one hand and the eternal cigar in his mouth. Billiards was his only exercise, except walking; according to Phelps, he used to say: "Never stand when you can sit down; never sit when you can lie down." Young Phelps nearly ran afoul of the great humorist when, at twelve, he acquired a shotgun. One day hunting in the woods along the banks of the Little River, he espied a flock of white ducks. "I let them have both barrels, killing two and mortally wounding three." A schoolmate came running up. "What have you done? Those are Mark Twain's prize ducks. If you are caught, he will put you in jail! Run for your life!" Phelps managed to get home safely, but the next day was terrified to learn that a price had been put on his head. A notice in the paper offered a substantial reward for the apprehension of the "miscreant" who had killed Mr. Twain's ducks.

On Nook Farm, the handsomest member of the distinguished Beecher family lived comfortably in the shadow of her famous brother Henry and equally famous sister Harriet. Isabella Hooker's attractive home on Forest Street was usually filled with chatty female guests who never questioned their second-class condition, content to let their menfolk run the world. In the fall of 1867 Frances Ellen Burr, sister of the publisher of the Hartford *Times,* called on her to enlist her aid in organizing a woman's suffrage association. For two years Isabella mulled over what she should do; she hesitated to become involved with the notorious Anthonys and Stantons; she knew she would be ostracized by her fashionable friends, but that was of no account. With the moral courage exhibited by all the Beechers she finally cast her lot, and once committed to the cause she never wavered an instant for the next thirty-seven years, despite the opposition of her relatives.

Immediately and vigorously she staged the first suffrage convention in Connecticut at the Roberts Opera House in October, 1869. A two-day affair, it was packed with Hartford's best people to hear such luminaries as Julia Ward Howe, Henry Ward Beecher, Susan B. Anthony, Elizabeth Cady Stanton, and William Lloyd Garrison. Isabella herself was too retiring to speak on the platform. But at the third convention in 1871 she raised her voice and was elected president of the Connecticut Woman Suffrage Association. To Miss Burr, who became secretary, she prophesied: "You and I will hold our office as long as we live." Isabella became a unique leader of the suffrage movement, unflinching in her stand, always aiming straight at the mark, original in her ways, and oblivious to public opinion. Unlike some early feminists, she was not supercilious, charming everybody with her refined manner, racy wit, and warm hospitality. One of her friends at church whom Isabella was trying to recruit begged off by saying she disliked the name "woman's rights." "But, my dear, don't you know you have none. You don't even own your own child." Her friend became a convert.

Mrs. Hooker and her followers never expected suffrage to blossom out at once. As Miss Burr philosophized, "one bobolink doesn't make a summer, nor one snowstorm a winter." On the contrary, they knew they were up against the "blue law" mentality of reactionary legislators. "This ingrained prejudice and inability to appreciate a true principle will require the battering rams of years to beat down," said Miss Burr. It took them seven years to achieve their first success: a law giving married women the same property rights as men, an equality denied the Christian female for 18 centuries. From then on it was an unrewarding struggle against the prevailing ideal of womanhood. She was too pure, too fragile, too ethereal to be vulgarized by exposure to politics. Horace Bushnell said woman suffrage was "a reform against nature. John Hooker, however, stood behind his wife. He thought the ideal woman could be an informed citizen without losing her wifeliness or motherliness. Her former neighbor Mark Twain appreciated her contribution, saying that her splendid energies had helped to achieve the only revolution for the emancipation of half a nation that cost no blood.

* * *

With the elderly Rev. William Jarvis and her brother Richard to keep her company, Mrs. Colt concentrated on making her home on the western edge of the Colonel's mile-square domain the center of Hartford's social life. The Colonel himself had called Armsmear his "shanty," but in fact it was one of the most elaborate residences in New England. The Colonel spared no expense and neglected no detail to make it the shining symbol of his ambitious soul. A hundred feet long, it reminded the sophisticated of an Italian villa,

Armsmear. (Courtesy Connecticut Historical Society)

Armsmear and the Colt estate looking north and east. The armory can be seen in the background behind his home, while Potsdam Village and the Willow Ware Factory are in the right-hand corner. (From *Armsmear*)

though it embodied other architectural styles as well. A pair of marble dogs, copies of the ones adorning the Uffizi Palace in Florence, guarded the main gate.

From her octagonal boudoir and veranda, Mrs. Colt could look over an immense lawn, past an artificial lake where her little boy loved to fish for trout and black bass, toward the great Armory, the German village, the dike, the Colt wharf and ferry, and the Connecticut River. On her left were the deer park, in which peacocks and swans wandered, and a half-mile of greenhouses, her husband's favorite indulgence. To the south stretched the orchard, cornfields, and meadows. Downstairs she luxuriated in her oriental conservatory, its glass panels set in foilated arches of iron painted red, yellow, and royal purple. Baskets of flowers hung from chandeliers above and the central dome was capped with a golden pineapple. In his picture gallery, the Colonel displayed all the precious gifts he had received from foreign potentates. He especially treasured the gold and jeweled snuffbox from a grateful Turkish sultan. There were remembrances from the royalty of Russia, Italy, and Siam. Of his medals of honor, he most prized the one from the London Institute of Civil Engineers, in whose august body he was the first American inducted. Here, too, was the cradle of his first-born made from pieces of the historic Charter Oak tree.

Mrs. Colt never gave a moment's thought to remarriage. Her emotions were completely absorbed in what her husband had created and left her to oversee. Anxious to enhance his stature — to make him in death larger than in life — she set about memorializing his meteoric career in ink and in stone. Behind a Victorian facade of modest dignity, she nurtured strong convictions about good and evil. The Colonel, she knew, had an ample measure of both, and she made it her mission to see that the world remembered only the good. Hartford's distinguished educator, Henry Barnard, was commissioned to write his biography, which he did with so much discretion that it read like a paean. Between her home and the Armory, she built the Church of the Good Shepherd, a unique Episcopal edifice that startled every churchgoer in the city. The architect was the distinguished Edward Tuckerman Potter, who later was responsible for Mark Twain's Hartford home. The largest stained-glass window featured the prosperous Joseph in a remarkable likeness to the Colonel among his sheaves and loaves of bread, standing alongside Jesus and his lambs. The arches of the doorway, even the sacred mottoes in stone, were adorned with various parts of the Colt gun and the machines which made it. Mrs. Colt also saw to the spiritual content: she insisted on previewing the sermons before they were delivered on Sunday.

At the same time, she had Potter design a library for Armsmear, an imposing room dominated by massive Victorian black walnut bookcases and

THE GREAT WEST WINDOW

In Mrs. Colt's Church of the Good Shepherd

The special memorial in the Church of the Good Shepherd erected by Mrs. Colt in memory of her husband and their infant children is a large window enclosed in a massive setting of stone. On the exterior, it stands beneath the cross at the peak of the roof. From the interior, the window has on one side the figure of Joseph in Egypt distributing food, while beneath is the Colt coat-of-arms with its motto: "Vincit qui patitur," he that can endure overcometh. On the other side is the figure of the Good Shepherd, bearing the legend "He shall gather the lambs with His arm," and beneath are both the Colt and Jarvis family coats-of-arms. Above the window is a representation of the Angel of Peace. The window was dedicated in 1886. Dr. Billy Morgan, who lived with Mrs. John C. Wilson, the daughter of Colt's president John Hall, told this anecdote:

> *"When the Church of the Good Shepherd was built as a memorial to him, a stained glass window was erected showing a reaper gathering sheaves of wheat as truly emblematic of his character. A witty old lady caustically exclaimed: 'The Harvester indeed...Sam Colt would have fallen for Potiphar's wife and the window should have shown him on Mt. Sinai breaking all the Ten Commandments!' "*

Church of the Good Shepherd. (Courtesy Connecticut Historical Society)

Lake behind Armsmear. (Courtesy Connecticut Historical Society)

a gas-lighted chandelier. Even when electricity came into vogue, she retained gas fixtures throughout the house.

As her hair with its topknot turned gray, then snowy white, she reigned over Hartford society, the ideal and idealized churchwoman, colonial dame, and benefactress. Unfailingly gracious and cordial, the queen hostess' engraved invitations in black were not to be lightly refused. Her parties were on such a scale of lavishness and variety as to both shock and amaze her prim, conservative friends. In her gallery, she staged elaborate tableaux. Every Fourth of July the proper families came for an evening of fireworks that were set off across the lake. It was nothing for her to entertain two hundred for lunch, dinner, or a lawn fete.

Her first extravaganza, one December afternoon three years after the Colt fire, was the marriage of her sister Hettie Jarvis to a wealthy Hartfordian. Over a thousand guests flocked to the wedding and reception at Armsmear. From abroad came Mrs. Junius Morgan, two Russian commissioners, and other dignitaries who stayed at the Allyn House and were transported by a procession of carriages to Wethersfield Avenue. There were several former governors, Colt officials, two of the eight Cheney brothers and their wives, and the daughter of Harriet Beecher Stowe. They all marveled at the splendor of the mansion and the bridal party. The choicest flowers from the Colonel's hot houses adorned the rooms, which were illuminated by hundreds of gas and wax lights. While the Colt Band played softly, the guests inspected the wedding presents displayed in the billiard room — paintings, books, laces, jewelry, and so much silver that one flabbergasted lady observed that it seemed as if the whole of Tiffany's stock had been transferred to Hartford. In the conservatory, rare exotic plants bloomed and song birds flew freely about. Mrs. Colt wore a magnificent robe of black velvet with a coronet of diamonds in her hair. She was still in mourning for her husband but out of preference she would continue to wear black the rest of her life.

Undoubtedly, the most spectacular of her affairs was the Martha Washington reception and tea held at the Allyn House for two nights in April 1875 for the benefit of her favorite charity, the Union for Home Work. Two thousand of Hartford's best people turned out and contributed

Caldwell Colt. (Courtesy Church of the Good Shepherd)

$5,000 to help those left destitute by the panic of 1873 and the resulting depression. In the banquet hall were thirteen tables decorated with artifacts representing the original colonies. The evening began with a concert by the Colt Band, but the highlight was a tableau depicting the leading personalities after the Revolution. Dressed in appropriate costumes, some fifty couples took various roles. Mark Twain was Governor William Rivington, Mrs. Colt was Mrs. James Madison, "Collie" Colt was Monsieur Otto, and Mrs. Charles Beach occupied center stage as Martha. After the tableau came dancing. For years, every charity bazaar and fair in Hartford reflected the widow's enthusiasm and organizing ability.

When Caldwell reached his majority in 1879, a thousand guests again celebrated at Armsmear. Over the entrance to the reception room hung an enormous "21" in red roses. As the evening wore on, a group of young ladies and gentlemen in costume, their hair powdered, descended the staircase arm in arm singing Mother Goose rhymes. In the morning, one guest who had imbibed too much found himself on the living room floor rolled up in a rug.

Caldwell, the only one of her five children to live beyond infancy, naturally could do no wrong. Tall, athletic, with a drooping mustache, he became an ardent sportsman and handsome wastrel after graduating from Yale. His eye was as sharp for the shape of a woman as for the sheer of his beautiful yacht, in her day one of America's fastest racing vessels. His crowning honor was to become commodore of the Larchmont Yacht Club. His deck parties aboard the *Dauntless* were wild enough to inspire tales of orgies.

In the era of great ocean schooners the *Dauntless* was one of the largest, nearly 121 feet overall, and luxuriously furnished. Built in Mystic in 1866, she was owned for a time by James Gordon Bennett, founder of the New York *Herald.* Caldwell acquired her in 1882 and five years later entered her in a match race, with $10,000 at stake, from Sandy Hook to Queenstown, Ireland. Her rival was the new and larger schooner *Coronet.* Caldwell engaged Captain "Bully" Samuels as master, a hard-driving veteran of the sailing packet trade. With a professional crew of sixteen aboard, the old schooner plunged through the wild March seas of the North Atlantic, at times under bare poles before hurricane-force winds. Disregarding the presence of icebergs and the cold water leaking through the hull, Captain Samuels never let up. His best day's run, 328 miles, set a record. At one point the ship's water tank ruptured, forcing the crew to quench their thirst on spirits for the rest of the fifteen-day voyage.

It was all in vain, however, for *Coronet* won by 30 hours.

* * *

When Mrs. Colt went to bed on Sunday, March 11th the weather was mild for that time of the year — in fact the mildest winter in 17 years — around forty degrees and raining. At two in the morning, awakened by a rattling of the window panes, she looked out and was surprised to see snow coming down in blinding sheets propelled by a fury of wind. The next morning, Hartford was being buried under three feet of wet snow. As far as she could see up Wethersfield Avenue toward Main Street lay enormous drifts, some ten to twelve feet high. Nothing moved. The silence was eerie. The Great Blizzard of 1888, New England's worst storm since the advent of the railroad and telegraph, had paralyzed the city.

The storm blew hard all day Monday and ended Tuesday noon, but the wind continued to howl until dark. Mrs. Colt wondered how the Armory was faring. Her coachman brought her the news that, like most other factories, it had been closed. Many workers, unable to get home, spent the night near their machines or sought shelter with strangers. Eight girls who tried to leave one plant stood helpless outside until, like Alpine climbers, they were roped together and pulled by men at the head of the line, who broke a path for them. Businessmen downtown gave up any thought of reaching home Monday night, even if it meant only a short journey, and crowded into the hotels. Milk sleighs were abandoned. On North Main Street, boys raided the cans and had ice cream for supper. A hearse bearing the remains of James Mullaly overturned, but the undertakers managed to find an express wagon that carried him to the Blue Hills cemetery where he was safely interred. Mrs. Charles Sealim was aroused by a loud crackling noise. Awaking her husband, who kept a livery stable, and two snowbound milkmen passing the night with them, they escaped from the house just as the roof and walls caved in. Their eleven horses were unharmed. Caspar Kreutzer, after enjoying himself at Koch's saloon, became so confused as to his whereabouts that he ended up in a deep snowbank where he was retrieved by two alert young men. The train from Boston was blocked by a snowdrift at Vernon, and fifty-two passengers were marooned in the local depot until Wednesday night.

Fortunately, Wednesday dawned clear and mild. The good weather brought people outdoors to marvel at the drifts and good-naturedly lend a hand where needed. Not a street or sidewalk was passable. Youngsters overcame this difficulty by making snowshoes out of boards or barrel staves. Eight-horse teams with plows began to clear the tracks of the horse railway. That afternoon, the Pratt & Whitney factory on Capitol Avenue exhausted its coal supply. In desperation a procession of several hundred employees, joined by others from the nearby shops of Weed Sewing Machine and Hartford Machine Screw, marched down to the Commerce Street coal yard. There they attached ropes to a sleigh laden with two tons of coal and dragged it back to the plant.

Good humor prevailed. In front of the Allyn House barber shop was an immense snow tunnel surmounted by a pole with a sign: "This Way to the Chinese Laundry." Another sign pointed north along the solid white mass that concealed Main Street: "This Way to Temple Street. Keep Off the Grass." Outside the opera house a pair of men's shoes, soles up, stuck up out of a large drift; some wag had placed a board behind them with the inscription: "Remains of Steve Clark."

Except for footpaths made by shoppers armed with baskets on their way to the grocery stores, most streets were still uncleared by Thursday. The Horse Railway Company had three hundred men clearing tracks, and Mrs. Colt observed a blue car pulled by four horses on a return trip from Asylum Street. The Jewell Belt factory dispatched a four-horse team to escort its president from an enforced stay at the Allyn House to his home on Washington Street. The Union for Home Work was besieged with calls for relief. Mayor Morgan Bulkeley paid a visit to its director and told her to spare no effort to provide the needy with coal and food and to send him the bills. On Friday the "Belle of Hartford" omnibus sleigh made it from downtown west to the city line, where in the vicinity of Mark Twain's house residents were finding that the easiest way to exit from their homes was by means of a ladder from their second-story windows. By Saturday, transportation within and from the city was running again and business was back to normal. In his sermon Sunday, the mathematical-minded minister of Center Church computed the volume of snow that had been dumped on Connecticut at 15.457 billion cubic feet.

* * *

In the Gay Nineties the skyline of Hartford hugged the ground, save for the church spires pointing hopefully heavenward. Aside from bicycling, the best way for a young man to entertain his girl was to ride the trolley. Young people took long evening rides, sometimes getting off to dance at a pavilion in Farmington or Laurel Park. They liked best the two-step to Sousa's marches and the waltzes of Victor Herbert and Strauss. They flocked to the new Parsons Theatre to see the latest plays. Downtown lawyers frequented the saloon run by Fritz Barby under the Opera House, sitting around a long table near the goldfish pool. Mark Twain still cut quite a swath as he rode about in his carriage, smoking his pipe. At Nook Farm, Harriet Beecher Stowe, now in her dotage, wandered aimlessly, picking flowers and chatting with the neighborhood children. The closing of Twain's great house for good in 1891 and his flight from Hartford signaled the end of the literary enclave.

Politicians and businessmen swept aside the intelligentsia as the leading lights. The city's power structure was dominated by such giants as James Batterson, president of the Travelers Insurance Company; the Rev. Francis Goodwin, who did well in real estate and did good by masterminding Hartford's park system; Colonel Pope and George Day, who were creating a bicycle and automobile empire; Senator Joseph Hawley, lawyer, editor, soldier, and — many claimed — statesman; and Morgan G. Bulkeley, who towered above them all.

Coming to Hartford as a young man before the Civil War, Hawley plunged into politics as a Free-Soiler and anti-slavery man. At the battle of Bull Run, he earned the nickname of "Fighting Joe." Later he was elected governor, congressman, and senator. In between, he became editor of the *Courant.* As chairman of the Centennial Exposition in Philadelphia in 1876, he achieved national prominence. In every Presidential campaign, he was drafted as a speaker. A magnetic personality who inspired men to follow him, he often appeared brusque and impulsive, either idealizing his contemporaries or judging them harshly.

Morgan G. Bulkeley was his political rival and far more able in everything he attempted. His father had been president of Aetna Life Insurance Company during its early years. As a boy, Morgan used to sweep out the small one-room office for a dollar a week. Following a career in trade and banking, he was made the third president of Aetna. He also had a natural flair for politics, serving eight years as mayor of Hartford, as governor from 1889 until 1893, and as senator for six years after Hawley's death in 1905. He was behind the building of the new bridge over the Connecticut River, the saving of the Old State House from destruction, the bringing of electricity to the city, the founding of the National Baseball League, and the development of an exclusive summer resort for the well-to-do at the mouth of the Connecticut River.

None of Hartford's leaders could be branded a greedy and ruthless exploiter. They agreed with Charles Dudley Warner that "in the United States...the labouring class is better...than it ever was in history, and there is little poverty except that which is inevitably the accompaniment of human weakness and crime." While Mrs. Colt and the Nook Farm residents, believing in the ideal of humanitarian brotherhood, felt compassionate over the city's poor, the businessmen tended to criticize charity as responsible for idleness and pauperism. The best way to overcome it, they asserted, was to let business continue to provide the benefits of material progress which eventually would filter down to the bottom. Not until the next century would the social justice of an unfettered economic system be called into question and rampant industrialism brought to heel.

Fourth of July brought out the populace more than any other holiday for an all-day celebration. In the morning a long parade preceded a concert featuring Colt's or Weed's Band, a balloon ascension in Colt Park, horse racing in Charter Oak Park, culminating in the evening with two hours of fireworks on the State Capitol grounds. The *Courant* described one year's finale as "a gorgeous temple of Corinthian pillars, surrounded by eagle and shield, Washington on horseback in the center, and flanked by a life-sized statue of Lincoln on the left and [President] Garfield on the right, with batteries and vases, all in colored lance-work. This piece terminates with a grand flight of 150 rockets and a brilliant illumination of the Capitol grounds."

During these years, Mrs. Colt hid her disappointment over "Collie's" long absences from the city and the tales of his expensive escapades by devoting herself to the welfare of Samuel, the Colonel's nephew and ward. Despite his unsavory inheritance, Mrs. Colt adored the unassuming young man, opened Armsmear for his fashionable wedding to a lass from Savannah in 1863, and presented the couple with a nice home across the street. Later, he became a gentleman farmer in Farmington, bred cattle, and raised a large family.

Under the strangest of circumstances Caldwell, at the age of 36, died in Punta Garda, Florida in mid-January, 1894. The cause of his death was reported as heart failure after a severe case of tonsillitis, but soon rumor circulated that aboard the ketch *Oriole,* which he kept in Florida waters for winter cruising, he had been shot by a jealous husband who caught him in bed with his wife. Recent research reveals a different and probably more accurate account: on the night in question, he was hosting a raucous party aboard *Oriole*, fell off, and drowned.

Speaking for the people of Hartford, Mayor William Waldo Hyde, a friend of Caldwell's since boyhood, praised the wealthy heir to the Colt fortune as "A large-hearted man with generous impulses." The body was returned to Hartford, with funeral services at Armsmear and the Church of the Good Shepherd, two days before his mother had planned to celebrate the 25th anniversary of its consecration. Five hundred Colt employees flanked the route of the hearse and carriages down Wyllys Street from Armsmear to the church. Two of the honorary bearers were the armory's John Hall and Colonel William Skinner. After the second service, the Colt's Band played "Home Again" and a hymn on the church lawn and accompanied the family to Cedar Hill cemetery where they rendered "Nearer My God to Thee" and "Rock of Ages."

Mrs. Colt's only surviving child was gone, but somehow the Colt name must go on! Grief stricken, the *grande dame* of Armsmear promptly built him an elaborate memorial next door to her church to serve as a parish house and recreation hall. Again she chose Potter as the architect. Costing $300,000, its design and decoration carried out the theme of "Collie's" love for the sea, like a great ship gone aground. Inside and out the building was studded with replicas of the prows of ancient ships. Instead of windows, there were portholes, and a ship's bridge ran along the ridge pole to the small spire shaped like a mast. The second floor was actually built like a deck, with a slight declination toward the port and starboard sides. The facilities included a bowling alley, library, lecture hall, and a full length portrait of Commodore Colt by Eastman Johnson.

At the dedication in September, 1896 the Rev. Leverett Bradley of Philadelphia, tutor and outdoor companion to Caldwell for three years during his mid-teens, recalled his generosity both in thought and deed: "He was not a student, not a lover of books... He was fond of sports and himself an ardent sportsman... He always insisted on fair play... He was absolutely fearless and would share with a friend in need though it were the last dollar, the last crust, or the last cigar."

Mrs. Colt refused to sell the *Dauntless* and in-

In the Gay Nineties, Hartford's well-to-do resided on Washington Street. (E. Irving Blomstrann)

Colt employees in the Gay Nineties. (Courtesy R.L. Wilson)

Caldwell Colt Memorial. (Courtesy E. Irving Blomstrann)

stead converted the vessel into a houseboat in Essex, its home port, where once a year without fail she retreated aboard for several days of contemplation. Not that she turned into a recluse, for she often remarked that her reliable cure for low spirits was to visit someone worse off than herself. But, as she approached seventy, her entertainments were infrequent. Armsmear took on a stern and gloomy cast; the trees along the driveway to the barn had grown so huge she could no longer see the Armory. Unseen, she thought, but not out of mind. What would become of it?

* * *

In the spring of 1901, as President Richard Jarvis impatiently awaited the day of his retirement and Mrs. Colt increasingly worried over the future of the Armory, the International Association of Machinists was flexing its muscles to fight for the nine-hour day. Fifty thousand machinists and metal workers went on strike across the country in May. Some 2,500 in Hartford joined the walkout, led by the workers at Pratt & Whitney and Electric Vehicle. The tough-minded president of Hartford Machine Screw, George Fairfield, countered this action with a lock-out. Colt's 750 workers stayed on the job. A few belonged to the union, but the majority were content with their wages and had no cause for complaint. Unlike the employees in the other shops, a large number had worked for Colt's all their lives, as did their fathers before them, and many still lived in Colt-built tenements behind the Armory.

Hartford manufacturers were thrown off balance by the concerted stoppage. Although convinced that the nine-hour day was an inevitable concession, they resisted the idea of paying ten hours wages for an hour's less work. George Fairfield, for one, let his views be known. "Why, that would be a 20 percent increase!" he told a reporter. Fairfield's parsimony was common knowledge. On one occasion, he was overheard arguing with one of his "hands" for more than an hour in

THE COLT PARISH HOUSE

Erected in 1895, the Parish House next to the Church of the Good Shepherd was built by Mrs. Colt as a grieving mother's memorial to her only surviving child. She called Edward Tuckerman Potter, architect of the church and the Mark Twain House, out of retirement to design the building. His conception was that of a ship to celebrate Caldwell Colt's love of the sea. The cost of construction was $300,000. Instead of windows, there were portholes and a ship's bridge ran along the ridge pole to a spire shaped like a mast. The building included a library, kitchen, small parlors, ballroom, bowling alley, and billiard room. Early in the 1960s the Church and Parish House renewed their ministry for the low-income residents of the neighborhood. In 1970s the Colt Bequest funded the Martin Luther King Housing Project in an effort to provide affordable housing. Both the Church and Parish House have been renovated in recent years.

his paneled office. Finally, the door swung open, and the president shouted at his bookkeeper: "Raise Clarence five cents a week." Assuming a statesmanlike pose, Fairchild told the same reporter he also opposed time and one-half after nine hours — another union demand. "Now, a machine doesn't earn any more at night than during the day; the screws we make after six sell for the same price as those made during regular working hours."

None of the manufacturers had any intention of giving the union recognition. Billings & Spencer decided to have a showdown when Superintendent F.C. Billings heard that his men were set to strike at five o'clock. After lunch he posted a notice offering a 54-hour week instead of 60, with a wage increase of 12½ percent. He also passed the word that any one leaving the job at five would be paid off for good. Around four o'clock, a crowd of strikers from the other factories gathered in front of Billings & Spencer to cheer the expected recruits to their side. It was a tense moment. The deadline came, but Billings' employees did not wash up. Billings had won.

Even so, the union refused to give in. There was no violence or picketing; the machinists merely stayed home. The union leader revealed that in addition to the nine-hour day, his members wanted a signed agreement, a restriction on the number of apprentices, and a grievance procedure. On the third day of the city-wide walk-out, Col. Albert Pope, then managing the American Bicycle Company, called a strategy meeting of fifty Hartford employers behind closed doors. George Fairfield presided. Pope closed his plant the next day. But a week passed with no progress; again the manufacturers gathered in Pope's office, mainly for the purpose of forming for the first time an employers' association to present a united defense against the union.

The president of the Central Labor Union, Ignatius Sullivan, now came forward with a peace plan. A persuasive Irishman from the East Side, he made the rounds of the employers and suggested that instead of outright union recognition, they sit down with a shop committee of their own employees. In this way, their differences could be discussed and resolved between themselves, without having union leaders present. His idea was well received by Colonel Pope, Cushman Chuck, and Pratt & Whitney. They did sit down and agree to a full ten hours pay for nine hours of work, but nothing more. Mrs. Colt had a similar notice posted at Colt's over her signature. The strike was broken; higher wages were of greater moment to the machinists than the other demands. On Monday every plant hummed again, except for Hartford Machine Screw where old man Fairfield still held out.

For Mrs. Colt, her brother's ill health was the last straw added to her burden of grief. During the last third of his tenure as president he had endured a great deal of suffering, and no sooner did he step down than he became an invalid at Armsmear. Vice-president John Hall was also unwell and anxious to return to Portland. The time had come not merely for another change of command but to sell the Armory. Before the strike, Mrs. Colt instructed her managers to find a private buyer. It seemed a better alternative to going public or selling her stock to employees. Hall and his right-hand, William C. Skinner, approached the Boston and New York financial house of Armstrong & Schirmer. Led by Morgans and Rockefellers, American business was being consumed by trust fever. In Hartford, Colonel Pope's bicycle trust had collapsed but he was striving to establish one for the gas buggy. Armstrong & Schirmer hoped to do the same for the munitions industry. Colt's capital stock amounted to a million dollars, but Elizabeth Colt received substantially more. Hall was induced to stay on as president at a salary of $20,000, with Colonel William C. Skinner as his back-up. In June the sale was consummated, and the Colt family ownership of fifty-four years ended. President Hall himself survived only one year, and the following January, on the ninth anniversary of Caldwell's death, Richard Jarvis died, leaving his sister alone in her mansion.

Plump and sedate, looking more than a little like Queen Victoria, Mrs. Colt still rode about the city in her carriage. Her Irish footman and coachman were equally corpulent. Just as she would have nothing to do with electricity, so she disdained the latest mode of travel the — automobile — ignoring the excitement created by her neighbor George Day's electric vehicle as he drove to work. She still entertained. The Taylor family across the street were invited to a luncheon, for ladies only, to honor Mrs. Wilkes and other guests from North Carolina. At 1:30 they were served, in order, grapefruit from Mrs. Colt's greenhouse, bouillon, lobster chops with cucumbers, creamed sweetbreads and rolls, breast of chicken and potatoes, jelly patties, creamed celery, tomato jelly salad, cheese sticks, charlotte russe, brandied peaches with cakes, bonbons, nuts, and other fruits. Sauterne wine accompanied the early courses and champagne the entree. Afterwards, coffee was served in the parlor.

In the summer of 1905, Elizabeth Hart Jarvis Colt knew she too was going to die. She paid one last call to the *Dauntless,* gave her blessing to the final details of Colonel Colt's statue being erected in Colt Park, even prepared little gifts as remembrances for her closest friends, boxed and tied with white ribbons. Many of her dearest possessions she willed to the Wadsworth Athenaeum — portraits, miniatures, marbles, snuff boxes, jardinieres, glass vases, and Dresden china — and, of course, the Colonel's personal collection of guns. She left orders that her five horses were to be shot and buried. On August 21st she died quickly at the summer home of her niece, Elizabeth Hart Beach Robinson, in Newport.

Compared to the operatic spectacular staged for Colonel Colt, her funeral at the Church of the Good Shepherd was spartan, though the Colt Band somberly played a march outside while the mourners emptied from their carriages. The minister, well aware she had bequeathed $800,000 to maintain the church and parish house, paid her a warm tribute: "Hers was an aristocracy of goodness, hers a nobility of Christian character. Do you not see, my brethren, what a privilege has been yours to worship side by side with such a woman and to witness the constant evidence of such practical and humble Christianity!" Her palace, Armsmear, became a home for the widows of Episcopal clergymen, and the likes of what Samuel Colt had wrought, and over which she had presided for nearly fifty years, would never be seen again.

CHAPTER V

THE HORSELESS BOOM

The colorful Colt Band, which played at every important function in Hartford including Trinity College commencements, was not the only extra-curricular activity of Colt employees. For a short while, another was the Colt Bicycle Club. It had been formed in 1890 at the height of the bicycle craze in America. There were thirty-two charter members, headed by L.C. Grover, then superintendent of the Armory. The enthusiastic wheelmen chose black and gold as their colors and spent $13.67 for each complete uniform. They made various "runs" and appeared in parades, winning prizes for "best appearance." Seven years later, they suddenly disbanded after a banquet at the Hotel Hartford enlivened by the Colt orchestra and Negro entertainers.

The bicycling fever during the Gay Nineties had all begun in Hartford with the founding of the Pope Manufacturing Company, which in its heyday was Hartford's largest industry and first monopoly. The capital of Connecticut might also have become the automobile capital of the United States had not Detroit existed, had Henry Ford remained a farmer, and had the Selden patent been upheld. Over a span of twenty years, Pope not only mass-produced the "safety" bicycle but also introduced the electric carriage, formed an automobile trust, and almost — but not quite — prevented Ford from becoming the kingpin of the gas buggy. The meteoric rise and fall of this newcomer to Hartford wrote a spectacular chapter in the saga of American enterprise.

Its founder, Albert A. Pope, was born in Boston. His father's financial reverses forced him to support himself from boyhood by peddling vegetables house to house after school and during vacations. At nineteen he enlisted in the Union Army, fought in many campaigns, commanded "Fort Hell" before Petersburg, and led his regiment in the last attack on that city. At the end of the Civil War he had risen to lieutenant-colonel. With $900 in his pocket, he plunged into the manufacture of slipper decorations and built up a successful dealership in shoe supplies.

Almost pure chance brought him to Hartford. The chain of events started at the Philadelphia Centennial Exposition in 1876, where Colonel Pope saw for the first time, as did many of his countrymen, the velocipede, that strange contraption with its enormous front wheel and solid rubber tire. Fascinated, he came back again and again to study the exhibit and to figure out how anyone could ride such an apparently unsteady machine. At the time only England made the velocipede, and it was touted as being twice as fast as a horse. As is frequently the case with a brand new technology, the public looked upon the vehicle with disdain. Horses didn't like it either. Municipal ordinances banned it from parks and avenues.

But Pope, on the lookout for a practical invention that he could turn into a profitable and useful product, believed he had found the perfect thing. He journeyed to England to learn more, bought patent rights for manufacture at home and imported a number of the machines. In 1877, the visit of an English cycle maker, John Harwinton, set his future course of action once and for all. Harwinton offered to make an experimental model, which he did at a cost of $338. It weighed about 75 pounds. Pope learned to ride the cumbersome machine and wasted no time in organizing the Pope Manufacturing Company.

Instead of building his own plant, however, he decided to contract the first order. In the spring of

1906 Pope-Tribune Touring Car. (Courtesy Connecticut Historical Society)

Pope-Hartford Touring Car 1909. (Courtesy Connecticut Historical Society)

1878 he approached George A. Fairfield, president of Weed Sewing Machine, which had a reputation for skilled craftsmen and machinists (many of whom, like Fairfield himself, had been Colt-trained), and for its ability to mass produce. Weed had been in Hartford since 1865, eventually occupying the Sharps Rifle plant. Fairfield had been the largest machinery contractor for Colt's until the close of the Civil War, and at the same time operated the city's first mechanical drawing school. In a few years he would leave Weed to run Hartford Machine Screw, which he had recently organized with his good friend Christopher Spencer. He had known the inventor since both were connected with the Armory.

The meeting between Pope and Fairfield was fortuitous in more ways than one. The sewing machine business had become fiercely competitive, threatening Weed's very survival. From an historical standpoint, bringing the bicycle concept to Weed was a logical step in the evolution of Eli Whitney's system of interchangeable parts, which had steadily advanced from guns to clocks and then to sewing machines, and which would reach its apex in the assembly of automobiles. On this occasion Pope even brought his model, riding it from the railroad station to the Weed factory, followed by scores of wide-eyed youngsters. Fairfield caught the Bostonian's enthusiasm and convinced a reluctant board of directors to accept the order for fifty machines. Some of his directors were certain the bicycle would never amount to anything more than an expensive toy, and the company would lose its shirt on what would probably be the last as well as the first order.

They were almost right. Weed encountered one difficulty after another: learning to forge the head, shaping the rims of the wheels properly so as to hold the tires, finding a cement to bind the latter to the flat sides of the rims, fabricating the handlebars and cranks without brittleness (by using Norwegian iron). Weed made every part except for the tires. Weighing in at sixty pounds, the production version was called the "Columbia," the first commercial self-propelled vehicle in America.

To the surprise of nearly everyone except Pope the machines sold readily. They proved sturdy yet extremely hazardous — unless the rider kept his weight back, he would be pitched forward over the wheel and land on his head. But a decade later Pope's introduction of the "safety" bicycle, with its equal-size wheels and chains, quickly made earlier versions obsolete. Until then, the Weed plant devoted most of its space to producing about a thousand a year of the "ordinary" or high-wheel type. Pope, in turn, set up six hundred salesrooms around the country, issued a catalog, and established a riding school in Boston. In 1882, he founded and supported the *Wheelman*, a magazine edited by S.S. McClure, while Thomas Stevens made history by riding around the world on a Columbia. Hartford's first bicycle parade in September 1885, featured three hundred uniformed riders on high-wheel Columbias, including Colonel Pope, who pumped along the dusty streets from the Capitol, led by a corps of buglers in an Irish jaunting car. Columbia became as generic a name for the bicycle as Kodak did for the camera and Singer for the sewing machine. In jig time the English monopoly was broken.

The spark plug of the Weed operation was George H. Day, a robust, mustachioed, dynamic man who lived next door to the Colts in a house built by Colonel Colt's brother James. His family came from the manufacturing village of Dayville in eastern Connecticut, where his great-grandfather had founded a cotton mill. He was also a descendant of General Israel Putnam. After several years as an insurance clerk, Day joined Weed and was soon in charge of the bicycle division. An enthusiastic cyclist himself, he formed the Connecticut Bicycle Club. Widely admired for his executive ability, warm personality, and unfailing tact, he was elected Weed's president in 1887. By 1890 the sewing machine market had collapsed, but Weed had six hundred men employed on safety bicycles alone. Colonel Pope, already part owner of the company, now decided he wanted complete control, and Day agreed to step down to the position of vice-president and treasurer. Weed's name was changed to the Pope Manufacturing Company.

In 1894, having erected a handsome, cream-colored office building on Capitol Avenue, with a paneled apartment for himself on the top floor, the Colonel moved his staff and clerks from Boston. Once a week he took the train down himself, arrived about noontime, worked until midnight, and returned the next evening. Year after year the company grew. New production methods were introduced for making pedals, hubs, spokes, and other parts. Pope set up the first metallurgical laboratory in New England; took over the Hartford Cycle Works,[1] a competitor; the Hartford Rubber Works,[2] which had pioneered the pneumatic tire in 1889; and built a separate facility for supplying nickel tubing. At its peak, the Pope complex occupied eighteen acres of factory space, in which nearly 4,000 worked; it was by far the largest factory in Hartford.

Cycling in those days was an adventure into a

wilderness of ill-kept dirt roads. Colonel Pope, aghast at the deplorable condition of the streets in Hartford and other cities, launched a campaign for better roads everywhere, spending $20,000 a year of his own money. To demonstrate what a good road should be, he built a section of macadam on Columbus Avenue in Boston, lobbied for a road engineering bureau in the U.S. Department of Agriculture, and aroused Congress and the state legislature. Pleased with his success in Hartford, and emulating the paternalism of Colonel Samuel Colt a generation earlier, he approved George Day's ideas for providing housing and recreation for his workers. Across Capitol Avenue, Columbia Street and Park Terrace were laid out and filled with attractive nine-room homes.[3] At this time, several wealthy public-spirited citizens were being persuaded to donate land for new parks in the city. Pope himself gave seventy-five acres to the south of his housing development for the creation of Pope Park — and $100,000 for its maintenance. In his offering letter to the city fathers he said:

I believe that a large part of the success of any manufacturing business depends upon the health, happiness and orderly life of its employees, and that in like manner a city thrives best by caring and providing for the well-being of its citizens. Your city is in need of open breathing places and pleasure grounds which should be scattered in different regions and so laid out and arranged as to afford the means of recreation and pleasure to all classes of law-abiding citizens.

There were now more than three hundred manufacturers of safety bicycles. Pope had geared itself to turn out one every minute — 50,000 a year. At least a million persons were awheel. Cycling clubs helped to open up travel between towns. Racing meets were held. On weekends in Hartford energetic young men engaged in "century runs — a hundred-mile jaunt through the countryside. Bicycle lawn parties were fashionable. One ardent wheelwoman who arranged such an affair at her home specified on the invitation that the guests wear "bicycle suits." Upon arrival, they surrendered their wheels to a young black maid who handed them a check. She was instructed to place a corresponding number on each bike, which she did by pinning it to the pneumatic tire. To their dismay, as they took their leave, the guests discovered that the front tire of every bike had a puncture.

The bicycle fad, however, peaked by 1896 and at the turn of the century was all over. Even so, there was no doubt that Americans were ready for the freedom of individual travel, and a bevy of inventors sought its fulfillment by means of a mechanized vehicle. A young engineer, Henry Percy Maxim, son of the inventor of the Maxim gun and an M.I.T. graduate, was one. In Lynn, Massachusetts he designed a three-cylinder gasoline engine and attached it to a Columbia tricycle. In 1895, he called upon his friend Hayden Eames in Hartford. Eames, a profane, blue-eyed down-Easterner, was then manager of Pope's tube division and eventually became general manager of Studebaker. Introduced to George Day, Maxim found his

[1] The Hartford Cycle Company, located at 75 Commerce Street, operated from 1890-95. Harry M. Pope was superintendent, David J. Post secretary-treasurer. They made models for men and ladies, with both solid and cushion tires. Their output approximated 40 a day compared to 100 a day for Pope Manufacturing. In February 1892, George Pope wrote David Post: "The Ladies Safety with pneumatic tires is the daintiest and best machine on the market at most any price. It ought to make a great seller and is good enough for the Queen to ride."

[2] During Colonel Colt's lifetime, another Samuel Colt was growing up in Hartford and years later bought the Rubber Works. Samuel Pomeroy Colt was born in 1852, the son of Christopher Colt — Colonel Colt's brother — and of Theodora deWolf, daughter of General George deWolf of Bristol, Rhode Island. Christopher Colt operated a silk mill in Ware, Massachusetts and died in 1855. Samuel P. Colt went to school in Hartford along with his older brother LeBaron Bradford Colt (1846-1924). Later they both settled in Bristol, practiced law in Providence and sired the Rhode Island branch of the Colt family. LeBaron became a U.S. district and circuit judge, and from 1913, until his death, served in the U.S. Senate.

Samuel P. Colt's career was equally distinguished. A graduate of MIT and Columbia Law School, he served as a state legislator and attorney general of Rhode Island. In 1887, the National India Rubber Company in Bristol went bankrupt. Colt was appointed receiver and, to everyone's surprise, soon had it making money.

In Hartford the next year, the Hartford Rubber Works was formed from the Gray Company, which in 1885 introduced the solid rubber bicycle tire for Colonel Pope's vehicles. Seven years later, in 1892, Pope acquired the Rubber Works. That same year the U.S. Rubber Company was organized as a holding company in New Jersey; by the turn of the century it controlled 15 manufacturers who accounted for 75 percent of all rubber footwear in the country, including the pioneer firm of Samuel J. Lewis & Company, which began to make India rubber shoes in Naugatuck in 1843 under Goodyear's patent.

(Footnote continued on page 78)

Hartford on Wheels

Colt Bicycle Club after winning first prize in a Washington, D.C. meet in July, 1892.

A Hartford-made Electric Vehicle.

(Courtesy E. Irving Blomstrann)

cordiality irresistible. He accepted an offer as chief engineer of a new undertaking, the Motor Carriage Department.

The first major decision was to develop an electric carriage, which Eames called a stop-gap until the gasoline engine could be perfected. Day journeyed to Europe several times to learn all he could about the French electrics. Maxim described the tremendous task: "Everything had to be created. There were no suitable bearings, suitable wheels, tires, batteries, battery-handling equipment, battery-charging equipment, brakes, or steering gears. Every detail of a motor vehicle had to be laboriously thought out and then worked out." In less than a year Maxim completed his first car, "a lovely little Mark I phaeton. It was quiet, reliable, easily operated, and fast enough..." The following year, May 1897, the Mark III electric was offered to the public at a price of $3,000. It had an operating radius of thirty miles and a top speed of twelve miles per hour, ideal for cruising about the city.

Under the headline "HORSELESS ERA COMES," the Hartford *Courant* welcomed the Mark III with this comment: "The idea of sitting in a smooth rolling carriage, nothing in front of the dashboard but space...is something exhilarating and fascinating." The rival *Times* stated that "its cost of maintenance and operation should be much less than that of a pair of horses." The editor added that he had "never found anyone so stupid that they could not run the carriage, but there are many who can't handle a horse." Among the early owners were the tycoons Andrew Carnegie, Thomas Fortune Ryan, and Harry Payne Whitney. Its debut marked the real beginning of the automobile industry in America, even though Ford had produced his first car, a quadricycle, a year before.

Meanwhile Maxim, and his crew had been working feverishly on the gasoline engine. In a few weeks they installed one in a Crawford runabout, the most advanced style of carriage, with ball-bearing wheels and rubber tires. In the initial road experiment, recalled Maxim, the buggy "shook and trembled and rattled and clattered, spat oil, fire, smoke, and smell." George Day "could not picture the possibility of perfecting such a terrible contraption." With his innate sense of marketing, Colonel Pope said: "You cannot get people to sit over an explosion. Until much improved, go ahead with the electrics — they're quiet, safe and easily controlled."

In 1897, Maxim successfully ran a Model Mark VII tricycle with a gasoline engine to Springfield, repeating the feat of Duryea's car four years earlier — the first to be built and operated in the United States. The next year, Maxim had on the road a four-wheel vehicle which traveled from Hartford to Boston, with repeated stops due to frightened horses and dreadful roads. It had a two-cylinder, air-cooled engine in front, hot-tube ignition, and foot pedal acceleration. George Day was still unimpressed. He feared that the clutch, gearbox, and necessary lubrication made it too complicated for the average person to drive. "We are on the wrong track," he told Maxim. "No one will buy a carriage that has to have all that greasy machinery in it." Later, he admitted his error. His daughter Josephine, however, was proud to be the first woman to operate her own gas buggy, although Hartford's high and mighty Park Commission chairman, the Rev. Francis Goodwin, refused to let her drive through Keney Park in what he condemned as "an abomination against nature."

[2] In 1901 U.S. Rubber chose Samuel P. Colt as its fifth president. Over the next 17 years, Colt directed the company's growth from $25 million in sales to $225 million, and its expansion into tires, chemicals, textiles, rubber plantations, and research. In 1917, it absorbed the old Hartford Rubber Works along with three other tire produces and adopted as its brand name "U.S. Royal." For its footwear it picked the brand name "KEDS." In 1919, after Colt's retirement, U.S. Rubber erected a six-story building on Park Street in Hartford for making 10,000 tires a day.

Thus, from 1857 until the Colonel's death there were three Samuel Colts living in Hartford: Colonel Sam Colt; his real nephew Samuel P. Colt, son of Christopher; and Samuel Caldwell Colt, either the son of brother John or the bastard son of the colonel. There are also two Colt Parks, the one given to Hartford by Mrs. Samuel Colt in memory of the Colonel and the other a state park in Bristol, Rhode Island created by the sale of 443 acres of farmland to the state by Samuel P. Colt's heirs. One of the latter's sons married the actress Ethel Barrymore.

[3] The 1892 Report of the Hartford Board of Trade (organized in 1888) reported: "The Pope Manufacturing Company have secured a body of 110 acres, of which eight have been reserved for the tube plant. The remainder...has been laid out in streets and residence lots... Here homes worthy of the name are to be built on a large scale for working people... They propose to sell homes to employees at cost... Tenements, a disgrace to civilization, have been built here and are rented at exorbitant rates. Women may sicken and children may die, but Shylock pockets his two percent a month... Our first-class builders have been powerless to stop the evil."

In one of the country's earliest motor car races, at Branford, Connecticut in 1899, Maxim's carriage surprisingly beat out a Stanley Steamer. The editor of an English technical journal, after an extensive tour of all the cities engaged in motor car production both here and abroad, concluded that "the town of Hartford, Connecticut is the greatest center of activity in the automobile industry today." Pope had now made and sold six hundred electrics — runabouts, dos-a-dos, surreys, buses, delivery wagons, and victorias. This same year, the Automobile Club of America was organized and the first automobile show, at Madison Square Garden, took place.

At the very moment that Colonel Pope's expectations stood at their highest, with the demand for electric carriages growing, the development of the gasoline engine progressing, and his own company on top, a financial storm engulfed him, of such force that even his resourcefulness could not prevent its bringing him to his knees. The main problem was the overproduction of bicycles; Pope had expanded too fast to meet the demand, and now it had been filled. In desperation the Colonel formed the American Bicycle Company, a trust of nearly one hundred manufacturers headquartered in Hartford, and retreated to Boston.

Meanwhile, in New York the Electric Vehicle Company was organized to provide cab service. John Jacob Astor and William C. Whitney, the father of Harry Payne and former secretary of the Navy, soon bought control and sought a supplier for 1,600 electric hansoms and broughams. Turning to Colonel Pope, they came to Hartford in April, 1899. With Captain Hayden Eames and George Day present at the meeting, Pope indicated that he wanted the business but lacked the resources. As the day wore on, a deal took shape. Whitney agreed to furnish a million dollars in cash to expand Pope's factories; the colonel threw in his assets which he valued at another million dollars; Whitney felt Electric Vehicle had the same worth. Thus was incorporated the Columbia & Electric Vehicle Company with a capitalization of $3,000,000.

Before signing an agreement, however, Whitney wondered about patent infringement should they decide to adopt the gasoline engine. Across the hall sat Herman F. Cuntz, Pope's patent attorney. Eames rushed into his office and pleaded for help. Cuntz produced the Selden patent. "For three years," he reminded Eames, "I've been warning you and Day that we ought to get a license, but you both never took me seriously." When Whitney examined the patent, he asked who owned it. Again Eames went to Cuntz, who gave him the information. As Cuntz later recalled, "In about five minutes Captain Eames came rushing back to me, jubilant and shouting 'we get the million dollars and must immediately contact that man Selden.' "

The merger with Whitney signaled the end of Pope's independence as a manufacturer and the plunge into the tumult of big business. Maxim called the event "the death knell of horseless carriage days." Whitney's group also owned the dominant Electric Storage Battery Company of Philadelphia, and the new combination now aimed to control electric cab service in every major city. Within two months, Pope and Day were expanding the Hartford facilities and bringing in new workers. They made the entire chassis and acquired William Hooker Atwood's carriage shop in New Haven to handcraft the body. The storage batteries alone weighed nearly a ton.

Directing this frantic activity was the chain-smoking, peripatetic George Day. On July 1, 1900, Whitney took over the Columbia part of Electric Vehicle from Pope, made Day president, and proceeded to consolidate all the related components. There emerged a trust embracing seventeen subsidiaries capitalized at almost $40 million, the largest enterprise of its kind. Yet, its stock declined sharply in value and dividends were never paid.[4]

Back in Boston, Pope bided his time until he saw the right opportunity for regaining control of at least the Hartford factories. It came with the bankruptcy of the bicycle trust. In a bold stroke, the Colonel picked up the pieces and moved his

[4] Commenting on the folly of trusts, the 1902 Report of Hartford's Board of Trade said: "As an independent enterprise the Pope Company held an impregnable position. With large reserves accumulated in the halcyon days of the trade, a magnificent series of plants, a highly efficient corps of men to fill its various departments, and a world-wide reputation for excellent work, it could meet this stage of the struggle for existence with absolute confidence... Instead, the several properties were allowed to be sunk in the swollen waters of big combines. The bicycle branch became a constituent of the American Bicycle Company...capitalized at $40 million, made up of ten millions of bonds, ten millions of preferred, and twenty millions of common stock. Last December [1901] the common stock was selling at two, and the preferred at ten dollars a share of $100 each, and the bonds at 55. Thus, in the estimation of investors, a capitalization of $40 million had sunk in value to less than $7 million. For such stuff a principality was traded."

headquarters back to Hartford. On a sweltering night in July 1903, the Allyn House ballroom blazed with light and reverberated with the voices of a distinguished assemblage gathered to celebrate the return of the city's leading industrialist. Amid the potted palms and floral decorations, the reception and dinner went on to eleven o'clock, and it was three in the morning before the last speaker had done. The head of the Hartford Businessmen's Association summed up the feelings of those present, declaring that "no greater good fortune could come to us as a city than to have Colonel Pope again in control of his splendid factories here... He made his name and the names of his companies and the name of Hartford prominent and respected in every country in the world."

The tall, white-bearded guest of honor was actually a stranger to most. Although his business interests had been centered in the city for almost a decade, he had never lived there. Generally admired for his vision and acumen and also for his philanthropy, yet at 60 he still retained the aloof bearing of a Civil War officer, and he was known for his quick temper and domineering manner. These qualities gave him an aura of mystery that few in the room had ever penetrated.

"Gentlemen," he said, "let me tell you that the automobile is as much bigger than the bicycle as it weighs more than the bicycle. The day is coming when you lovers of the horse won't see him in the streets. Horses have got to go just the same as they went from the street car." Hartford, he was sure, "would be the booming capital of the automobile industry."

Pope, however, did not count on Henry Ford. A month prior to the testimonial for Pope, the Ford Motor Company had been incorporated and the first Ford car appeared almost as he spoke. There were some seventy plants experimenting with motor cars, mostly of the electric or steam type. Pope's output still led the pack, and New England accounted for one-half of all motor carriages. The Pope-Tribune, a six horsepower runabout with a front-mounted engine, sold for $650, while the ten horsepower Pope-Hartford, with its detachable tonneau (a rear seat for two), cost $1,200. Olds had produced 4,000 one-cylinder roadsters; Ford netted nearly $100,000 in ten months from the assembly of 658 cars. Yet the automobile remained a rarity, unseen by millions, exciting both wonder and derision, still looking like a buggy without a horse. And most of the carriage power was still being furnished by over twenty million horses.

"The beginning of the end," as Hiram Maxim put it, for the rejuvenated Pope Company was the acquisition of the Selden patent. George B. Selden was a moody, irascible patent lawyer from Rochester, New York. Two decades earlier he foresaw that the horseless carriage would revolutionize American transportation. In general terms, he sketched out a vehicle powered by a motor that contained most of the essential features of the internal combustion engine: a compression cycle, clutch, gear train for reversing, and the differential. He applied for a patent in 1879 but, aware his idea was far ahead of its time, cleverly delayed its issuance by filing a series of minor changes. When finally granted in 1895, the patent stirred up a controversy that lasted sixteen years, earning for itself a place in patent history comparable to those of the Bell telephone and McCormick reaper.

It was left up to Day and Eames to negotiate with Selden after Whitney's infusion of new capital. The inventor gave them an option on an exclusive license, and for several months they delved into the patent's validity. Sir Dugald Clerk, considered the world's gas engine expert, encouraged them. Early in January 1900, Pope decided to buy the rights for the sum of $10,000 plus royalties. Upon his return from a vacation in the Bahamas, Day, as president of Electric Vehicle, was instructed to enforce the patent by bringing suit against any and all competitors suspected of infringement. To prove Selden's claims, Maxim and Henry Cave, another of Pope's engineers, were assigned the arduous task of constructing, at great expense, a vehicle that would run just long enough to be exhibited to the court. The contraption was driven only two miles and then cast aside forever to gather dust. Maxim, from the beginning, had insisted that "the engine...was utterly impractical and a joke...the claims were so broad they were ridiculous."

As a result of winning the first legal round, there came into being in 1903 the Association of Licensed Automobile Manufacturers, twenty-six companies who paid royalties to Electric Vehicle, A.L.A.M., George Day, and George Selden. The latter two men received one-fifth of the $6 million collected. George Day resigned his position with Electric Vehicle to head the Association. "We intend to oppress no one," he promised, but "to prevent mushroom concerns from coming in with freak machines to impose on the public..."

One of these "mushroom concerns" refused to join. Previously, recalled Hiram Maxim, "little attention had been paid to him, as his carriage was a very cheap one, and he was not regarded as an important figure in the industry." His name was Henry Ford. In the summer of 1903, A.L.A.M. ran

Factories of Pope Manufacturing Company. (Courtesy E. Irving Blomstrann)

an ad in the Detroit *News* warning the public that nobody was entitled to sell, buy, or use a car not licensed under the Selden patent. There followed a stormy meeting at which the president of A.L.A.M. threatened to put Ford out of business. It did look like an unequal contest, with the millions behind the budding trust pitted against a neophyte whose working capital was only $28,000. But Ford jumped out of his chair and shouted: "Let them try it!"

In October, Electric Vehicle and Selden filed suit against the "cocky" upstart and his New York agent in the U.S. District Court of New York. The suit relied on the Patent Commissioner's statement of 1895 that viewed Selden's conception as "the pioneer invention in the application of the compression gas engine to road or horseless carriage use." A.L.A.M. denied it sought to become another monopoly like Standard Oil, which Ida Tarbell was muckraking in *McClure's Magazine*, only to deny licenses to uncooperative infringers. It solicited public support through an advertising campaign, to which Ford responded with the assertion that "we are the pioneers of the Gasoline Automobile."

The lengthy trial consumed 14,000 pages of testimony — five million words. Ford's lawyer was Ralzemond A. Parker, a bearded and burly bulldog. Now 60 years old, with gray mustaches and steely eyes, the Rochester inventor watched the proceedings intently. Dugald Clerk was supposed to be the plaintiff's chief witness, but he hardly helped matters by admitting under cross examination that all the devices described in Selden's patent had been known before. In his testimony, Maxim ignored the inventor's contribution to the development of motor carriages, unwittingly contributing to Parker's strategy of showing that the art had advanced without regard to Selden.

Before the trial's conclusion three disasters struck. In August of 1907, Pope and the Electric Vehicle companies failed. They were overcapitalized and suffered not only from the rapid decline of the electrics but also from the financial panic of that year. At the same time in Detroit, Henry Ford introduced his Model T. Finally, the immensely able and affable George Day, the victim of overwork, died of a heart attack in November at the age of 56. Henry Ford referred to Day as "a gentleman of whom personally I have the greatest respect" and even had taken him on a tour of his plant the previous year.

In 1909, however, Judge Hough upheld A.L.A.M. and Selden. The feisty Ford refused to give up, even though the suit had already cost him $200,000. He appealed to the Circuit Court which, in January 1911, ruled that Selden's liquid hydrocarbon gas engine offered no novelty and that Selden himself had failed to build a car that would run. Ironically, his patent was due to expire the next year.

For Henry Ford, the victory was over the twin foes of monopoly and Wall Street. "If we had not won the suit," he confided to his family, "there could never have been in this country such an automobile industry as exists." Selden he regarded as "a decent old fellow" who had been duped by those wanting to "exploit the industry by claiming tribute from every motor car manufacturer." During the eight year period of this litigation, the industry had grown from $97 million to $500 million. Trusts were fast becoming outlawed; not only was the automobile trust stopped in its tracks, but two months later the Supreme Court dissolved the Standard Oil combine.

Detroit, of course, was far better suited than Hartford to be the automobile capital. For years the buggy makers had flourished there. Its foundries were 700 miles closer to the iron mines. Machine shops abounded, and their mechanics had been putting together marine engines since the 1880s.

The month before Judge Hough's favorable decision, Colonel Pope died of pneumonia. By 1914, his factories were silent. They were sold to Pratt & Whitney, the machine tool builders, and to Billings & Spencer, drop forging specialists. Hartford had lost forever its hold on the automobile.

CHAPTER VI

A REPUTATION FOR EXCELLENCE

"Hartford has a great future. As the capital of Connecticut, it should inevitably be a great city great in its population, in its industries, in its wealth, in its public undertakings for the general good." So spoke its mayor the year that Mrs. Colt died, and a young salesman named Samuel M. Stonc came to the Armory from St. Louis. The mayor's main concerns for his burgeoning metropolis were the lack of a municipal charter that would ban party politics, the urgency for a new city hall to replace the cramped quarters of the Old State House, and the necessity for further protection of the East Side against flooding.

Otherwise, everything did look rosy. Between 1890 and 1910, the population doubled to nearly 100,000; nearly one in three was foreign born. Jobs were plentiful and paid well — relatively speaking. In fact, the average annual earnings of $452 in 1900 had almost the same purchasing power as the average in 1955 of $3,935, although the work week was sixty hours as compared to today's forty hours. Lunches could be had for 50¢ or less; beer was a nickel, including cheese and crackers; one dollar was enough to buy a dress; a pound of coffee cost 25¢ and a 100-pound barrel of flour sold for $5.40; rents were available at $10 a month, and a two-family house downtown ranged in price from $2,800 to $4,150.

Extension of the trolley service to outlying towns had already made Hartford the metropolitan shopping center for the entire valley. Twenty-one lines ran all the way from New Haven to Springfield, south to north, and from Rockville to Unionville, east and west. For its size the city was unique in having a network of parks, 1,200 acres in all, thanks to the persistent efforts of two ministers. The great liberal preacher Dr. Horace Bushnell, a half century earlier, had persuaded the city fathers to acquire the slum area around the Little River and to make it the first municipally-owned park in the country. In his footsteps followed the Rev. Francis Goodwin, who envisioned a ring of open space around the city and as park commissioner obtained donations of land from such wealthy men as Colonel Pope, Henry Keney, and Charles Pond. The most recent gift, in the will of Mrs. Colt, provided for converting most of the Colonel's estate into Colt Park.

On both sides of the river there was keen interest in the construction of the new stone bridge named after Hartford's leading citizen, Morgan G. Bulkeley, who headed the bridge commission. A towering, dynamic figure, he was now a U.S. Senator, while still holding sway as president of the Aetna Life Insurance Company. Later, he would become a Colt director and major stockholder. For a hundred years the fire and life insurance business had been nurtured in the city, becoming as vital to its prosperity as manufacturing. The insurance fever had been inspired by the maritime trade of the early 19th century on which local merchants risked their capital and reputations. Now the river trade had vanished, except for steamboats carrying passengers and freight to New York and barges bringing coal and lumber upstream. The General Assembly had chartered well over a hundred insurance companies state-wide, most of those surviving being headquartered in Hartford. The policies issued amounted to four billion dollars and their assets far exceeded those of the manufacturing sector, although their employment was much less.

The Hartford Board of Trade set forth the city's advantages as a manufacturing center in a book full of fine engravings. At that time, there were over 130 factories. It recognized Colt's as leading the way in technological know-how and workmanship and in fostering other successful enterprises. "The lessons inculcated in the Armory a generation ago, and since taught by its graduates, have been largely instrumental in stimulating other manufacturers here to set up similar standards, and in winning for Hartford a world-wide reputation for the excellence of its manufactured goods."

Two years before, Colt's had obtained the rights to manufacture the English Vickers-Maxim automatic machine gun. The agreement in effect gave the company control of all machine gun production in the world. The new management had also invested in new machinery during the years 1901 through 1903, increasing output by 40 percent. In 1902, needing more space, it had to displace its tenant Atlantic Screw, and in 1907 another tenant — Whitney Manufacturing — moved out of the Armory to new quarters. Yet, there was no new construction in contrast to the feverish expansion of other manufacturers in the city like Pope, Pratt & Whitney, and the two typewriter companies, Royal and Underwood. Total capital investment in the manufacturing sector doubled to $55 million. Colt's, with employment ranging from 600 to 800, had actually declined in relative size until it ranked as only the fourth largest. Altogether, 18,000 wage earners were making — besides firearms, machine tools and typewriters — automobiles, boxes, cigars, clothes, electrical switches, horseshoe nails, leather goods, organs, screws, tires, and valves.

The Board noted that the city had escaped the contagion of labor strife which had caused great waste of capital and bitterness of feeling in other places:

The principal streets are for the most part broad, well-paved and lighted by electricity... It has a paid fire department, with seven steam fire engines... Gas is furnished at $1.40 per thousand feet. Two electric light companies provide both the arc and incandescent systems. There are about twelve and one-half miles of street railway... The police has long been noted for its efficiency, and...here many thieves who came to prey have remained to plead.

Besides the city's public schools, theological seminary, and liberal arts college, the book listed a number of benevolent institutions, including the Old Peoples' Home, Orphan Asylum, Retreat for the Insane, and the American Asylum for the Deaf and Dumb.

The principal concern of Hartford in 1905, however, was business. Opportunities seemed unlimited for newcomers. They struggled upward with the encouragement and help of the parish priest and the ward boss. For the rapidly expanding factories, there was an abundant supply of willing hands and backs to fill the stoop and bull jobs. Ambitious young men who saw more education as the quickest stepping stone to promotion filled the evening classes of Hillyer Institute at the Y.M.C.A. to study mechanical drawing, plumbing, wiring, and automobile mechanics, or they attended the Huntsinger Business School, the third largest of its kind in New England, which placed two hundred graduates every year in local offices.

The factories like Colt's depended for entry workers on the thousands of immigrants who poured into the city in an unending stream from 1900 to 1930. Besides the Irish and Germans there now came Russian Jews, Italians, Swedes, and many other nationalities — numbering over 30,000 by 1910. In search of better housing the largest group of foreign-born, the Irish, had begun to move out of the East Side. Frog Hollow near Park Street became the foremost Irish ghetto, a closely-knit neighborhood with strong loyalties for church, party and each other. Many were skilled machinists and toolmakers in one of Colonel Pope's nearby factories. A political breakthrough was achieved in 1902 when Ignatius Sullivan, who the previous year had successfully mediated the machinists' strike, became mayor. Genial and silver-tongued, Sullivan bent over backward to place his followers in every possible job the city offered. His version of the spoils system made a mess of the local government and alienated the old-line Democrats, resulting in his overwhelming defeat two years later. A young Irish lawyer named Thomas J. Spellacy, a product of Front Street and a graduate of Holy Cross, was about to begin an illustrious political career that would extend over four decades, including eight years as mayor from 1935 to 1943, during which time he was also the undisputed boss of the Democratic organization in Connecticut.

The East Side, in turn, became "Little Italy," a vibrant self-sustaining community, noisy, aromatic and colorful. One of the last descendants of the founders of Hartford, Miss Frances McCook, loved to walk through the area:

You'd go down Front Street and see the old grandmas with shawls, and not a word of English out of them, and the old men with their pipes and their curious caps, and carts of vegetables, carts of flowers sitting out in the sun.

Colt took part in the 1908 dedication of the Bulkeley Bridge across the Connecticut River with a float displaying machine guns.

A 1902 Colt advertisement for pistols, revolvers and machine guns.

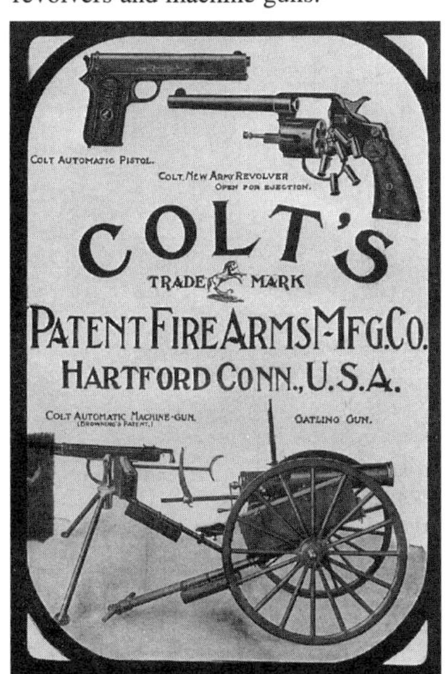

Colt's main office for many years, which was connected to the armory by a bridge. Note the wooden single-action army revolver hung over the front entrance.

Newcomers learning English in night school. (Courtesy E. Irving Blomstrann)

Even more so than the Irish, they crowded their broods into the well-worn tenements, six families to a floor and to a single bathroom. The less fortunate *paesani* used the public bathhouse, paying a nickel for a towel. Day and night, the streets teemed with children playing; pushcarts lined the gutters; on the sidewalks were piled crates of Sicilian fruit, rare *verdura*, chestnuts, and snails in sawdust; in the store windows hung *provolone* cheeses, *pepperoni* sausage, *proscuitti* and Genoa *salami*; knots of *padres* engaged in heated conversation on the corners; the *mammas* shouted the news from one open window to another amid the frequent blowing of police whistles and the clanging of fire trucks. The saloons, which provided a free meal with a 10¢ stein of beer, were also favorite places to congregate. The *padre* was monarch of his home; he ruled his children with a firm hand, arranged marriages, and tended to the making of the family's red wine. The women were devout church-goers, their husbands preferring the excitement of religious festivals with their parades and fireworks.

A new wave of poor and oppressed Jewish immigrants from Eastern Europe, many skilled in furring, iron-making, carpentry, and shop-keeping, and all passionate Zionists, were making Hartford their home. Like their German brethren, they shared a deep-seated tradition of mutual aid and founded many charitable societies. Unlike the Catholics, the Jews embraced the public schools and provided for the religious education of their young separately. But socially, they were looked down upon by their more affluent predecessors. They lived alongside the Irish and Italians in relative harmony, except for teen-age gang fights, and the East Side united to elect Herman P. Koppleman, a popular newspaper and magazine dealer, to the city council in 1903, and, years later, to Congress.

Hard on the heels of the Eastern European Jews followed the Poles, dispossessed peasants lured by the steamship advertisements promising cheap land in America. Even poorer than other immigrants, they congregated in the area around the Colt Armory. Their living conditions were the worst; more often than not, the only bathroom was outdoors, and the Irish landlords exacted an exorbitant rent. Lacking any skills, Poles gravitated to the factories within walking distance. As the church had been the center of village life in Poland, so it was here; on the corner of Charter Oak Avenue and Governor Street, once the center for Hartford's well-to-do, they scraped together enough money to build a small wooden church known as Saints Cyril & Methodius, and also their own school which taught their children to fear God, remember their mother country, and become good Americans.

Colt workmen in 1909.

As time passed, the Irish and Italians gradually moved to the South End. Eventually, after World War II, they would become home owners in the suburbs with the help of GI loans and FHA mortgages, leaving behind the blacks and other minorities to occupy the decrepit tenements that had withstood the abuse of one tide of immigrants after another for a hundred years. The domination of Hartford by Anglo-Saxon Congregationalists and Episcopalians would last only a few more decades. As the original Yankees, they inspired in the newcomers mixed feelings of awe and spite. Now, those who had at first been stepped on as "Micks," "Polaks," or "Wops" were unwittingly beginning to turn into Yankees themselves as they climbed the ladder, rung by rung, to respectability and influence.

* * *

On April 26, 1906, there occurred a little-noticed ceremony which added a final halo to the Colt legacy. At Armsmear gathered the mayor, park commissioners, and the executors of Mrs. Colt's estate for the unveiling of the memorial to her husband, her last effort before her death to immortalize him. Her cousin, the Rev. Dr. Samuel Hart, delivered the main address which extolled the man "who gave the example of precision workmanship which is followed in the great workshops not only of this city but also of the country and of the world. Long shall this mansion provide a home for the gentlefolk whose path adversity has crossed." The statue was located on the site of the graves of the colonel and three of Mrs. Colt's children who had since been removed to Cedar Hill Cemetery. It showed Sam Colt as a sailor boy whittling the first wooden model of his revolver and as a manufacturing tycoon. Two bas reliefs recreated his presentation to the Russian Czar and the demonstration of his gun to the British House of Commons.

In the background watched an elderly, bewhiskered gentleman, a stranger to most of the other spectators. He was the Colonel's "nephew" and Farmington squire, Samuel Caldwell Colt, who had served as a Colt's director from 1866 to 1901.

Also present at the unveiling was the president of Colt's who lived next door to Armsmear. Lewis C. Grover would have appealed to his predecessor Elisha K. Root because of his training as a machinist and his rise to manager of the Whitney Arms Company in New Haven, where he caught the eye of John Hall. In 1886, the latter invited him to join Colt's as assistant superintendent. He went on to become general manager and, when Hall died, succeeded him as president in July 1902. Grover was an indefatigable worker with few outside interests.

Samuel Colt's memorial in Colt Park. (Courtesy E. Irving Blomstrann)

As head of the Board of Park Commissioners, he directed the improvements in Colt Park after the city accepted it as a gift from Mrs. Colt.

Grover's ill health forced him to step down in January 1909, and he lived only until the following September. Fortunately, another able executive was waiting in the wings: Colonel William C. Skinner, who had been induced to come to Colt's three years after Grover. A big-hearted, eternally cheerful man, Skinner had graduated from Trinity College in 1876. Settling in Hartford, he formed a partnership with General Henry C. Dwight. Dwight, Skinner & Company became one of the leading firms in the wool trade; Skinner retained his interest until 1899. In July 1901, he was elected a director and vice-president of the Armory.

The year that Skinner took over the reins, an outsider — except by marriage — moved into the top management as vice-president. He was Charles L.F. Robinson of Newport, a wealthy yachtsman and the husband of Mrs. Samuel Colt's niece, Elizabeth Jarvis Beach. Robinson's father had made a fortune in mining and shipping coal. Charles had a degree from Yale's Sheffield School of Engineering. A partner in Robinson, Haydon & Company, he also served as president of the Maryland Coal and Gatling Gun companies. He managed nevertheless to devote a great deal of time to sailing. He was a member of the America's Cup Committee for three years and had cruised extensively in European and Caribbean waters, following which he wrote a book entitled *30,000 Miles In The Wanderer.*

By the end of December 1908, at the age of 34, Robinson and other investors had in effect taken over financial control. The Boston and New York interests that had bought out Mrs. Colt in 1901 formed a holding company, Colt's Arms, in New York state, although the Armory retained its identity as Colt's Patent Firearms Manufacturing Company. All but five of the 10,000 shares of stock outstanding were held in trust by the American Loan & Trust Company of Boston. The holding company issued $1,200,000 in bonds, half of

Lewis C. Grover

which had already been retired. Now, two of the outside directors gave up their seats on the board, leaving only Treasurer Frank W. Schirmer, a principal in the original acquisition. At Robinson's request the management was changed to include a chairman, president, two vice-presidents, treasurer, and secretary. Robinson moved his residence from Newport to Hartford.

For two years Colonel Skinner ran the Armory, receiving a salary of $7,500. Much to the board's regret he begged to be relieved of the presidency in January 1911. "I've been in the business harness for over 30 years. I hope the Board will elect Charlie to take my place, as he is eminently fitted for this position in every way." Robinson agreed to do so, at a salary of $10,000, only if Skinner would consent to become chairman and first vice-president. Skinner was also given the unusual designation of the company's "superior officer." At this time the holding company was dissolved, the remainder of the bonds paid off, and the capital stock increased from $1 million to $2.5 million. The 15,000 new shares were distributed to the stockholders of the holding company.

For the past tax-free decade Colt's had been enormously profitable. Although no figures were published "owing to keen competition in the firearms business," annual dividend payments ranged from 13 to 35 percent and averaged 22 percent. The amount declared was based on earning the dividend twice over. The year 1911 was noted as the best in forty years, and appropriately a total of 40 percent in dividends was paid. Robinson concentrated on cultivating the foreign market, making several trips abroad and giving Fabrique Nationale of Liege an exclusive license to sell Browning's automatic pistols in Europe (except England). Thanks to government orders for the new .45 cal. automatic, sales shot up 44 percent in 1912 to almost $2 million, returning a profit of 34 percent.

In 1914, on the occasion of the 100th anniversary of Sam Colt's birth, the *Courant* featured an elaborate two-page spread. President Robinson's picture revealed a pale, round face, a nearly bald head, and sported a long mustache, while Chairman Skinner's, also with mustache, impressed one as a handsome man of character and charm. According to the article, Colt's had enjoyed four years of prosperity. Employment had doubled to 1,200. Much of the equipment had been modernized, and a sprinkler system had been installed in the Armory's 350,000 square feet. The Colt dock was still in use. To improve employee welfare, management had erected a clubhouse and established one of the first group insurance plans — with benefits ranging from $300 to $800 depending upon length of employment. As a seller of arms world-wide, the company had direct representatives throughout the United States and in Central and South America, China, Australia, and New Zealand. In addition, there were resident agents in Cuba and Mexico. Recently, the Greek government had ordered 10,000 revolvers.

Robinson was actually in poor health. The year before, in March, he had been badly hurt in an automobile accident while driving to church, lacerating his scalp and suffering a back injury. Now he breathed with difficulty, devoting as much time as he could to his yacht and to his collection of Americana. In July 1916, he was vacationing aboard *Savarona* and anchored in Woods Hole. On the morning of July 6th a crewman entered his cabin and found him fully dressed in a chair dead. He left an estate of approximately half a million dollars, including fifty shares of Colt stock valued at $40,000. His collection of Americana sold at auction for $66,204.

A week later Colonel Skinner was again elected president. Upon his shoulders now fell the entire burden of steering Colt's through a war that seemed certain to involve the United States soon. Skinner, like Sam Colt, had never fought for his country; his colonelcy, like Colt's, was a political favor bestowed on him by former Governor Morgan G. Bulkeley, now a Colt director, on whose staff Skinner served four years from 1889 to 1893. Skinner was extremely popular both within the Armory and outside in the business community. He held directorships in three Hartford insurance companies and two Hartford banks. For eighteen years he was a conscientious trustee of his alma mater, Trinity College. His cheerful disposition, however, was not enough to protect him from the strains of being president of Colt's in wartime and having two sons and a son-in-law in the front lines overseas. A widower since his wife's death in 1904, he had no one with whom to share his worries. He was also undoubtedly affected by the loss in action of his predecessor's son, Lieutenant Caldwell Colt Robinson. Lieutenant Robinson died in France in his 21st year, in June 1918. Named for Colonel Colt's son, he had been born at Armsmear, graduated from Yale, and worked at Colt's.

Skinner's ordeal was mitigated by having at his right hand a highly competent sales manager, who became vice-president in 1916. Samuel M. Stone was destined to be the head of Colt's longer than any other president except for Richard Jarvis — a span of twenty-three years. Born in Urbana, Ohio, Stone had earned a reputation among suppliers of

Col. William C. Skinner

Col. Charles L.F. Robinson

The President's office.

guns, sporting equipment, and hardware as the southwest's ablest salesman. For fourteen years he was associated with Simmons Hardware, St. Louis wholesalers, where he eventually managed all but one of their departments. His competence attracted the attention of both Stanley Works in New Britain and Colt's in Hartford. In 1905 both offered him a job, but Frank Nichols then the Armory's sales vice-president — won out. Stanley Works, however, did not lose out entirely because they later hired Sam Stone's younger brother who rose to a vice-presidency. As a salesman for Colt's Stone traveled country-wide, spending as much as nine months of every year on the road. Nichols also sent him abroad, where he called on potential customers across the continent from France east to Russia and Turkey. Upon his return he took over Nichols' position.

Making and selling munitions was a business like any other. Occupied with problems of design, production, marketing, and profit, those who managed the Armory seldom worried about the moral implications of their occupation. Upright and conscientious men like Skinner and Stone could attend church on Sunday and deal with weapons of destruction the rest of the week without a sense of hypocrisy. Most of the leading businessmen in 19th century Hartford had been raised as Episcopalians. To be an Episcopalian was to reach the pinnacle of social success — no nearer God perhaps than were the members of other denominations, but certainly closer to those who composed the power structure of the city and to their wives who dictated social behavior, like Mrs. Samuel Colt. As long as Mrs. Colt lived, it was a sensible idea for Colt executives to belong to the Church of the Good Shepherd.

Sam Colt himself had been a convert to the Episcopal Church, and it would not be uncharitable to surmise that he did so in order to please his wife and father-in-law. For Colt was essentially an amoral person. Even so, Hartford did not regard gunmaking as a sin — not in a state that had been the arsenal of the nation since colonial times. It is tempting, too, to compare Colt with the character of Andrew Undershaft in Bernard Shaw's *Major*

Target practice.

Chinese visitors apparently interested in buying the Colt machine gun at the left.

The Colt dock on the Connecticut River, from which guns were shipped by steamboat. (Courtesy E. Irving Blomstrann)

Revolver and rifle assembly room in East Armory about 1898.

Advertisement for the Colt revolver adopted by the armed services in 1911.

Barbara. There are certain amazing similarities between the real Yankee munitions maker and Shaw's fictional creation of the millionaire dealer in death. Both were equally direct and simple in their motivations, unashamed of profiteering, selling arms to opposing armies, willing to use any means to gain their ends, and mindful enough of their worker's welfare to build them model villages. Colt would have agreed with the imaginary Undershaft that poverty was the worst of crimes. The two things necessary for salvation, he said, are money and gunpowder. Without enough of both, no one can afford the luxury of honor, justice, truth, or love.

Yet a closer look at Colt forces one to conclude that he had been no Undershaft. For one thing, the Colonel was basically patriotic, with a sentimental attachment to democracy and saving the Union; he did not place himself above the law, nor try to push around presidents and kings, even though he was not adverse to bribery and chicanery to get his patent renewed or to acquire land for his Armory. He was indifferent to the outcome of most causes which his arms reinforced — except slavery, which he considered an economic waste. Colt was the archetypal Yankee who loved work, success, wealth — a doer who preferred "to be at the head of a louse than at the tail of a lion."

Sam Stone, who came to Hartford the year of Mrs. Colt's death, unwittingly broke with the Episcopal tradition that had dominated the running of the Armory. His family had been staunch Presbyterians, but he joined the Windsor Avenue Congregational Church because of its proximity to his residence on Evergreen Avenue. Connecticut Congregationalists had always been reformers — liberty-loving individualists who since the time of Thomas Hooker had espoused the political doctrine of free consent, and who in 1775 opposed the English king and helped to create a new nation. On the other hand, during the Revolution, Episcopalians mostly represented the *status quo* and the well-to-do. In hindsight, if they had predominated in America at that time, instead of being discriminated against and exiled, there might never have been a successful rebellion.

Stone liked the Congregational idea of subservience to none and skepticism of any authority other than that to which the individual willingly acceded. The Old Testament reinforced his conviction that the only true authority was God — not king or man. With regard to the morality of warfare, he found contradictory and confusing answers in the Bible. The Jews, of course, believed in holy wars. Jesus never spoke directly against fighting, possibly because war was the business of the Roman emperor, and most of the battles fought during his lifetime occurred far away on the frontiers of the empire, while Jerusalem remained at peace. Yet the New Testament also said: "Blessed are the peace makers: for they shall be called the children of God" and "Love your enemies, do good to them that hate you." Nowhere did he find any excoriation of weapon makers.

Thus, from Sam Colt to Sam Stone, the presidents of the Armory considered their business as worthy and decent as any other. They were just as patriotic, too — in fact, they presided over a company that always stood ready to perform a vital service when the country had to be defended. Yes, they may have had qualms about selling arms to tin-horn generals and dictators such as came and went in Central and South America, but doing so was strictly a business proposition, cash on the barrelhead, and the responsibility for keeping Colt's prosperous and its stockholders content had to take priority.

Except for the millions made by Sam Colt over the last fifteen years of his life, none of his successors waxed rich from selling arms. True, the company itself earned handsome — some would say exorbitant — profits year after year until the end of World War I, and liberal dividends were paid to the stockholders. But the men who managed Colt's and the inventors who kept feeding it new ideas did not become multi-millionaires. In no way could they be stereotyped as "greedy robber barons" or "unprincipled merchants of death."

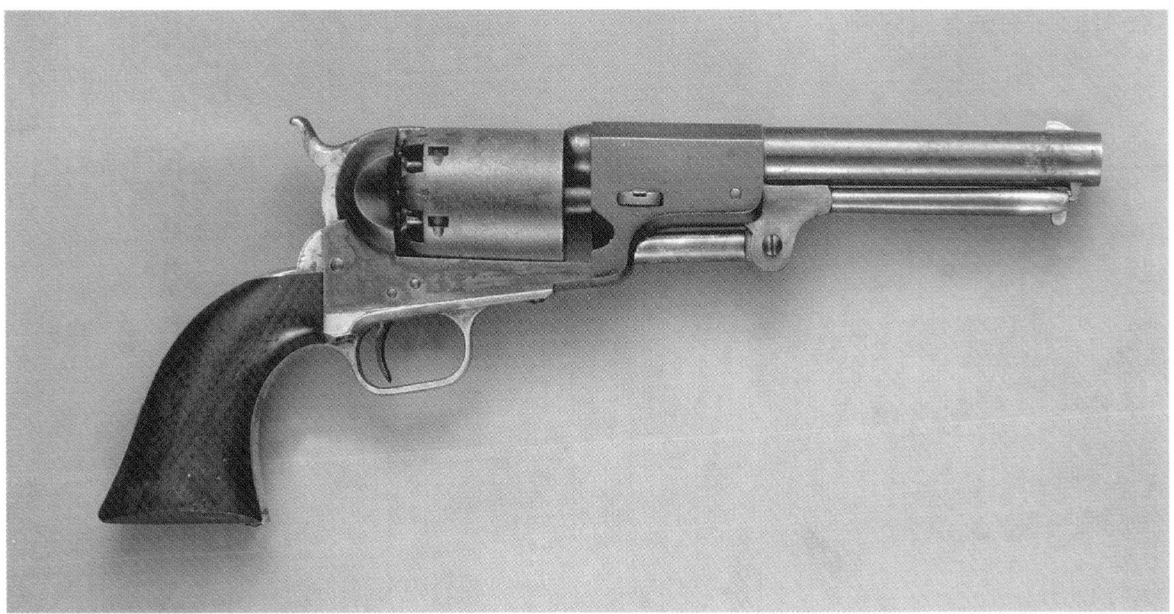

A Colt Hartford English Dragoon revolver. Pistols of this type, a variation of the highly successful Third Model Dragoon, are of special interest since they were assembled in England during the mid-1850s from parts manufactured in Hartford. Note the British proof marks on the cylinder. *Courtesy of Clark V. Cail, photograph by G. Allan Brown.*

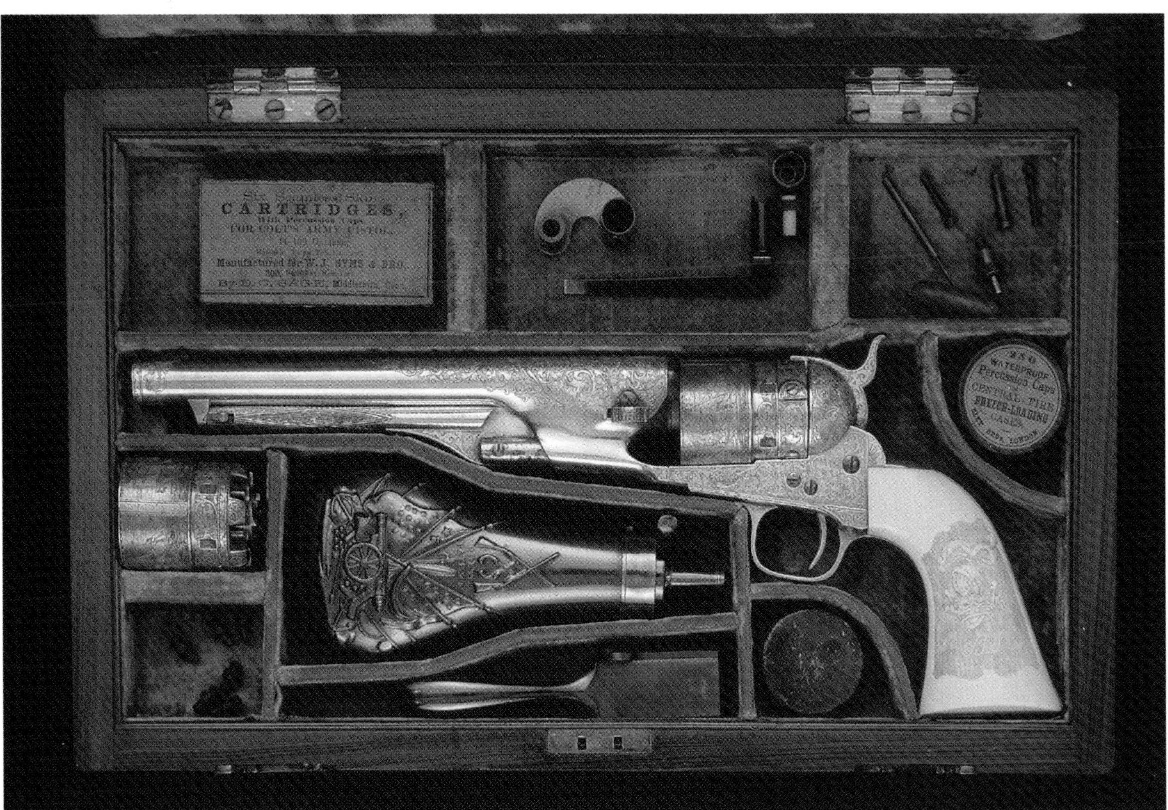

A deluxe, cased Colt Model 1860 Army revolver. This exquisite example features the Thuer Conversion, prized by collectors as Colt's first production experiment with adapting metallic cartridges to their revolvers. The Thuer's characteristic "conversion ring" is clearly visible at the base of the cylinder mounted on the pistol; the spare cylinder, stored near the bottom left-hand corner of the case, allows percussion loads to be used...no doubt a comforting feature during the early days of fixed ammunition. Finished in gold and silver, and decorated with elaborate engraving by the famed Gustave Young, this pistol was made for Don Louis Laureano Sanz, the Marquis de San Juan and Governor General of Puerto Rico.
Courtesy of the fine art auctioneers Butterfield & Butterfield, San Francisco, CA.

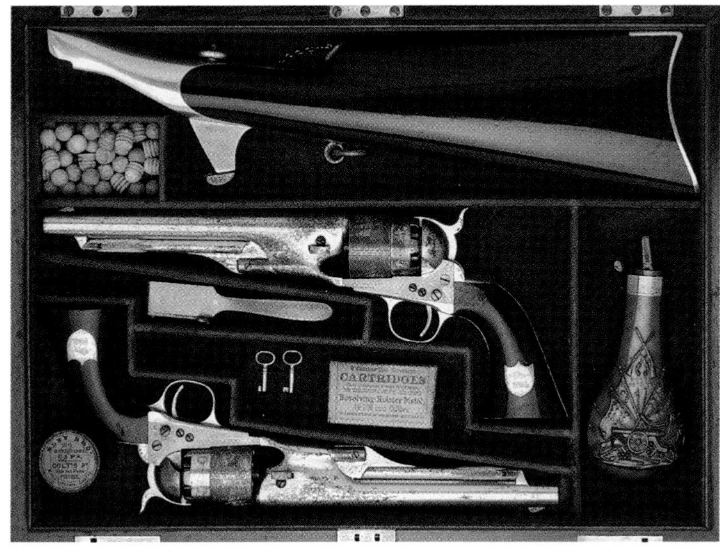

A cased pair of gold-finished Colt Model 1860 Army revolvers with matching attachable rosewood canteen shoulder stock, made for Eustace Barron.

Courtesy of the fine art auctioneers Butterfield & Butterfield, San Francisco, CA.

A Colt Model 1862 Police revolver, cased with accessories and featuring a round barrel conversion with ejector. This fine pistol, serial number 1859, has a 5½" barrel and semi-fluted cylinder.

Courtesy of Horace Greeley, IV. Photograph by G. Allan Brown.

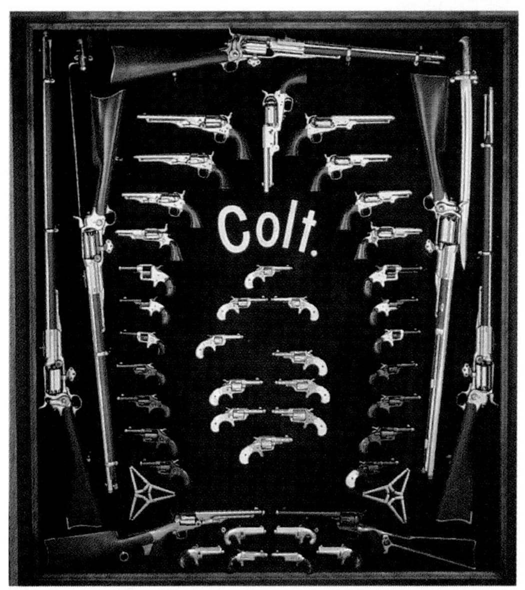

A remarkable Colt factory display board, made for the prominent distributors Hartley & Graham of New York City, c.1877. The board, which contains examples of forty-six handguns and longarms representing twenty models and variations of Colt arms, is a powerful reminder of the depth of the Colt firearms line. When the Hartley & Graham showroom was closed, the board took up a new residence at the Remington Arms Co. headquarters in Bridgeport, Connecticut. During World War II, it was suggested that the contents of the board be broken up for scrap, but scandalized Remington employees managed to save this unique historical item by hiding it in the ladies room (facing the wall) until the war was over.

Courtesy of the fine art auctioneers Butterfield & Butterfield, San Francisco, CA.

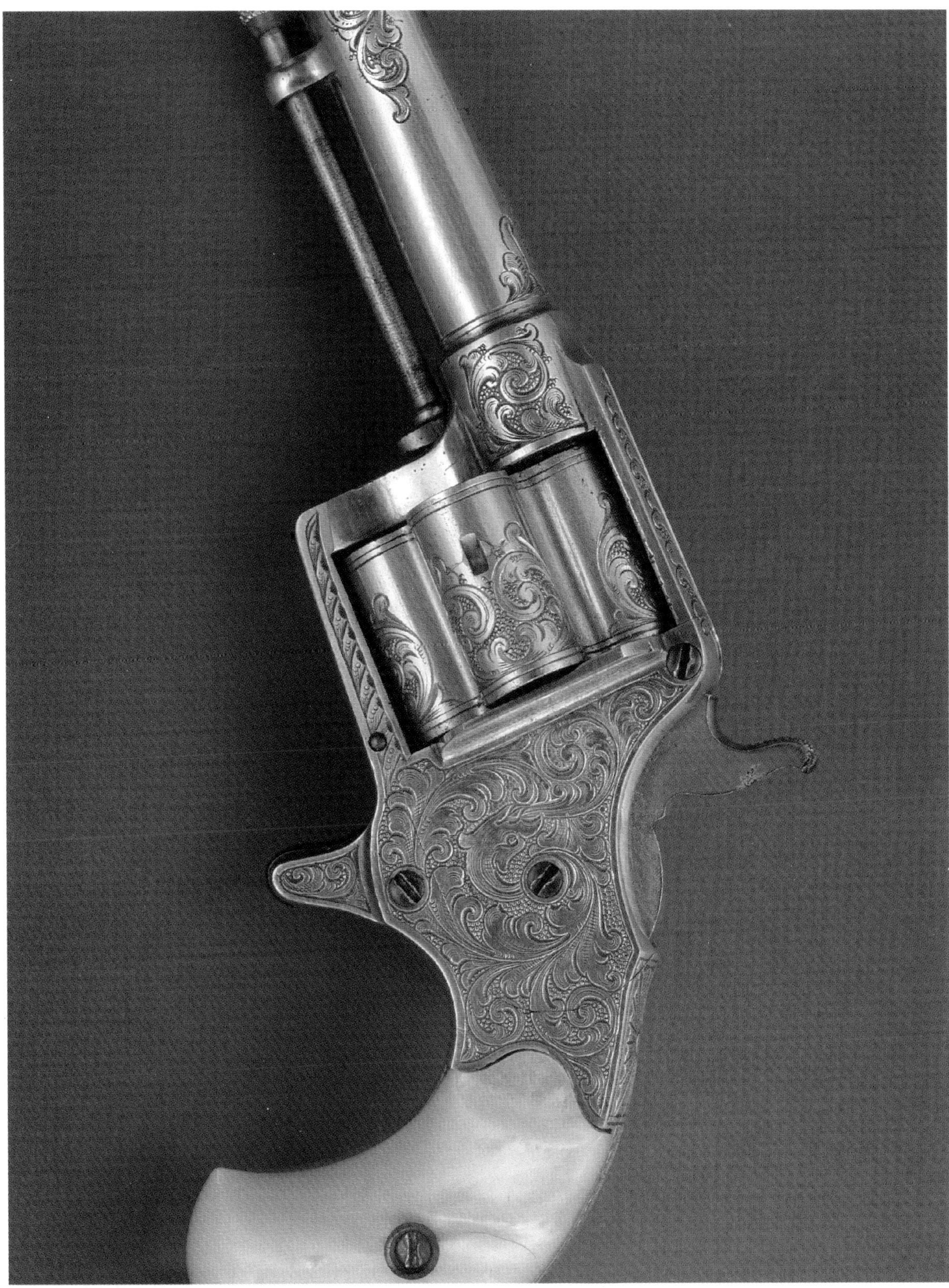

Colt "Cloverleaf" House Model Revolver, c.1871, serial number 187 with 3" barrel. The "Cloverleaf" House Pistol, which earned its nickname from the clover-like appearance of its four cylinder openings, is historically important since it was the first Colt revolver specifically designed and manufactured for use with metallic cartridges. This exceptional specimen, one of the very finest of its type, has a gold-plated cylinder, silver-plated frame, mother-of-pearl stocks and lovely engraving by the celebrated New York City master Louis D. Nimschke.

Courtesy of Horace Greeley, IV. Photograph by G. Allan Brown.

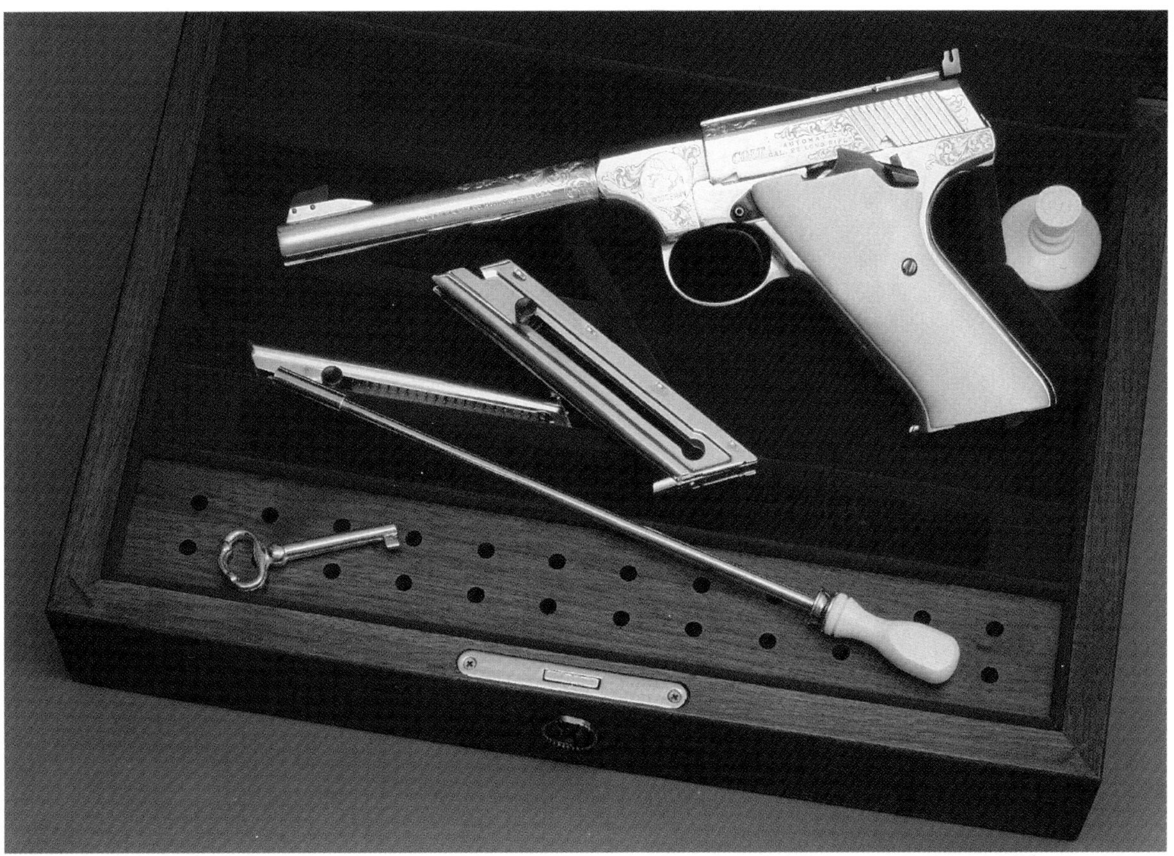

A Colt Woodsman Target Model, with silver plating, ivory grips and class "A" engraving by Colt Master Engraver George Spring. Serial number 101340SHG, it was specially crafted for its owner by the Colt Custom Shop.

Courtesy of Horace Greeley, IV. Photograph by G. Allan Brown.

A charming .25 caliber Colt Automatic Pistol with silver plating and pearl grips. This factory-engraved example was shipped on December 13, 1924.

Courtesy of Horace Greeley, IV. Photograph by G. Allan Brown.

A dramatic view of the design prototypes for Colt revolvers presented to Presidents John F. Kennedy and Lyndon B. Johnson. These paragons of the gunmakers art were once in the private collection of movie star Gene Autry.
Courtesy of the fine art auctioneers Butterfield & Butterfield, San Francisco, CA.

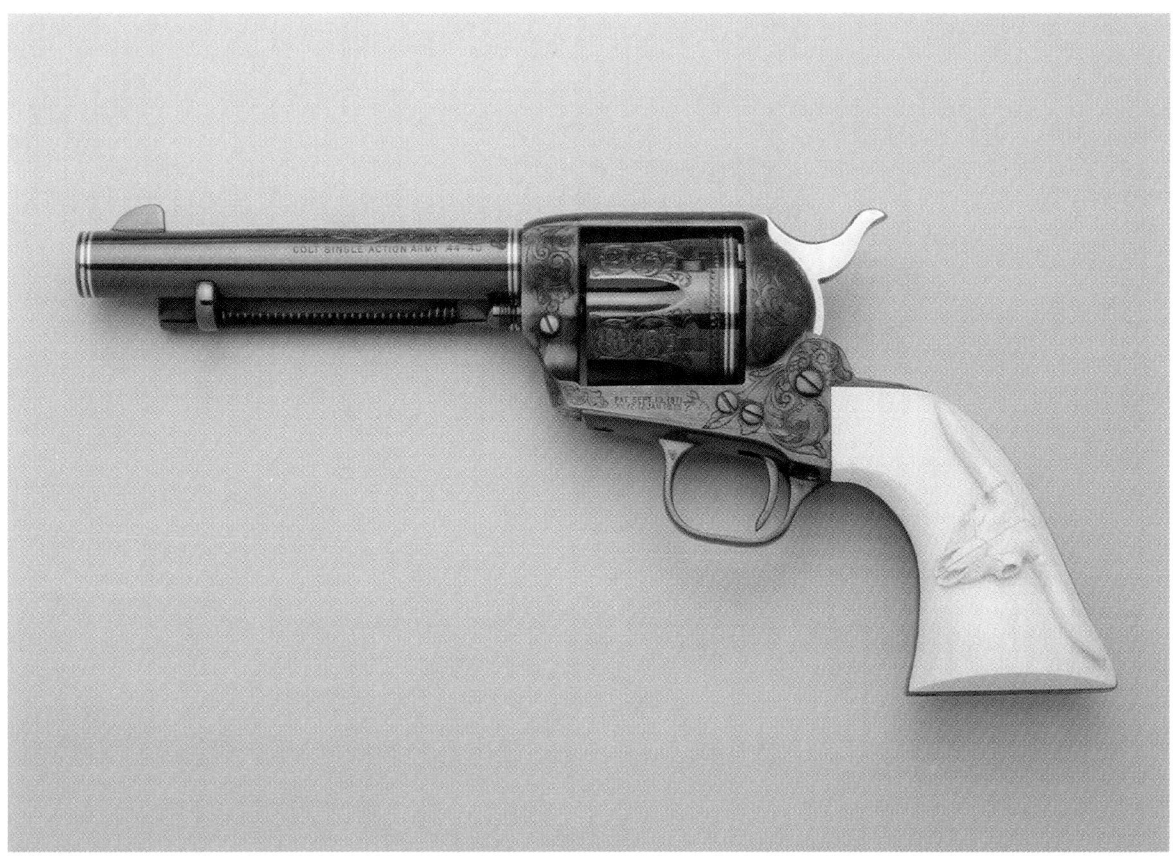

The "End of Trail Gun." Radiating the spirit of the Old West, this elegant product of the Colt Custom Shop was sold for charity, raising money for the Children's Hospital of Orange County, California. *Courtesy of Colt Manufacturing Company, Inc.*

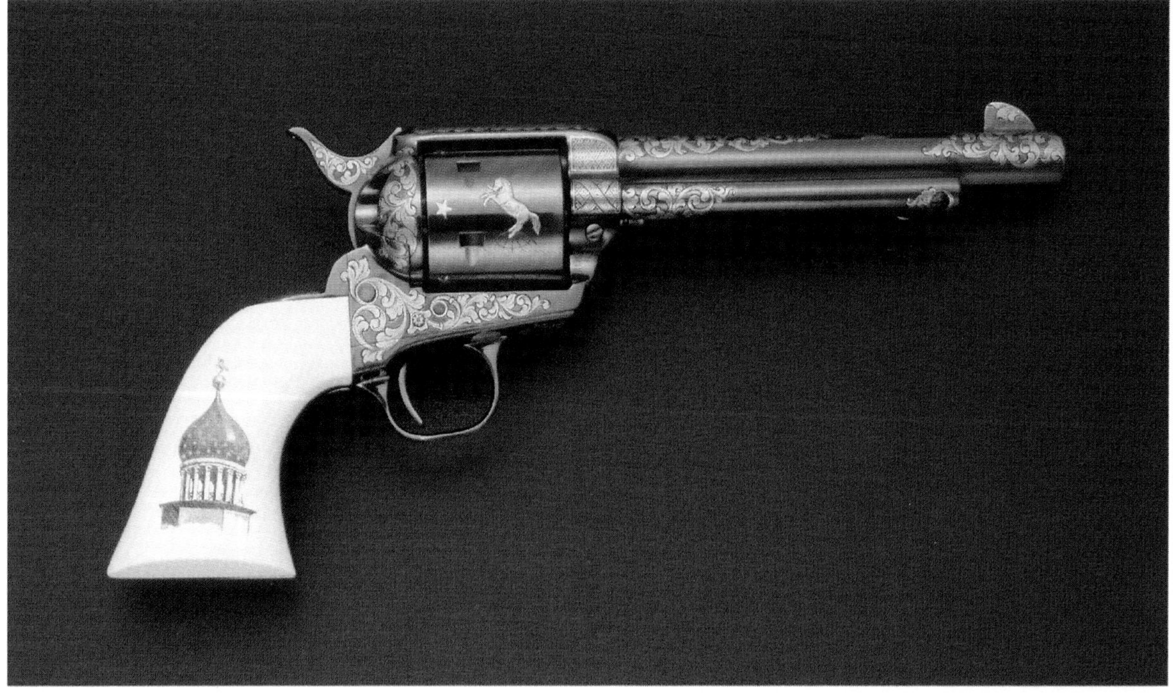

Colt Single Action Army, serial number SA 7, in .45 ACP caliber. With engraving and gold inlays by Colt Master Engraver Dennis Kies, this Colt Custom Shop creation (shipped Sept. 26, 1989) features a striking Royal Blue and French Gray finish combination. The scrimshawed stocks illustrate the Colt dome on the right and the Statue of Liberty on the left.
Courtesy of Horace Greeley, IV. Photograph by G. Allan Brown.

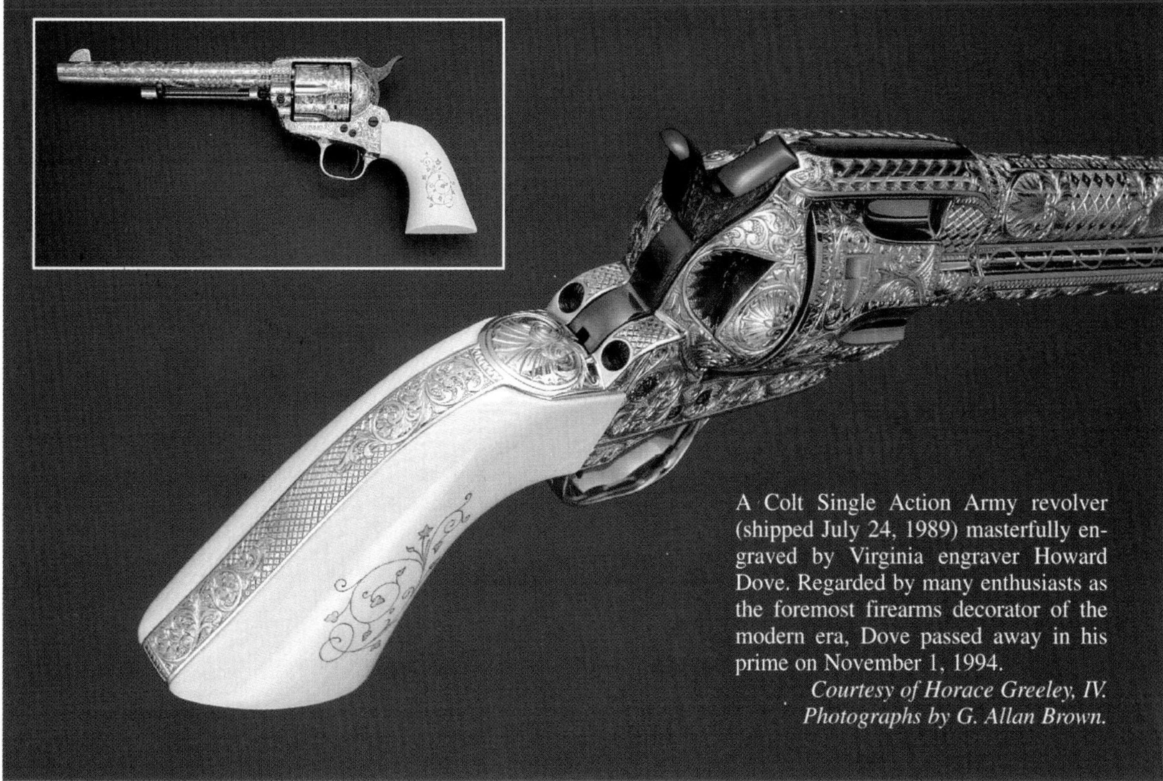

A Colt Single Action Army revolver (shipped July 24, 1989) masterfully engraved by Virginia engraver Howard Dove. Regarded by many enthusiasts as the foremost firearms decorator of the modern era, Dove passed away in his prime on November 1, 1994.

Courtesy of Horace Greeley, IV.
Photographs by G. Allan Brown.

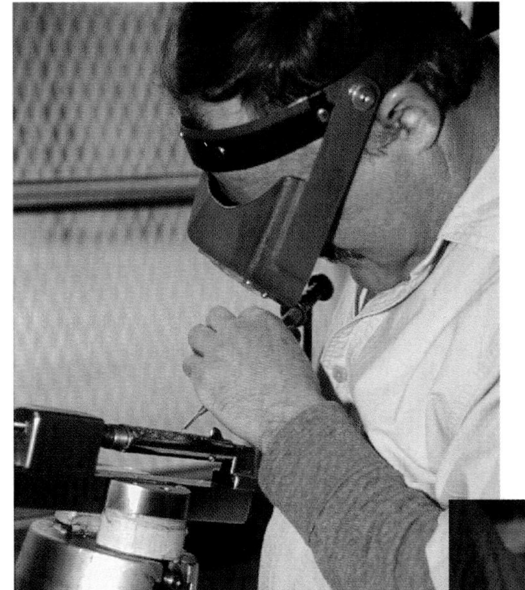

One of the greatest Colt success stories of the modern era has been the Custom Shop. Even during times of great uncertainty, the Shop has flourished, continuing to produce the finest decorated firearms available in the world. As can be seen from these two photos of Custom Shop craftsmen at work, a great deal of hands-on labor is expended at the Custom Shop to achieve the highest level of quality and artistic beauty.

Photographs courtesy of Colt Manufacturing Company, Inc.

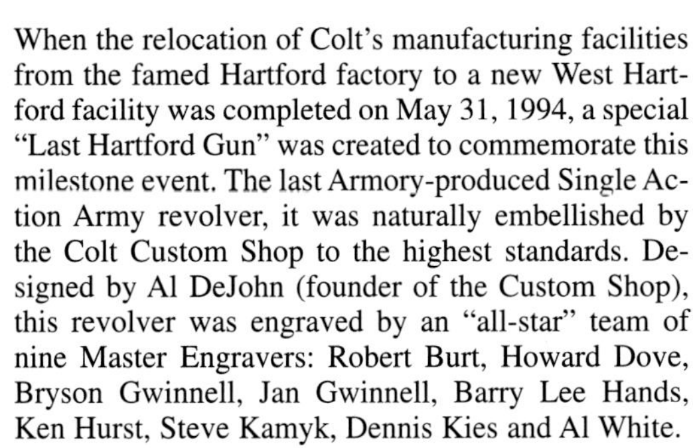

When the relocation of Colt's manufacturing facilities from the famed Hartford factory to a new West Hartford facility was completed on May 31, 1994, a special "Last Hartford Gun" was created to commemorate this milestone event. The last Armory-produced Single Action Army revolver, it was naturally embellished by the Colt Custom Shop to the highest standards. Designed by Al DeJohn (founder of the Custom Shop), this revolver was engraved by an "all-star" team of nine Master Engravers: Robert Burt, Howard Dove, Bryson Gwinnell, Jan Gwinnell, Barry Lee Hands, Ken Hurst, Steve Kamyk, Dennis Kies and Al White.

CHAPTER VII

MAKING THE WORLD SAFE

Hartford had never been busier that spring. Anticipating America's entry into the war that was raging in Europe, most of its seventy factories throbbed with urgency on war-related products. "Help Wanted" signs hung on every gate. From Canada, northern New England, New York, the mid-Atlantic states, even from Kansas, a constant stream of job seekers, hungry for fat paychecks, poured into the city, squeezing into already over-crowded, unsanitary tenements and boarding houses and forcing rents to double and triple. Beginners could earn $27 to $30 a week, while the highly skilled took home up to $200 weekly.

The city was in the midst of its fastest decade of growth, from 100,000 to 138,000. The black population alone more than doubled. Most of the newcomers were sharecroppers from Americus, Georgia, its rusty red soil still clinging to their overalls and aprons. The Yankee blacks who had lived in Hartford for generations resented the arrival of these "Southern Negroes," looking down upon them as boisterous country bumpkins who competed for the limited supply of rents and the domestic service jobs which, for the majority, were the only ones open. Unfortunately, no new housing of any kind would be built until the 1920s, and equal opportunity was denied to blacks in the very factories that had the greatest need for manpower.

As Colt's annual meeting convened, the hundred or so stockholders were all smiles, confident of hearing good news. For almost three years the Armory had boomed, expanding its facilities and work force to fill orders for guns that were secretly routed through Canada to supply the armies of Great Britain. In the past twelve months alone, employment had doubled to nearly 4,000, while the market value of its stock had risen from $160 to $775 per share. It had been able to retire all of its bonded debt of $1,200,000 and to write off another million of obsolete assets. In 1914 it had earned almost a million dollars on sales of only $2,284,000. In 1915 its earnings jumped to $2.5 million, an astounding profit of 50 percent after spending $700,000 on new equipment.

In the front row sat Colt's six directors. Frank Schirmer represented the New York financial house that had negotiated the sale of Mrs. Colt's stock back in 1901. Lewis Sperry was Colt's counsel, a former state legislator and congressman and also the Hartford County coroner who had spearheaded the investigation of the Park Central Hotel fire in 1889. Louis R. Cheney, son of one of the eight Cheney founders, was treasurer of the Austin Organ Company. He had moved to Hartford after working a number of years for the silk mill and devoted most of his time to good works like the Hartford Hospital and the American School for the Deaf. Charles M. Jarvis who had made his mark in business as head of the Berlin Iron Bridge Company, later merged into the American Bridge Company, a large combine of structural iron and steel fabricators. Jarvis was now a vice-president of American Bridge. D. Newton Barney was treasurer of the Hartford Electric Light Company. Hartford's most distinguished elder citizen, Morgan G. Bulkeley, now in his 80th year, had joined the board in 1913 and was Colt's largest stockholder.

Cheney and Bulkeley represented the alliance between business and politics that still dominated the city, even though the Democrats controlled the board of aldermen and council. When Cheney ran

Colt never left the Army's side.

". . . The board therefore recommends that the Colt .45 automatic pistol . . . be adopted for use by foot and mounted troops in the military service in consequence of its marked superiority . . . to any other known pistol . . ."

Report in the Army and Navy Journal, April 1, 1911

In 1911, the United States Army adopted as its official handgun the Colt 45 caliber automatic, designed by John M. Browning . . . and for 70 years, no American military force has found a better side-arm. Since the doughboy days in World War I, the famous "GI 45" has seen more action than any other military sidearm in modern times. Colt now honors this tradition with a custom-etched and selective gold-plated Commemorative in a limited public offering of 3,000. This one-of-a-kind Government Model features historical moments in the life of this modern classic: the American Eagle grasping a 45 ACP bullet from an early Colt ad; a motif of an American doughboy leading an attack in WW I; and a symbolic motif of John M. Browning, America's premier gun designer, shaking hands with Charles L. F. Robinson, Colt president 1911–1916, upon turning over all rights and patents of his invention to Colt.

This unique Commemorative is a handsome expression of the Colt Government 1911 Automatic that embodies many of the features of the original issue, and some historical additions that trace the origins of this milestone sidearm. This Commemorative is accompanied with a custom french-fitted American walnut presentation case with a brass exterior name plate and interior commemorative plate. To own one is to possess a part of America's history, and to honor a great American. Contact your nearest Colt dealer. (Important product and service literature accompany every Colt sale; be sure to ask for yours.)

COLT - an American heritage

Advertisement for Colt Model 1911 commemorating the inventor, John M. Browning. Appearing in 1981, the ad takes artistic license with the World War I background photo introducing, through retouching, a Colt automatic into the sergeant's hand.

(Courtesy of Naftzger & Kuhe, Farmington, Connecticut)

for mayor in 1912 he was endorsed by the *Courant* as "a gentleman of highest social standing and fine business connections." That year Colt's annual meeting, normally held on the first business day in April, was postponed until after the election the following week. Cheney defeated Thomas J. Spellacy, the Democrat candidate. Upon being sworn in, he said: "the affairs of a municipality are very largely of a business nature, and I trust that they may be kept out of politics as much as possible." Two years later he was reelected by a narrow margin but resigned the next day because he lacked a plurality of votes cast, apparently due to a "defect" in the voting machines in the Fourth Ward.

President Skinner gave a glowing financial report. The backlog of orders exceeded $30 million — three years' work. Two and a quarter million dollars had been spent on new equipment and buildings; the plant would soon have to be enlarged again. In cash and securities, the company had tucked away $11.5 million. Then his climax: since Colt's net profit had soared 160 percent to $6,346,000, the directors had voted to declare a dividend of $75.00 a share on the present stock and to recommend the shares be split eight for one. All the 21,112 shares represented were voted affirmatively, and the meeting ended with cheers for the management.

Five days later, on April 6, 1917, Congress declared war against Germany, and the United States joined the struggle to make the world safe for democracy.

For the purpose of defense, the country had been divided into thirteen ordnance districts by the War Department. The Bridgeport District covered all of Connecticut and Western Massachusetts. Pre-war, besides government arsenals, the only other major munitions area was located in the mid-Atlantic states, led by duPont and Hercules Powder. Within Connecticut, five firms were the principal suppliers; in addition to Colt's, the Remington Arms & Ammunition and Union Metallic Companies, Marlin-Rockwell, and Winchester. With the nation at war the lid of secrecy over their activities had been lifted; the ordnance districts became an arm of the Interallied Munition Pool; everyone had to work closely together. Forgotten in the common cause were commercial rivalries, production secrets, and profits — in fact, most of the war plants lost money. Colt's was a spectacular exception. Forming a trade association, the munition manufacturers shared designs and methods, performed engineering work for each other without charge, and exchanged plant visits.

As the second largest, the Bridgeport Ordnance District, employing at the peak some 400,000 persons round the clock seven days a week, achieved an astounding record. In the nineteen months of America's participation in World War I, the five private arsenals alone produced 181,662 machine guns. Most of the other factories in the state tooled up as fast as possible to contribute a variety of machinery, parts, and other equipment for use in the war machine. The brass industry in Waterbury consumed 67 million pounds of that raw material; with 15,000 workers Scovill Manufacturing made millions of time fuses, projectiles, and brass cartridge cases. Ensign-Bickford in Simsbury supplied two and one-half million feet of detonating fuse for mines and forty million two-inch hand grenade fuses. Cheney Brothers in Manchester spun silk yarn for parachutes and powder bags. Thousands of feet of elastic textile cord from the Russell Manufacturing Company in Middletown were used for pistol and cartridge belts, gas masks, canteen covers, and bayonet scabbards. The Hartford Rubber Works made rubber boots and tires for military vehicles, as well as 55,000 gas masks; Jewell Belting made 200,000 bayonet scabbards. As the largest machine tool builders, Pratt & Whitney furnished machines to government arsenals in America and England for manufacturing rifles; they also equipped Colt's production lines and those of other plants along with the hand tools and precision gauges required.

Labor-wise, it was the hey-day of the open shop. Employers called the tune on wages and working conditions. Any attempt to strike was quickly smashed. The threat of the military draft quieted most would-be troublemakers, and turnover among the newer workers was too high ever to solidify the work force. In the Armory there were two abortive strikes — once when thirty-six assemblers demanded higher wages, and again after the company cut its piecework rates. In both cases the men involved either returned or were replaced. In Bridgeport, 5,000 machinists employed by Remington and its satellite shops made a concerted effort, in 1918, to achieve more money, an eight-hour day, and union recognition. They resumed work only after the War Labor Board promised to hear their case, but struck again when the terms of the award failed to meet their demands. Finally, President Wilson himself intervened and ordered the men back.

For the first time, women were entering the factories. Before they had worked only in textile mills like Cheney's. "Making munitions is a woman's job" proclaimed posters and advertise-

The Park River and Sheldon Street tenements. (Courtesy Connecticut Historical Society)

Construction of new armory during World War I.

Colt foremen held a banquet at the Bond Hotel in May, 1917. Two of those seated at the head table are President Skinner and Vice-President Stone.

Many of Colt's old-timers boasted of a half century or more of service. *Standing:* Ted Stevens, Richard Broomhall, Jim Shortell, Dave Ahearn, William Morrow; *Seated:* George Green, C.J. Ehbets, Dave Jordan, and Ed Williams. Ehbets was Colt's patent king.

In the old armory Root's system of shafting and belts, made by the Jewel Belting Company of Hartford, operated the machines until the Second World War.

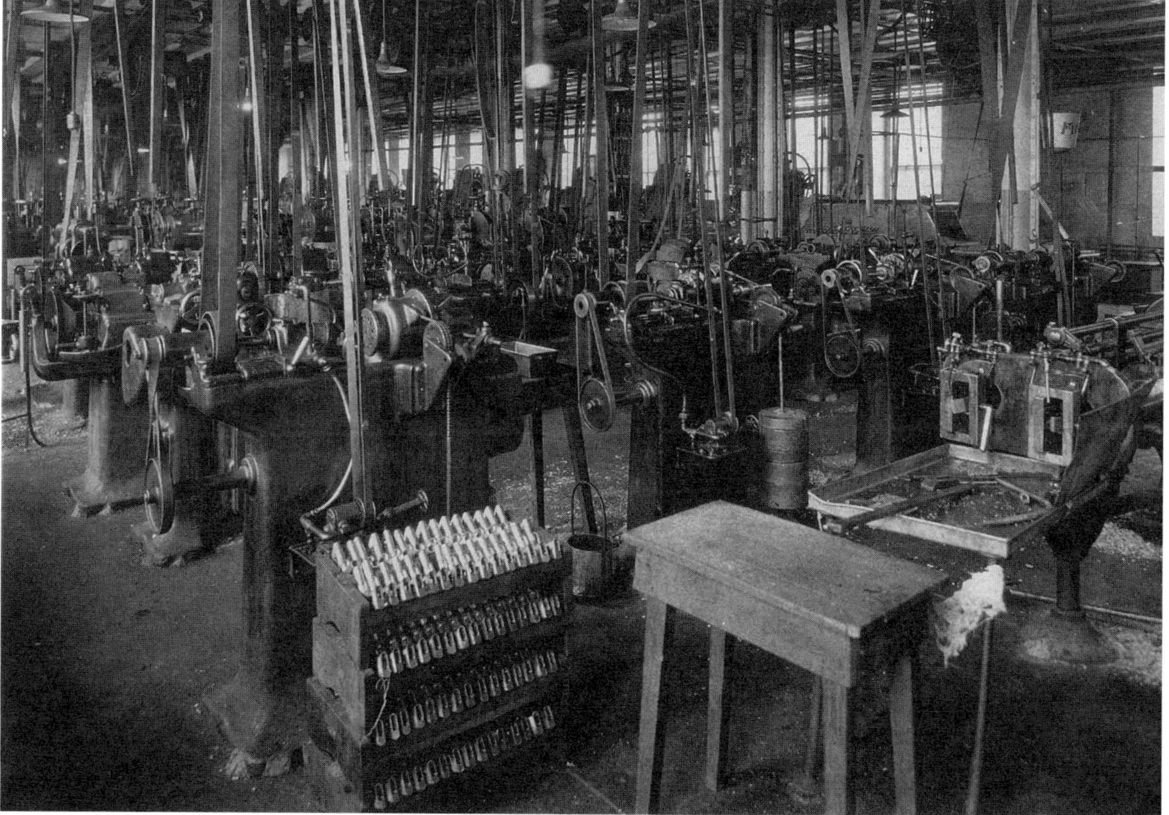

Milling .45 cal. receivers in World War I.

Rifling barrels.

Loading a rack of revolver frames into a gas furnace. The "blueing" operation was continued up to World War II.

Final inspection.

ments. Patriotism as well as the promise of good pay lured housewives into becoming machine operators on both day and night shifts. Some companies tried house-to-house canvassing to find women who would work part-time. Rest rooms, cafeterias, dispensaries, and safety devices had to be provided. At Colt's, women drilled, polished, inspected, and ground barrels to close tolerances. Remington had 4,000 making cartridges. Employers were surprised at their ability to produce as much as men; they adapted quickly to repetitive jobs, lost fewer days due to illness, and stayed longer. Altogether, the introduction of females into factories was a revolutionary change in the industrial employment picture that survived the end of the war.

Sam Stone more than once commented on the desperate need for help as the Armory strove to double its employment again. It was a worse situation than during World War II, a generation later. One morning as he strolled down Sheldon Street along the Little River toward his office, he met a group of Polish women sitting on the front steps of a tenement.

Around them played small children; several held babies in their arms. On an impulse, he inquired if they would like to work in his factory. He had considerable difficulty in making himself understood. At first they thought this well-dressed gentleman had in mind an immoral purpose. He pointed toward the Armory and kept repeating the words "machine" and "money." Their eyes lit up, but they shook their heads. "No work in factory, take care of kids." He looked at their strong arms and wondered what he could do. Before noon, he had the answer. In a few days a saloon-keeper nearby was offered a handsome sum to sell out. The saloon was cleaned and painted, a sandbox installed, and a sign hung in the large plate glass window. It read "Colt Day Nursery." In charge was a registered nurse. Soon the young Polish mothers on Sheldon Street were learning to run machines inside the Armory.

Not only was Colt's plagued with a shortage of workers and a high labor turnover, mainly due to the lack of housing for their families, it had problems getting enough steel for its gun barrels and slides. In January 1918, the Armory also faced a coal shortage. New England was burning three million tons of coal every month, most of which came by water. The railroads were jammed with wartime goods. Coal was piled high around the mines in Pennsylvania. Washington ordered special trains to carry it to Hampton Roads where nine steamers waited to transport it north. In the meantime, Fuel Administrator Garfield closed all factories east of the Mississippi for a five-day period. For ten weeks Monday would be a meatless holiday. Skinner could not believe that the government meant to stop vital war production. The heads of the five Connecticut arsenals quickly won an exemption, and three days later a steady flow of coal began to arrive in Hartford. Emergency crews were assigned by the mayor to deal with the congestion in the freight yard and 160 cars were speedily unloaded. The crisis was over, but throughout the war those on the home front were urged to observe a meatless Tuesday, a wheatless Wednesday and a porkless Saturday.

* * *

From the start of the conflagration that swept Europe in 1914, the machine gun became the most important infantry weapon other than the doughboy's rifle. There were two models in use — the lightweight air-cooled Lewis and the heavy .30 caliber Maxim-Vickers. When America entered, the Army was woefully understocked with obsolete weaponry, despite the fact that Colt's had pioneered the machine gun in America. The Army had 670 old machine rifles; 282 Maxims, 1904 model; 353 machine rifles; and 148 of the outmoded "potato-digger" 1895 Colts. Only two armories were equipped to make machine guns, and the first American division landing in France had to be supplied with French armament. The previous December the Secretary of War had contracted with Colt's for 4,000 Vickers on top of its foreign orders. By May 1918, Colt's was turning out fifty per day. In addition, it began to convert several thousand more for airplane use, the Vickers being the only weapon that could be synchronized to fire through whirling propeller blades. By the end of the year the company had delivered some 13,000.

Soon after the American declaration, there arrived in Hartford a tall, slim, ram-rod straight man with a bald dome and the eyes of a sharpshooter. He found an apartment for his wife and children and at once proceeded to where a desk in an obscure corner of the Armory had been reserved for him long ago. For the next two years he stayed close to the work he loved, dreading the limelight. John Moses Browning was now in his early sixties, still quiet and unassuming, although — unlike most inventors — immensely rich from his lifetime of perfecting firearms. He had worked for two of Colt's biggest competitors, Remington and Winchester, but his longest and last association was with Colt's — one that extended over a period of nearly thirty years.

Though never one for idle talk, John was completely at ease with the workmen. One operator complained to him that he made the same part over and over but had no idea how it fitted into the whole. The inventor paused to give him a lesson on the part's importance, so that at the end he had a clear picture in his mind of the gun he was helping to fabricate. If an engineer ran into an irksome dead end, like as not he brought the problem to John. Once asked where he had acquired his wealth of technical knowledge, Browning replied: "In my father's shop; he was a gunsmith." Then, seeing the young man's embarrassment, he added: "But I've been taking courses ever since in colleges like this." John himself frequently solved a pressing engineering problem on his early morning walk to work. Upon reaching his office, he would rough out a preliminary sketch in pencil, so simple yet so precise that rarely did it require refinement.

The following month, Browning put the finishing touches on his latest and most powerful weapons — a 37-pound heavy machine gun and a light, rapid-firing 15½-pound automatic rifle, both .30 caliber. The Browning machine gun contained 236 component parts that required for manufacturing 1,250 different fixtures, 1,600 cutters and 2,800 gauges. The Army was desperate to get both into production. Apologetically, the ordnance officials approached Browning with a request that he assign full rights to the government for both weapons, as well as his .45 pistol, for the duration of the war and also supervise production in every factory. "We know our offer is only a fraction of what you would receive from royalties on orders already booked, and it may not be acceptable," they said. They agreed to pay him $750,000 — less than six percent of what he normally would have been entitled to. "Major," the inventor promptly answered, "if that suits Uncle Sam, it's all right with me."

Because of its own heavy backlog of orders for Maxim-Vickers machine guns and Browning-designed pistols, Colt's was compelled to depend upon Marlin-Rockwell, Remington, and Winchester to fill most of the contracts. The first BAR's

John Browning with his Model 1917 .30 cal. water-cooled machine gun.

reached France with the 79th Division in July of 1918, and, strange to relate, Lieutenant Val A. Browning, the inventor's son, was the first to fire the weapon against the enemy, as he also did the .30 cal. machine gun in September. By the end of November, Colt's sub-contractors had completed 41,000 machine guns, compared to only a thousand from Colt's, and 43,000 automatic rifles, compared to Colt's 9,000.

Four days after the Armistice, Browning ran a successful test of a .50 cal. machine gun, which General John J. Pershing had demanded to penetrate the heaviest German armor. This water-cooled gun later became one of America's basic weapons in World War II and Korea, both on the ground and in the air. The BAR, too, continued to be used throughout subsequent wars. A reporter who wanted to know how Browning achieved such miracles got this reply: "One drop of genius in a barrel of sweat!" While Browning was regarded by the experts as "the foremost living perfecter of modern firearms," Colt's could take full credit for overseeing their tremendous output in only eighteen months.

Equally in demand were pistols. Five times as many American soldiers carried pistols as the Germans or Allies. Over 150,000 Colt .45's, designed by Browning, had been assembled since their introduction six years earlier. Colt's production manager, Fred Moore, and President Skinner had attended the unprecedented trial in 1911 and would never forget the perfect score of 6,000 rounds without a malfunction which the inventor racked up. Nine days afterward the Army adopted the gun as the standard sidearm for thc armed forces, and fifty years later it still held that honor. The record made on that March day was not challenged or repeated until May of 1917, when Browning's recoil-operated .30 cal. machine gun fired 20,000 rounds without stopping. Now Colt's had a contract for a million more .45's at a price of $14.50 each. At the same time, it assisted Remington in gearing up for 150,000 model 1911 Colt automatics. Their manufacture depended mostly on the skilled hands of old-timers who knew every trick of fitting and assembling — methods never incorporated into the shop drawings. It took six months to revise the blueprints so as to create maximum interchangeability between the parts made at Colt's and those at Remington. Colt's had 3,500 men at work on handguns alone, and by the time of the Armistice, 2,200 a day were being shipped.

Lieutenant Val A. Browning demonstrates his father's automatic rifle (the B.A.R.) which he was the first to fire in France.

Fred Moore, Colt production manager during World War I.

* * *

On Thursday, November 7th, from early in the afternoon until midnight, the city went wild. As soon as word of the armistice bulletin posted in front of the *Courant* building on State Street spread, thousands rushed into Main Street, shouting, cheering, waving flags, forming impromptu parades. Church bells, auto horns, and factory whistles joined the clamor. Workers from Colt and other shops poured into the streets, hatless, coatless, still wearing their aprons and overalls. Colt employees held aloft partially completed machine guns and beat in unison with hammers and other tools on tin pans. The Colt Band followed. Soon there were several enormous processions marching in different directions downtown, brandishing not only Old Glory but the Italian and French tricolors, the Union Jack, and the red and white flag of Poland. As they passed City Hall, Mayor Richard Kinsella, with the insight of the astute Irish politician, observed: "Money could not buy such a demonstration." With great hilarity, Jewell Belting's work force marched boldly through the east door of the Capitol and out the west side. But the celebration, which almost ended in a riot, was premature. The peace announcement flashed by the United Press was false, and even after the belated official denials it was impossible to stem the tide of rumor.

Four days later, at 2:45 in the morning, news of the signing of the real armistice reached Hartford, and again the whistles blew. Before dawn the parades had formed again. Italians from the East side crowded around the *Courant* building, bringing flagons of wine and bursting into song. They sang "Hail, Hail the Gang's All Here" and "The Star Spangled Banner," led by a nurse in full uniform. "Today is Liberty Day," shouted one stalwart East Sider. As the sun broke through a leaden sky, the Main Street area resembled a Saturday afternoon. By 8:30 the trolleys were unable to move, the factories had closed for the day, and people of all stations swelled from every direction. Pushcarts dragged by urchins carried a load of cheering celebrants. Two jubilant old men amused the crowd by shouting over and over in Italian "Hooray for Wilson, hooray for the U.S., Hooray for the Allies," and then hurling their hats to the sidewalk.

That evening a mammoth parade through the city was organized, partly well-drilled and partly spontaneous. For two hours ten thousand officials, soldiers, workers, volunteers, and gleeful youngsters — headed by the Colt Band and the State Guard — marched from Main Street to the Capitol. A reviewing stand was hastily thrown up in front of Morgan Bulkeley's house on Washington Street. Every nationality was represented, "one of the finest demonstrations of Americanism ever seen in Hartford," enthused an observer. Effigies of the Kaiser were strung up by the neck, nailed in a pine box, dragged along, or held high by the head. Decorated trucks carried workers from the various plants. Seven hundred men from the Armory carried Browning gun posters, and the guns themselves were displayed on an elaborate float. It all ended with band concerts on the Capitol grounds, and the next morning an exhausted, yawning citizenry returned to its normal routine.

Colonel Skinner was satisfied. Colt's had managed to deliver 425,500 automatic pistols, 151,700 revolvers, 13,000 Maxim-Vickers machine guns, and 10,000 new Brownings, while it handled smoothly the sub-contracting of nearly a hundred thousand more. The Armory had gone all out to meet every demand placed upon it. Peace was welcome. But he doubted that it would make the world safe for democracy or for anything else. In fact, he had only to contemplate the transformation which had taken place in the distaff side of Hartford to realize that the world would never be the same again.

* * *

Like most men of that era, Sam Stone underestimated the importance of the vote to women. In fact, he hardly thought about it at all. He knew there was something called the Connecticut Woman Suffrage Association which had its headquarters on Pratt Street in Hartford. The pioneer organization, founded by Isabella Hooker in 1869 and presided over by Mrs. Hooker until a few months before her death in 1907, now claimed 18,000 members. The president was Mrs. Thomas N. Hepburn, wife of a prominent Hartford surgeon. While Mrs. Hooker had been an elitist who looked mainly to her own class to free women, Mrs. Hepburn appealed to the disenfranchised at every level, winning the support of the State Federation of Labor and thousands of working women. Another ally was the clergy-led temperance movement.

In January 1916, several of the ladies in the Stones' social set were aroused by the speeches of Helen Todd of California, a former state factory inspector who had been successful in winning the vote for her sex in that state. On a whirlwind tour of Connecticut, she stressed the necessity for women to organize politically and fight for the

The Colt Band. (Courtesy Connecticut Historical Society)

vote, rather than try to convince their menfolk of its moral righteousness. In addition, she said, laws were needed to protect women and children working in factories. Hearing that made Stone bridle; he pointed out that Colt's had many women doing men's work, and they weren't being exploited — in fact, he even had a nurse taking care of their infants.

By this time six western states had granted women suffrage, but it had met with defeat in the legislatures of Massachusetts, New York, and Pennsylvania. The main thrust of the suffragists now was to persuade Congress to pass the constitutional amendment drawn up by Susan B. Anthony in 1875, which stated simply that "the right to vote shall not be denied by any state on account of sex." The Senate in 1914 had passed it by one vote, but it lost in the House. In Connecticut, the C.W.S.A. staged in May its biggest demonstration of strength yet, with a colorful pageant through downtown Hartford. In the face of a stiff breeze, past a curious crowd, paraded a thousand suffragists afoot, in automobiles, and on floats depicting women in various professions. "Joan of Arc" led on horseback. An oxcart rumbled along bearing a sign "Connecticut Trying to Catch Up." They ended their march at the Park Casino on Elm Street. There the spectators were amused by a float that reproduced a colonial kitchen, in which a Puritan mother sat by the fireside, her daughter at her feet, rocking a cradle. On the side of the float hung a large sign:

Mother mends our stockings;
Mother mends our coat.
Perhaps Mother would mend some laws
If Mother had the vote.

Just as it reached the Casino, the ubiquitous Colt Band escorting it broke into the ragtime strains of "Oh, You Beautiful Doll," causing the mother to make a hasty departure.

At the mass meeting held in the Casino, Mrs. Hepburn predicted that "suffrage is coming to Connecticut just as surely as the sun will rise tomorrow... The vote will not bring the millennium [but] opportunities for education and advancement and race betterment." A factory worker from

New York, Rose Winslow, captured the hearts of the many union members present as she spoke on what the right to vote would mean to the girls who slaved in mills and factories: "A great majority of these women who do not want the vote...do not know what it is to earn a cent for themselves. The fact that they have chosen the American Beauty rose as their flower...shows they are women of the leisure class...we cannot live on the toil of another...we want a square deal, not praises, but wages!"

The following March, the suffragists focused on the State Legislature. Jeannette Rankin, the nation's first congresswoman and a Republican from Montana, was welcomed in Hartford and escorted by a thousand women to the Capitol. She was introduced to Governor Holcomb and Republican Chairman J. Henry Roraback, both of whom snubbed her. Before a full house at the Parsons Theatre that night, Mrs. Hepburn attacked the state's "extreme variety of boss rule" which made it impossible for the suffragists to get fair play.

On the day of the hearing to consider a referendum on the Anthony constitutional amendment, some six hundred women and their male supporters jammed the Capitol corridors, armed with a petition containing 43,000 names, waving flags of purple, green, and yellow, and wearing a tricolor knot on their hats — the same colors as those of the Pankhurst militants in England. The Hartford *Times* said the scene "resembled the crowded deck of an overladen transport — the vote-desirous ladies swarmed like bees, but they didn't sting." While the *Times* was sympathetic to their cause, the rival *Courant* gave them short shrift; its editor, Charles Hopkins Clark, grumpily held the view that women were well enough represented by men, a view shared by the powerful Republican machine.

The following day the anti-suffragists had their turn. Claiming the majority of women didn't want the vote, they said their ideal was the conservation of womanhood — not the destruction of its special glory by seeking to make it masculine. "This progressive age has produced a type of feminist whose grievance is satiety of ease, freedom her pain, and plenty her disease." George B. Chandler, the state's compensation commissioner, went even further: "They have certain exotic vices like free love and feminism at one end of their propaganda and socialism at the other end — we are asked to add to the laws and take away from the home." In rebuttal, Mrs. Hepburn stuck to the political realities; it was clear the Democrats were going to repudiate their party platform favoring suffrage, and she exposed their deceit. She related her encounter with one member of the Democratic state committee who had pledged his support earlier but now had changed his mind. "Why, what difference does it make?" he said. "We all know that a party platform is merely an advertisement to catch votes!"

It was no surprise when the legislative committee issued an almost unanimous adverse report and the House voted 124-106 to accept it. The margin of defeat, however, was smaller than in the 1913 session. Mrs. Hepburn was far from discouraged: "We are going to keep right up with our fight. There will be no let up."

Enthralled by the dogged spirit of liberated women like Mrs. Hepburn, more and more proper ladies gave up their bridge parties and teas and devoted their time to the suffrage movement. They addressed and distributed pamphlets, raised money and helped the Association organize the state by district and county. The battleground shifted to Washington. Senators Brandegee and McLean were pressed hard to vote for the constitutional amendment. The former was an adamant foe, basing his opposition on the doctrine of states' rights. Throughout the war the barrage of suffragist propaganda never ceased: petitions were circulated through the factories, lectures on citizenship widely given, and by early 1919 nearly 90,000 signatures had been obtained from Connecticut women. Labor and the Democrats were solidly on their side, while the anti's struck back by accusing suffragists of shirking their patriotic duties to sell Liberty Bonds and otherwise assist the war effort.

That spring the suffrage committee of the General Assembly issued its first favorable majority report, but the bill died in the Senate for lack of a two-thirds majority. Earlier, the prohibition amendment had slid through the legislature without trouble. Senator Bower of Hartford, noting that twenty-nine states now permitted women to vote, recalled his conversion to woman's suffrage thirty years before when he attended the Hartford High School. His classmate was Edward Beecher Hooker, son of the great feminist Isabella Hooker. In those days, the subject of women's rights was considered a joke, and as a result, Hooker was teased unmercifully. Bower, however, became a believer, and he assured his fellow senators that woman's suffrage was no joke now.

At the 50th convention of the C.W.S.A. in Bridgeport the following November, the main speaker was Grace Thompson Seton, her words a stirring call to action: "I feel like saying with Job,

'Oh Lord, how long?' Nineteen states have ratified the 19th amendment, yet here we are in Connecticut knocking our determined knuckles at the door of an obdurate, but otherwise perfectly nice governor who has three times declined to call a special session… Fifty years is a good apprenticeship. It is high time the suffragist was graduated into the voter."

The year 1920 was the crucial one and it looked as if Connecticut might be the linchpin state. Twenty-seven others had now ratified the Susan B. Anthony amendment, nine short of the necessary two-thirds majority. In January, the "drys" savored victory with the passage of the 18th Amendment on Prohibition. Afraid of defeat for suffrage at the last moment, the national leaders appealed to their brethren in Connecticut to take emergency action. Although both houses and both political parties favored a special session of the legislature, Governor Marcus H. Holcomb and a small coterie of Republican diehards dared to flaunt the wishes of those who had put them in power. By the end of March, only one more state was needed for ratification. The best possibilities were Vermont and Connecticut, the legislatures of which stood ready and willing to ratify. For the C.W.S.A., the week of May 3rd was Armageddon. A motor corps visited forty towns; a mass meeting was held on the Capitol grounds. But Governor Holcomb maintained his ostrich-like pose: "The desire of a few women does not create an emergency."

Resentment and indignation soared. Alice Paul of the National Woman's Party insisted the legislature could convene itself, but former Governor Simeon E. Baldwin, who was regarded as the state's constitutional authority, rejected the idea. During the summer, ratification by Tennessee and Vermont assured passage of the 19th Amendment and relieved the pressure on Connecticut. The diehards capitulated, and in September, by an almost unanimous vote, the legislators made Connecticut the 37th and last state to ratify. While the victory was superfluous, it still vindicated those who had struggled for fifty-one years. In the November Presidential election, 150,000 women (41%) voted for the first time, a few thousand more than the total number of working women in the state.

A nation yearning for "normalcy," tired of war, reform, the Red scare, and foreign involvement, gave a landslide to Harding and the Republicans. Connecticut suffragists, however, had the satisfaction of seeing Senator Brandegee run far behind his ticket. Its crusade won, the C.W.S.A. held its last convention soon after, and its veteran campaigners formed the League of Women Voters to educate the newly franchised on political issues. The dire consequences predicted by the anti's — of women being able to vote and work as they pleased — never materialized. To the chagrin of the suffragists, the politicians, as they reluctantly admitted the opposite sex to their domain, chose not them but their former opponents. The most conspicuous change of all, noted and applauded by apprehensive males, was in the realm of fashion. At last the emancipated woman shed her Victorian corset and floor-length skirt. A new age had arrived.

CHAPTER VIII

INSIDE COLT'S

The Armory ended World War I stronger than before. Not only had it shipped $66 million worth of munitions, it had earned $21.5 million from 1914 through 1918. Its surplus swelled to over six million dollars. Sales in the last year of the War alone were nearly $32 million and the profit exceeded six million dollars. Employment peaked at 10,000, of whom 2,220 had worked in the Meriden plant on Browning automatic rifles. This satellite facility was now for sale.

At the annual meeting of stockholders in 1920, President Skinner proudly announced that "the company doesn't owe a dollar to anybody and the whole plant is now equipped with the latest machinery." A year later, however, the surplus had shrunk by $800,000 for several good reasons. Having accepted no commercial business during the War, Skinner's first peacetime move was to fill the accumulated back orders for handguns, and he felt a moral obligation to do so at pre-war prices — even though wages and materials had, in the meantime, risen sharply. The Colt .45 was still the Army's standard automatic as well as the favorite of police departments. Moreover, reconversion caused extensive changes in the plant. A large investment was made in tools, fixtures, and gauges for another police weapon, the rapid-firing machine gun, and other new products. Even so, the combination of military and commercial orders left vacant 100,000 square feet of factory space.

Suspecting a severe drought in military sales for the next several years, Skinner and Vice-President Stone set in motion a diversification program — Colt's second. They obtained contracts for adding machines and commercial dishwashers to be marketed under other than Colt's name. Relations with the Federal Adding Machine Company, however, proved disastrous. For some inexplicable reason the management of that firm dissipated two million dollars in cash, forcing the Armory to halt production. In 1920, Stone also acquired a company engaged in molding hard plastics; the material, which he renamed "Coltrock," was used in making electrical plugs and switches. Later, buttons, tobacco humidors, and other products were added to the line.

Nevertheless, during the early 1920s the erosion of Colt's surplus continued and employment dropped to a low of 900. Yet, the New York *Financial World* enthused over the company's prospects, calling Colt's "one of the most successful in the world in its field — high-grade firearms. Investors who have pinned their faith to this company have been well rewarded, for the stock sells at three times pre-war prices and dividend returns are exceptional." The article, however, didn't mention that the price of Colt stock was only a third of its wartime high.

Six weeks after the 1921 annual meeting, Colonel Skinner, wearied from running the Armory during the War, again resigned as president. "I've been in harness since 1880," he told his directors, "and I feel the need of relief from the details involved in my office." Vice-President Stone, in his 52nd year, succeeded him. Frank Schirmer of Boston also resigned as a director. There were now three vacancies on the board, which were filled by President Stone; Frank C. Nichols, vice-president; and Walter Penfield, vice-president and treasurer. Fred Moore, who as a young toolmaker had been Browning's protégé, was elevated to works manager. Colonel Skinner stayed on as chairman but died the following March in his Allyn House apartment at the age of 67. His estate probated at $613,000, including 8,401 shares of Colt stock valued at $201,624.

Bolstered by a million dollar contract from a foreign government, the machine gun division soon revived. The real excitement in the Armory centered around the development of John Browning's latest and last invention — a .37mm anti-aircraft cannon. At the Aberdeen Proving Ground in the summer of 1921, with President Stone and Fred Moore looking on, it was successfully tested. Eventually Browning refined it to the point where it could fire a larger cartridge with a velocity of 3,000 feet per second. But Washington had no interest in, or money for, new military weapons. Colt's itself was trying to stay solvent by manufacturing anything but guns. So Browning's drawings and three working models were filed away until war again threatened the world. John Moses Browning died five years later, having 128 patents on eighty different firearms in his name. His record was perfect: every arm he entered in a government trial had won over all competition, a worthy successor to the crown of Colonel Colt.

In 1923 Colt's established an electrical division by acquiring the assets of the Johns-Pratt Company, for years a member of the Capitol Avenue manufacturing community. The purchase price was $1,237,000. Johns-Pratt made service installation devices, enclosed fuses, Vulcabeston packing, and hot molded products; their marketing was handled by Johns Manville. Moving their production equipment to the Armory filled up 200,000 square feet (out of a total of 900,000) and added over 500 workers to the Colt force.

By 1926 Stone could feel more optimistic. Earnings were a healthy $662,000 that year. He settled a dispute with the government over Colt's wartime taxes, having to pay less than a quarter of the two million dollars claimed. The Chileans came through with a contract for the improved Browning automatic rifle, after holding a competition in which Vickers, Hotchkiss of France, Mapsen of Sweden, and gunmakers from Germany and Italy also took part. The demand for revolvers was running 15 percent above the pre-war level. Equally pleasing was the fact that the diversification program seemed to be paying off. Both the electrical and dishwashing divisions were expanded.

As president, Sam Stone, deceptively mild, upright, and unshakable, followed the old Yankee business maxim of the less said, the better. He believed the 3,600 stockholders were entitled to know only the barest essentials of the company's operations, and his reports were purposely terse. During his long tenure sales figures were not revealed. Occasionally, he would comment on the Armory's problems, such as the nagging one of surplus space which, in 1928 he referred to as "a heavy overhead burden." Apparently responding to outside criticism, he cautiously stated it would be occupied "if suitable lines somewhat kindred to those we now manufacture could be installed with an assurance of profitable returns." But other than the dishwasher, electrical, and plastics divisions, on which he spent $150,000 for new equipment in that year, he said diligent research had so far not resulted in uncovering any additional lines or products in which he would recommend investment.

Through the boom and bust year of 1929, Colt's kept right on paying the $8.00 annual dividend. The Plastics Division, now considered to be first in custom molding, was enlarged, using up a quarter of the vacant production space. At the start of the Great Depression, the Armory employed 1,581, of whom 120 had service of twenty-five years or more, and ten could look back on a half century in the Armory. The first three years of the Depression affected Colt's just as severely as it did most manufacturers in Hartford; three of its divisions worked a four-day week; revolver sales in 1932 were the smallest of any year. The executives had their salaries reduced ten percent, but President Stone did his best to keep as many working as he could. Although employment fell to about 1,200, the decline was much less than in other local shops. In fact, some 200 more men than necessary were retained in order to spread the available work, and neither day nor piecework rates were cut. The company's humanity was costly: a million dollars came out of surplus to maintain employment and wages.

Optimism was a scarce commodity in those dark days. But Stone did not let the dismal present obscure his vision of the future. Colt's obligation — and his own duty — was to be ready to meet the defense requirements of the country whenever world events made them apparent. Americans, however, had turned their backs on the rest of the world, refusing to join the League of Nations and retreating inside a transparent shell of false security. The armed forces of the United States barely existed; in 1930 its standing army of 30,000 soldiers was smaller than Poland's, Spain's, or Turkey's. Surveying the firearms capacity of the nation, Stone realized there were only six government-owned arsenals, and they had capacity for producing less than five percent of what would be needed should a major war occur. Full preparedness would call for a three billion dollar investment in plant and equipment. He saw to it that as

President Samuel Stone (Courtesy Taylor Stone)

President Stone, Vice-President Dwight Phelps and associates on the boardwalk at Atlantic City during a convention.

much new equipment was bought during these years of declining sales as could be wrung out of the depreciation account. Come what may, Colt's house would be in order.

Despite the fact that earnings were near zero, Stone also insisted on maintaining the record of paying an annual dividend that had stood ever since the Colt family sold the Armory in 1901. Even reduced to four percent, however, the dividend payments, added to the capital expenditures, ate up nearly a million dollars of the company's surplus.

Starting in 1933 shipments and earnings rebounded; employment, too, climbed back to the 1930 level, and all workers received bonuses. For the next ten years, Colt's would be riding its last crest of prosperity. Neither profits nor dividends would be as spectacular as those made or paid before 1920, though, because of two natural disasters, higher production costs, and the first Armory-wide strike.

* * *

As late as 1930, when war clouds were gathering again in Europe, Colt's was Hartford's largest manufacturer as well as its oldest. It would soon be surpassed, however, by Pratt & Whitney Aircraft in East Hartford, which at that time had 2,700 employees making 600 engines for the French government. Situated as it was along the city's waterfront at the junction of the Connecticut River with the Little River — where Dutch traders had encamped 300 years before — the Armory made an impressive sight. The long, four-story brick structure in the shape of an inverted "H" that had been erected after the Civil War formed its center. On the east side were concrete additions with saw-toothed roofs; on the west, a two-story brownstone office with an inviting porch; to the south, rows of tenements that were once company-owned. What held the eye longest were the curved arches of the factory windows, so typical of New England mills, and rising over all — supported by twelve slender columns — the blue, onion-shaped dome atop which perched the rampant stallion clutching a broken spear. This was the Colt symbol and a Hartford landmark.

Ever since the feverish days of World War I, Colt's had maintained an employment office which was then managed by Herbert Walker. Employment departments came into being to deal with the manpower shortage. Often the man in charge had been a foreman or an old-timer who no longer fitted in anywhere else. Department heads tended to resent his existence as a dilution of their authority to hire and fire. He was an appendage without influence. With the liberalization of the workmen's compensation law originally passed in 1913, the employment manager frequently took on the additional duty of safety director. Sometimes he directed in-plant training programs. During the late 1920s and early 30s he also became involved in discouraging union organization and nurturing instead a docile employees' association.

Coddling the worker in any way was considered a sign of weakness, an invitation to trouble. Management could not be wrong. The irony was that on the one hand department bosses opposed anything that smacked of treating employees like children, while on the other they feared their becoming self-respecting individuals with feelings and rights of their own. Not only did this attitude define the accepted concept of the boss-worker relationship; it was also the essence of the line-staff rivalry that prevails today in large organizations — a never-ending struggle for power between doers and advisers, those on the firing line every day and those who sit in offices and back them up with a variety of services.

In general, until collective bargaining legalized an authority other than management's to speak for the worker, the personnel function received little attention. For a long time it was like frosting on the cake, the first excess to be lopped off come a retrenchment. The Second World War forced more and more companies to recognize its importance and to make it as indispensable a component of the management process as engineering, production, finance, or marketing.

The weakest link in the management chain was the foreman. From the days of the independent inside contractor in the Armory, there still lingered the tradition of the department autocrat. Tell him what you wanted to produce and when, but don't tell him how. He was the proverbial bull in the shop, only now he had become an anachronism. To his way of thinking an employee was merely another kind of machine; either he produced, or he didn't. Between top management and the foremen, a considerable void existed. A kind of caste system divided the plant, with the hourly workers at the bottom and their immediate supervisors in the middle; the latter were socially much closer to their subordinates, though, and hardly considered themselves a part of management. The root of the problem was the failure to treat foremen as managers; their pay differential was too little, they enjoyed few extra benefits or perquisites, and they received little or no training in management.

Most foremen, of course, were chosen for their technical expertise. Some were also natural bosses, considerate of their men's welfare. Tom Roche, for example, had already celebrated his 50th anniversary, and for the past thirty years had been a respected supervisor. As a thirteen-year-old boy in County Cork, Ireland, Tom heard about the great Armory and decided to join his two sisters living in Hartford. He almost didn't make it. Coming up the Connecticut River, the steamboat *Granite State* caught fire near Goodspeed's Landing and he had to be hauled out of the water.

Lawrence Appley, when he headed up the American Management Association, used to say that "the basic function of management is the development of people and not the direction of things." Yet, for the average supervisor to be personnel-minded is quite contrary to his nature or training, since to gain his position he necessarily had to be concerned primarily with things. Production, however, depends upon people. Sam Stone, like many self-made executives with an instinctive appreciation of the human element, had little patience with engineers and their black or white view of what made business tick. It particularly irked him when some bright young engineer would boast of his latest mechanical innovation by saying: "We're trying to take the human element out of it, so the job will run smoothly." He knew as well as anybody what mechanization had accomplished in American industry — that it had provided the highest standard of living anywhere in the world. Colt's machines performed over eighty percent of the operations, just as they had done in Colonel Colt's lifetime. Yet, people were still important; machines couldn't assemble, inspect, or test guns. Machines didn't run by themselves, and sometimes eliminating the human element in the quest for absolute automation made the job worse from a management standpoint. Yes, worse, if the change alienated the worker or did away with his job entirely. One day a small group of engineering trainees was brought to Stone's office to meet him. He took them over to the window and pointed at the Armory. "See all those buildings? Suppose you took all the men and women out of them and lined them up along the street? What would you have left? Only empty buildings and idle machinery which can't produce a damn thing. Don't ever forget that when all's

Edwin Williams

said and done it's people who count!"

President Stone liked to think of Colt's as one big family; he knew hundreds by their first name. It was an axiom that if a new employee lasted his first year, he was assured of a job the rest of his natural life. When he became too old to run a machine, he was still kept on as an elevator operator or janitor. Stone was especially proud of having two or even three generations of the same family employed simultaneously. But, although Colt's may have been more cohesive than most shops of its size, even Stone's personal touch was no longer sufficient to permit individual recognition or treatment in every case. Over twenty different nationalities made up the work force, half of which was divided equally among Italians, Polish, and Anglo-Saxons.

Anyone could walk unannounced into the president's office. One morning before the eight o'clock start of the office workday, a powerfully built woman carrying an infant framed his doorway, flustered and incoherent. Stone invited her to sit down. From her mixture of rapid Russian and broken English he gathered she desperately needed a job; her worthless husband had left her with two children to support. With a big smile, he took the baby out of her arms and directed her to the employment office. "I'll hold her until you return," he said. She didn't get the job that day or the next, but she kept coming back until she succeeded. Years later at Mr. Stone's funeral, Pauline Malik, tears streaming from her eyes, said that there would never be another boss like him and never a better home to work in than Colt's.

Long service was a cherished Colt tradition about which the management frequently boasted. It was their firm conviction that only through the eyes and hands of assemblers and inspectors who learned their skills through years of on-the-job experience could tolerances be held as closely as required, the 800 inspections made on every gun, the accurate firing of the finished product guaranteed. At this time, Colt's had sixteen employees with over a half-century of service. One, with 64 years, continued to work until the day before he died. The dean of this group was Leron H. Robertson, who had been one of Sam Colt's first "hands" when he began making revolvers on Pearl Street in 1847. Robertson stayed on the payroll through four wars — in 1848, 1861, 1898, and 1917. At the age of 94 he had accumulated 77 years of service to the Armory.

In 1933 Herb Walker and Arthur Ulrich, the company's longtime secretary, counted 104 employees in the factory who had passed their 65th birthday. "Most of them are experts in a particular phase of gun-making," they said. "We couldn't afford to dispense with their services. Some of them could do their jobs blindfolded!" It certainly seemed true when one watched them working to the thousandth part of an inch with a sense of touch that was almost miraculous. Billy Cluff, at 81, was then the oldest in both years and length of service. Short, white-haired, keen-eyed, for some sixty years he had been assembling shell ejectors into gun cylinders. The rod and ratchet that make up the ejector must fit perfectly. Cluff would tell by the feel whether it was snug or not. Deftly using a file and buffer, he could size a ratchet within a hair's breadth in a few expert strokes. Billy also enjoyed serving as president of the Twenty-Five Year Club, each of the 143 members of which wore a silver pin with a star for every five years of service over 25. Every year they were entertained at a banquet at Colt Memorial Hall.

In the same room, John J. Cavanaugh showed off his skill at straightening barrels. Picking up a reamed barrel, he dropped a plug gauge into it; if the gauge stuck, the barrel was crooked. In front of his window was a small, square-framed, opaque glass with a narrow black line running diametrically across it. Johnny squinted through the crooked barrel at the black line and determined where it needed straightening by noting the point at which the penciled lines inside the barrel deviated from a parallel course. Placing the barrel in a vise, he made the corrections with a few skillful hammerings. He had been doing this operation for twenty-five of his forty-eight years in the Armory.

Charlie Coles, later to become curator of the Colt gun collection under President Stone's auspices, was — along with Vice-President Fred Moore — a recognized authority on machine guns. He joined Colt's in 1892, worked on the old Gatling gun, and then followed the evolution of John Browning's gas-operated machine gun through its water-cooled to the present air-cooled stage of development. Coles's father, employed in 1876, had been foreman of the machine shop.

Arthur Ulrich himself was an old-timer, still spry at 77. He began as a stenographic clerk in 1886 and rose to secretary of the company in 1903. He prided himself on being the Armory's historian in charge of its oldest and rarest firearms. He remembered Mrs. Colt vividly. He and the other young clerks used to vie with one another for the privilege of opening the door for her when she made her periodic visits, or assisting her into the carriage waiting to drive her back to Armsmear. The coachman, an intriguing Irishman named Mike Tracy, had been hired by the Colonel. One day Sam Colt had asked to be picked up at the Hartford Club at seven o'clock in the evening. Mike arrived a half hour late, but his employer was nowhere to be seen. In cold weather, until nearly midnight, Mike walked his horses up and down the yard. Finally, the Colonel came out and got into the coach without a word. As they neared home, he said: "Well, perhaps after this you'll get there on time."

In a small room on the first floor of the office, Ulrich hoarded his collection of gun models. The oldest was one of the first revolvers Colt made in the ill-fated Paterson, New Jersey plant in 1836. There were examples of the Colonel's "calling cards," handsomely engraved and inlaid revolvers which he handed out to friends. One striking model sported mother-of-pearl likenesses of Lincoln and an American eagle, while the stock was made from a piece of the famous Charter Oak tree.

On the second floor was President Stone's spacious but somewhat cluttered office. Various pictures and awards covered the walls. A well-worn couch occupied one side, and from the creases in it one might suspect that the president was accustomed to taking frequent naps. Stone sat behind the same rolltop desk on which Samuel Colt used to scrawl his letters and memorandums. The role of a chief executive is often a lonely one, especially when it comes to decision-making. Before

Arthur Ulrich

Mike Tracy

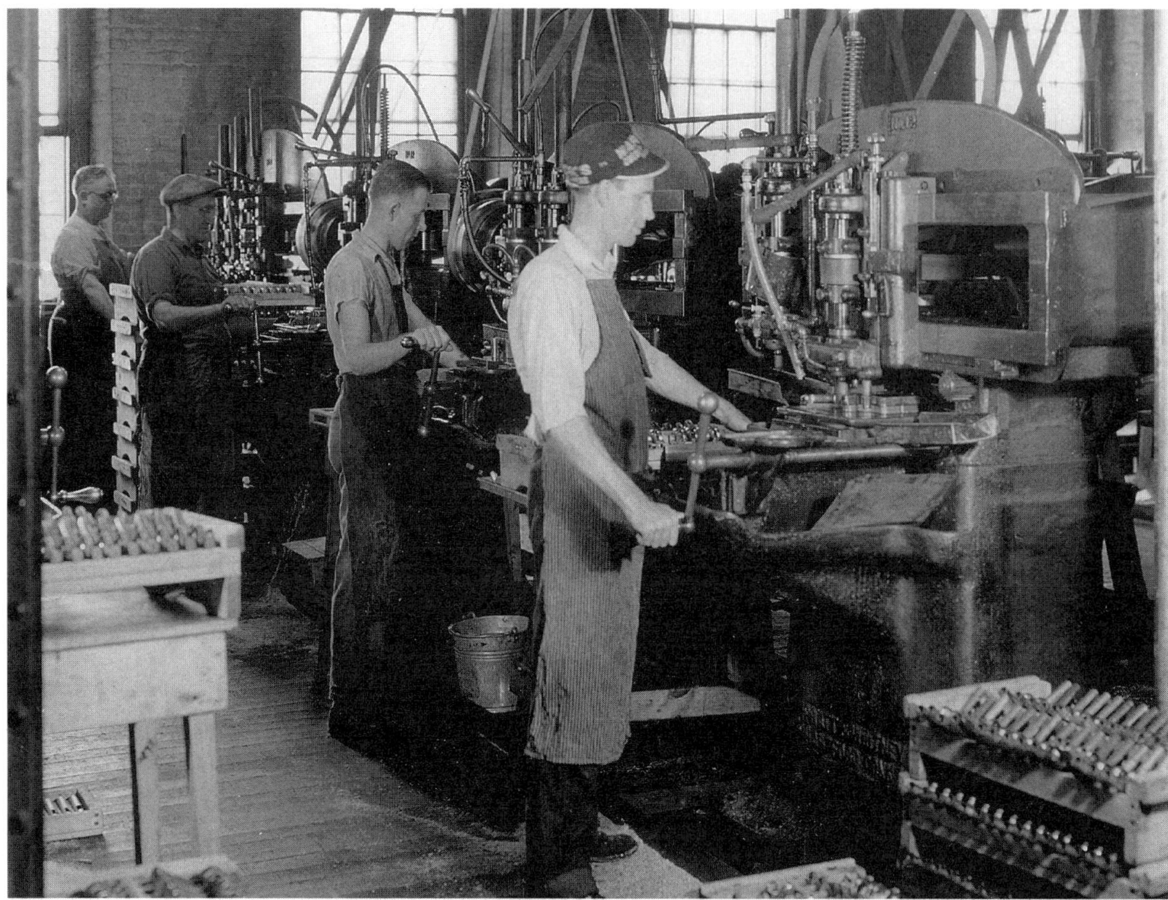

Profiling receivers.

the days of specialized staff support and data processing it was even more so, and decision-making had to be a subjective, seat-of-the-pants function. Like most of his contemporaries, Stone judged his effectiveness by two simple axioms: one, never to let himself be surprised; the other, to be content if he made the right decision fifty-one percent of the time. The wrong forty-nine percent he might regret, but then he realized no one — not even a president — was perfect.

If you had visited the Armory in 1940, say, and been given a conducted tour, you would have been told that over a thousand separate operations were involved in making a Colt revolver or automatic pistol. It was literally carved out of steel, and the steel had to be machineable — not too hard, nor too soft. The first stop was usually the forge shop, the modern version of the blacksmithy, a terrifying, ear-splitting place — where red hot blanks were placed with tongs on the forge and a giant weight pounded the raw steel between two dies in the shape of a gun frame. Tripped by a foot pedal, the 500 pound weight dropped six feet, sending sparks flying high into the air. Across the alleyway a battery of punch presses trimmed off the excess metal. After being tumbled in drums to smooth their surfaces, the frames were ground to their proper thickness. Then they passed on to the heat treating department for annealing. This operation softened the metal enough for machining. After completion of the finishing operations the parts came back again to be hardened.

Besides forging and annealing, the most important operations included drilling the cylinder, rifling the barrel, filing, fitting, assembling, testing, finishing, and bluing. At first glance the machining rooms reminded one of a labyrinth, intricately yet rationally laid out, the result of years of planning and experience. Side-by-side were the rough and finish millers. The frame must be shaped on a profiler, the barrel drilled and counter-bored, the trigger hole cut, and more than a hundred other fussy operations performed, some to tolerances as close as one thousandth of an inch. On the inspectors' benches lay a variety of gauges, "go" and "no go" they called them, to make sure every part was accurate. Split a hair six times, and you have some idea of the maximum

Polishing the sides of the "Woodsman" automatic pistol.

Hand checking stocks for revolvers and automatic pistols. Selected walnut was used for the grips.

precision required.

Drilling a five-inch barrel was a delicate process. Each reaming under a continuous flow of oil to remove the tiny chips made the hole microscopically larger. A drop or two of hot lead was squirted inside and wiped through to give it a high polish. A special machine rifled it, making a left-hand spiral so the bullet would spin straight to its mark. On the cylinder alone there were sixty separate operations; first the rear, then the front was bored to form six chambers of absolute accuracy.

Certain things could be done only by hand or eye, such as filing the slide and receiver of an automatic pistol, fitting the two parts together, determining the height of the firing pin, or fitting the cylinder of a revolver to its frame. Only the most skilled were entrusted with the latter step, or with the equally demanding task of "facing" the barrel hole. The visitor watched an old-timer fit the barrel to the revolver frame so that when screwed up tight, the front sight would be in alignment. After a few deft touches of his file, the craftsman would screw the barrel to the frame. Holding it to the light, you could see that the front sight was perfectly true.

Polishing was such an exacting manual operation that nine out often polishers, even though carefully trained, could not do the work. Ernie Holmes, then the foreman of finishing, led the visitor through his room of sparking wheels. "There's John Dumbrosky," he would say, "one of the dozen best finishers in the entire country." Walking over to his whirling wheel, he would ask John: "Will you finish up the side of this revolver frame? I want this man to see you do it." But neither John nor the observer could see anything, because he had to work blindly on the upper side of the wheel, only his dexterous fingers guiding him.

After polishing, frames, cylinders, barrels, slides, and receivers traveled to the bluing room, where a battery of furnaces slowly revolved. The parts were bathed in hot gasoline, placed on racks, and loaded into the furnaces. There they remained for five hours in a secret mixture of primer and charred bone, coming out with the distinctive dark blue finish of Colt guns. After the firearms were assembled and tested, they received a final examination. Men like Ed Kelly, the foreman, and Axel Hallstrom spent a lifetime upholding the reputation of Colt products. Theirs was the last word on whether a finished gun met the exacting standards for quality and perfection.

CHAPTER IX

THE STRIKE

The American working man was desperate, insecure on his job if he was lucky enough to have one, scared of losing his self-respect and going on the breadline, enraged at bloated bankers and hard-nosed employers, even close to contempt for the capitalist system itself. Thirteen million were unemployed when Franklin D. Roosevelt launched the New Deal during his first hundred days in office — a whirlwind of activity that resulted in twelve landmark acts of Congress. To the barons of business and finance he became "That Man," "that Madman," or "that Traitor to his Class"; to the poor and dispossessed, he was a messiah, the greatest President since Lincoln.

The legislation which most bedeviled businessmen was the National Industrial Recovery Act, its symbol a blue eagle clutching a cogwheel. It applied codes to 700 industries that forbade child labor, regulated prices, set up maximum hours of work and minimum wages, and encouraged collective bargaining. The latter provision, known as Section 7-A, was looked upon by organized labor as an open sesame to mass unionism and the closed shop, but it proved to be the most controversial in the entire act and a catalyst for warfare between labor and management.

There was no doubt the company union and the yellow-dog contract were fast becoming bygones, yet employers in general were emotionally unready to embrace arms-length collective bargaining and federated unions that insisted on exclusive representation of all employees and signed contracts...unions they feared would inevitably be more hostile than cooperative. Strikes and lockouts swept the country. Labor, believing it had government support, pushed hard and antagonized the public. Management retaliated by resorting to strikebreakers, injunctions, and hastily-formed company unions. A nation-wide textile walkout and a general strike in San Francisco were smashed by militia and vigilantes. Yet, two years later, four million had been re-employed, the staid American Federation of Labor had recouped its losses during the 1920s, and a new, dynamic international union attuned to the needs of unskilled and semi-skilled workers had emerged — the C.I.O.

For many years Colt's had enjoyed a company union which called itself the Independent Association of Colt Employees. It was more of a club than a union. No major policy was ever challenged, the foreman ruled his department, and if a complaint did reach the factory manager or even Mr. Stone, one or the other was the sole arbiter. In the spirit of the times, however, this comfortable state of affairs terminated in 1934 when the employees voted 813-153 to disband the association. Two months later, in May, three craft unions affiliated with the A.F. of L. organized, formed a joint council, and attempted to bargain with the company. There were frequent meetings, but Colt's refused to make an agreement or offer counterproposals. Doubtful that the joint council represented the majority, it did its best to ignore the bargaining committee altogether. If a proposal had merit, it would adopt it quietly and then out of the blue announce it to all employees as its own idea. This cat and mouse game was played for ten months, when finally the National Labor Relations Board ruled that Colt's had refused to bargain collectively. It gave the company ten days to recognize the joint council.

The dispute was destined to attract national attention because the Armory at the time was a major supplier of munitions to the War Department — in fact, the only one with contracts for machine guns, which, because of its patents, no other manufacturer could produce.

Mr. Stone, like most older chief executives, was hostile to unionism in every fiber of his body. The whole idea went against the grain — a fear of strangers telling him how to run his business, of constant bickering and opposition, of lower production, and even the loss of management rights. He worried, too, about the effect on the large number of old-timers, with twenty-five up to fifty years of service, whom he felt sure wanted no part of an "outside union." They were mostly a dying breed of craftsmen whose skills were needed less and less as new machines and production techniques were introduced.

"It's the younger crowd, the new fellows, who are causing all this trouble," he used to say. "They want to change the whole social order, at least they listen to those damn organizers who preach such nonsense. Men like Hurley and Fenton are misleading them, filling their silly heads with all sorts of impossible promises and taking them right down the road to disaster. You can't any more run a factory like a democracy than a ship can be navigated by majority vote of the crew and without any captain to give orders."

Not even Section 7-A of the NRA was a deterrent for him.

"The law says nothing about majority rule or the closed shop. It's that radical Biddle who runs the Board who talks that way. Under no circumstances will I submit to the demands of outsiders. We're willing to deal with our employees individually or collectively, but not to let a couple of new unions think they're going to represent everybody, and I'm not so damn sure they do represent the majority anyway. Our policy has always been fair, we've never stopped employees from doing their own thinking. But I'll tell you one thing: Colt's is going to stay an open shop come hell or high water."

Francis Fenton and Daniel Hurley were tough, determined Irishmen. In charge of organizing activities in New England for the A.F. of L., Fenton saw an opportunity for promotion, perhaps even recognition by national president William Green, if he could crack the Colt fortress. He was convinced, not incorrectly, that the Manufacturers Association of Connecticut supported and perhaps even directed the defense tactics of Colt's and other manufacturers in the state then being organized or struck. "It's a conspiracy against collective bargaining," he charged. "The Association keeps a black list of those they think are pro-union, conducts a secret employment service and works behind the scenes to keep its members in line." Dan Hurley was head of the joint council, a good Colt employee somewhat overwhelmed by the leadership role into which he had talked himself, and frightened, not so much by the possibility of losing his job if management dared to retaliate, but by the spectre of radicals horning in. Hurley, though blustery and aggressive, was a regular churchgoer and true blue American; he wanted no truck with the commies.

The ten-day grace period set by the NLRB for Colt's to comply with Section 7-A came and went with no move by the company. On Wednesday morning, March 13, 1935, soon after the first shift reported for work, over a thousand men and women walked off their jobs and stationed pickets in front of the office. There was no disorder. "It's surrender, or strike," was Hurley's parting remark to his foreman. The strike leaders set up headquarters in a tenement close to the factory. Its main attraction was an always bubbling coffee pot. On Saturday afternoon they organized a parade through the city. Led by the American flag and a rag-tag band, 600 marched, carrying one sign which read "Strike to Enforce Section 7A of NRA."

The first of many mass meetings was held at the Odd Fellows Temple on Main Street. Hurley and Fenton did most of the talking. "We've got to hold a united front and maintain a big picket line," they urged. "The bosses will try every trick in the book, so stay on guard. We've already heard a rumor that strikebreakers are going to be brought in by truck. And you gals watch out, the bosses will come around to your homes and try to persuade you with sweet talk to go back." Fenton claimed the eyes of the whole country would be turned upon their moral struggle to win recognition and higher wages.

Several hundred Colt employees were brave enough to remain on the job, and Stone was determined to keep the plant open as long as he could. To make entering easier, Herb Walker persuaded the police to alter the picket line. At first the pickets had walked in a large circle in front of the office. Now the police restricted them to two abreast outside the main gate. They sang labor songs, booed and jeered those going to work, but nothing more. Wisely, the company continued its policy of paying a quarterly bonus of five percent. It was sure the strikers would be unable to stay out more than a few weeks. "They'll give in after missing a payroll or two," several in management predicted.

Others disagreed, feeling there was too much strike fever in the air, the leaders were too militant, and they had succeeded in stirring the fighting instincts of the majority.

* * *

Sam Stone stood, legs apart, feet firmly planted, an unlit cigar clenched defiantly in one corner of his mouth. The windows were open, heads thrust out, the machinery throbbing behind them. On the sidewalk swarmed the pickets. Some were passing out miserably printed broadsides. Frank Fenton faced the president, hands in his pockets, relaxed and smiling. But not Mr. Stone. He glared at the organizer and lost his temper. "Get the hell out of here," he roared.

"Why, Mr. Stone, this is public property. I have every right to be here."

"You're a trouble-making outsider, and I'll get the police to run you out of town."

"Just try, Mr. Stone. Just you try. It's obvious you know nothing about the law and workers' rights. I suggest you hire yourself a lawyer. Otherwise you may be in big trouble."

"Threatening me?" Stone looked more defiant then ever, as if in another moment he would take a swing at his adversary.

"No, I'm giving you some good advice. Like all reactionary employers, you're taking this thing too emotionally. Better calm down and get some help."

Sam Stone moved toward the entrance. "We'll see," he mumbled. "You haven't won yet."

* * *

Sunday night Andrew Adams walked down to the neighborhood grocery store to get something for his wife. As he emerged, four men jumped out of a car parked at the curb and knocked him down. "You dirty scab," they shouted, "are you going to work again tomorrow?" They kicked him viciously, got back into the car and drove off. It was the first of many such incidents, all of them repudiated by the strike leaders. "We are absolutely opposed to violent measures of any kind," said Dan Hurley, and he implied that a number of strange men had slipped into the city who were undoubtedly responsible for beating Adams.

Management was quick to react. The violence stiffened its resolve to resist. One Colt director, Samuel Ferguson, chairman of the Hartford Electric Light Company, spoke out at the annual meeting. "These strikers are being instigated by some outside agency to damage the company. I will support the management even if it means operating in the present crippled condition for an indefinite period. Our cash surplus is ample to pay losses for the next two years, if necessary. I favor the complete elimination of all government contracts, if pressed. The margin of profit is low, anyway. There can be no compromise with those using force for ulterior motives not in any way connected with the welfare of our valued employees." That statement, loudly applauded by the stockholders present, served to polarize the situation. Now there was no doubt it would be a fight to the finish. The company made preparations for a long siege, bringing cots inside and arranging to feed non-strikers who dared not go home. The unions were thrown off balance; Frank Fenton raged that "turning the factory into a hotel violates the health and sanitation laws," and rushed off to City Hall to stop it. He never did.

* * *

Colt foremen began visiting strikers at their homes to lure them back to work without success; a few more non-strikers crossed the picket line each day, yet the line itself grew bigger, reaching a peak every Monday morning. Most of the action, however, shifted to Washington. Backed by President William Green of the A.F. of L., Fenton and John McCurry, another field organizer, decided that only government pressure would force Colt to capitulate. They found a friend in Senator Gerald P. Nye, the liberal Republican from North Dakota, who was chairman of the Senate Munitions Committee. Because of national security, the government, he said, would be justified in taking over and operating the Armory. "They ought to confiscate its patents as well." Two weeks after the strike began, the NRA, failing to work out an amicable settlement between the parties, announced it would suspend the company's Blue Eagle, thus making it ineligible to receive additional contracts. The NLRB meanwhile debated whether to ask the Justice Department to prosecute Colt's for violating Section 7-A.

At the next mass meeting, Fenton hailed the Washington moves as "a victory for labor." Scoring Colt's "holier-than-thou" attitude toward the A.F. of L. organizers, he told the cheering and foot-stamping workers that "you've got to have outside leaders to get economic justice, men who don't owe the company anything and can't be fired. Now we've got the feds behind us...even the President said he was going to prosecute NRA

Colt strikers picketing outside the armory in 1935.

violators. If any of you go back now, the company will roll up an inventory, and then you'll be out on the street."

Two other voices, one a prominent Socialist, the other a New Haven clergyman who headed up a left-wing organization called the Workers Education Bureau, joined the fray. Norman Thomas, speaking under the auspices of the Hartford Central Labor Union, told several hundred strikers they were fighting for American rights and the privileges of life which could be won only through collective bargaining. The Rev. Nelson Cruikshank was more inflammatory: "Colt never considers itself an outsider in any country which has cash to buy its arms. It talks about outside agitators — doesn't it belong to an association pledged never to recognize unions? Your strike is for a better day for the workers of America!" Another radical organization, the American League Against War & Fascism, declared that defeat against "this most strategic war industry would prove a serious blow to the effort of the working class to mobilize against the terrific war danger now threatening the world."

With renewed energy the strike progressed. Three thousand tickets were sold for a dance at the Polish National Home to raise funds. Other local unions began making weekly contributions. Food packages were distributed to the needy. The Hartford Federation of Churches decided they had a moral obligation to look into the causes of the strike, but their report was never published. A gang was seen throwing bricks through the windows of a Colt official's home. Five women were found guilty of breach of peace for attacking Rosanna Mador and her sister Gertrude. One incident that nearly resulted in serious injuries occurred when six strikers, returning from a fund-raising visit to Springfield, decided on the spur of the moment to frighten Mary Lynch, a non-striker. Parking in front of her South Windsor home, they threw several cobblestones into her bedroom window, narrowly missing the heads of her brother and sister. In the Colt parking lot tires were slashed and sugar dumped into gas tanks. Gustave Johnson, an inspector with thirty-four years of service, was not intimidated: "They broke seven windows in my house, but I'm going back to work just the same. I can't afford to be idle the way things are now. Unemployment ain't going to pay for my food and my mortgage."

Fenton laid plans for getting financial support from the national unions, promoting a union boycott of Colt products, organizing a general strike in the city, and obtaining welfare aid for those in need should the relief fund be exhausted. At the start of the fourth week 500 manned the picket line. Some two dozen policemen were on duty to protect non-strikers arriving by trolley car or taxicab. The pickets vented their wrath especially on those living inside the plant, who went home on weekends and returned early Monday morning. The company claimed that 725 production workers were now back at work; the unions, hotly disagreeing, said the number was more like three hundred.

* * *

Senator Nye was furious. Chairman Donald Richberg of the NRA, a former labor attorney, had delayed notifying the War Department that Colt's was no longer in good standing. Nye threatened to appeal directly to the White House. Richberg replied that he would not declare the company ineligible for new contracts until he had studied the legal angles thoroughly. He summoned Samuel Stone for a conference, while the strike leaders met with Nye. Afterwards, Nye held a press conference: "For more than a week Mr. Richberg has failed to notify government departments that the Blue Eagle has been withdrawn from the Colt factory for refusal to negotiate, with the result that this company is going right on selling its munitions while it starves its striking workmen into submission or compromise."

The NRA chief wasted no time in going to the White House and telling President Roosevelt that Senator Nye's intervention would do nothing but thwart his efforts for a settlement. On Friday, April 12, the President called the senator and persuaded him to calm down. "All right, Mr. President, I'll agree to postpone my committee's investigation of the NRA for a few days. But I want you to know that next Wednesday is zero hour." Richberg again conferred privately with Stone. The meeting lasted all day and into the evening.

"Mr. Stone, I'm trying to understand just what the nub of this problem really is. We don't want to remove your Blue Eagle; we need your guns; there's trouble brewing in Europe. God knows what this Hitler will do next."

"My company has been in business for 87 years, and we have always treated our employees fairly. We're willing to bargain with this joint council — in fact, we have been meeting with them for nearly a year. But we think the right to work is even more important than the right to strike."

Richberg looked puzzled. "If you are willing to bargain, then why don't you recognize them and sign a contract? Other companies are doing that."

"We don't think the unions' position constitutes fair treatment of those who are not union members — and there are at least seven hundred of them. Until the strike broke out, we were prepared to recognize the joint council, but since then they've called in outside organizers, indulged in violence, and they tell those who are working that they will lose their jobs when the union wins. There has been no election, so how do we know if the joint council represents the majority? And you know as well as I do, that there's a serious question as to whether the whole NRA is constitutional."

While Mr. Stone was talking with the NRA chairman, Francis Fenton was presenting his side to other members of the Board: "The fact is that 1,350 employees walked out — that's the best evidence that the unions represent the majority."

"I am well aware of the weakness of Section 7-A," Richberg sighed wearily. "It's ambiguous, and it can't be enforced. But that'll all be changed if Congress passes the Wagner Act."

Stone replied, "Our position is this, sir: the law as written now says we can bargain collectively or individually. It does not say there must be an exclusive agreement. Therefore, we will not sign any agreement to which the signatures of the officers of the three unions in the joint council are affixed, because that would mean no recognition of the rights of those who don't want to belong to any union. Also, you have overlooked the fact Mr. Fenton and Mr. Hurley are insisting on a 25 percent wage increase."

Richberg bridled. "It doesn't make sense to me that the question of a signature ought to be the basis for continuing a strike and keeping a lot of people out of work. Now. Mr. Stone let me suggest a way out for both sides. Would you be willing to submit this matter to arbitration?"

"Never!" replied Stone.

"All right, I then propose that the Board set up an impartial fact-finding committee with the chairman to be named by the President. Will you accept that?"

"No, sir."

The next day Donald Richberg revealed that his mediation efforts had failed because of the stubbornness of both sides, and he would proceed to notify the War Department of Colt's ineligibility for munitions contracts. But his ire was directed mainly at Senator Nye and the Munitions Committee, whom he accused of making a peaceful settlement impossible by their inflammatory statements.

By April 27th, however, Richberg had changed his mind again. Attorney General Homer S. Cummings of Connecticut, known for his aversion to any form of collective bargaining, convinced him that Colt's had not violated the law. Richberg dropped his bombshell in testimony before Nye's committee. Questioned why he hadn't spoken out before, he lamely replied: "With the strike on we didn't think it fair to bring out that the NRA and Department of Justice were holding one opinion, and the NLRB another." The senator was bitter: "Mr. Richberg today finally admitted the NRA and Department of Justice don't believe that under Section 7-A they can legally compel employers to bargain with union representatives. It has taken the Government almost two years to make this admission." Francis Biddle said he hoped Congress would now give his agency enforcement powers. There was consternation and despair at strike headquarters. Fenton telegraphed President Roosevelt "we have been led up a dark alley by the Government, to be slugged by Mr. Richberg at its blind end," and appealed to him to decide who was right — the NRA or the NLRB. Before a cheering assemblage of strikers that overflowed Odd Fellows Hall, he branded Richberg "the greatest arch traitor to labor this country has ever know," and reassured his audience that the company was licked and would give in soon.

Now the joint council frantically tried to bring the widest pressure possible against Colt's. The leaders beseeched their brother unions in Hartford to join in a general strike. The president of the Hartford Central Union, William Kuehnel, agreed that "we are obliged as a last resort to use mass economic pressure," but the I.A.M. and other local unions with contracts were not anxious to take such a drastic step. They knew it would create more bitterness and more violence, and they were uneasy about the participation of the radicals, who were denouncing "rotten capitalism" wherever they could find a platform.

Secretary of Labor Frances Perkins decided to try her hand and dispatched P.W. Chappell, one of her conciliators, to the city. He saw Fenton and Stone to no avail. She then tried without success to get the President to intercede. Governor Wilbur Cross, a prudent old Yankee Democrat who welcomed federal largesse but resented any attempt to exercise control over the states, also dallied briefly with the idea of intervention, but after meeting separately with Stone and John Egan of the Connecticut A.F. of L., he bowed out. Wisely recognizing his lack of experience in labor matters, he determined instead to set up a state board of mediation and arbitration. Chappell returned to Hartford on May 4th and brought both sides together for the first time.

The strike leaders were wary and sullen; they let Fenton do the talking. Chappell began by recommending that the company agree to recognize the joint council as exclusive bargaining agent for all employees. The company's attorney, Lucius Robinson, accepted the idea in principle but added a qualification.

"We may agree to that, provided the non-union workers have the right to negotiate with us individually or collectively. For that purpose we insist they have representation on the joint council."

Fenton shot back: "That's no good — you still want to have your lousy company union, and we won't let you."

Robinson was unperturbed. "Further, we will not agree to any wage increase. We are confident that our rates are as high, if not higher, than those prevailing in Hartford. We have no objection to appointing an impartial fact-finding committee to determine if our rates are equal to the average ones paid for similar jobs in the area."

Fenton didn't like that suggestion any better; pounding the table, he said: "We want wages settled *now* before we go back to work."

"And," Robinson concluded, "the company will agree to take back all those on strike, as fast as work schedules permit, except those who are charged with or convicted of violence."

The committee members shook their heads in unison. Fenton rose, and they all walked out of the conference room. At a mass meeting Sunday night, Fenton termed the company's offer "unconditional surrender." "Are you going to accept this kind of agreement?" There was a resounding chorus of no's and a thunderous stamping of feet. "We demand either a 25 percent wage increase or arbitration," he shouted, "and all strikers must be reinstated. The company is being arbitrary and uncompromising; it's gone back on its statements to the government that it would recognize the joint council. Listen, all we have to do is hold out for a few more weeks; we won't let the bosses starve us into submission!"

The strike had now run two months, and the public's attitude was swinging against it. At the beginning, there had been widespread sympathy for the rights of the unprotected and underpaid workers to organize so as to have more effective control over their jobs and equal bargaining power with management. But many were tired of reading about it, dismayed by the swelling of the relief roles, outraged by the increasing number of violent incidents, and fearful of its impact — if allowed to continue — on other businesses. Moreover, the unions' funds were near exhaustion and the welfare department was feeding more families every day. Stone saw that the time had come for Colt's to make its move to end the strike. He took full-page ads in the Hartford newspapers explaining Colt's position and last offer. The ad said 800 had returned to work and 500 had signed a statement to the effect that they had not chosen any union to represent them — all of which was true. Finally, May 15th, one week ahead, was set as the deadline for the strikers to register for work, or the company would feel free to hire new employees.

To make sure every striker got the information, postcards were sent to their homes. Fenton denounced the advertisements as "the last act of a tyrant — a deliberate stand to see if they can break our ranks." The postcards, he said, amounted to intimidation.

The zero hour for the strike started at six a.m. on Wednesday. Fenton told a reporter "the time has come to get militant," as he lined up two thousand pickets around the entire Armory. They were by no means all Colt employees; at least a third came from other factories. Some three hundred female garment workers snake-danced down the street before leaving for their jobs. Despite a beefed-up police force, the pickets prevented many non-strikers from entering the gates.

Samuel Stone rose early that morning to watch what he felt would be the unions' last demonstration. He noticed a sprinkling of college students in the ranks and spoke to some of them, trying to find out why they were there. Surrounded by a group of pickets, he singled out one who was being especially noisy and aggressive. He identified himself as a graduate student at Yale who was protesting the company's despotism. The encounter grew heated, the young man called the president a skunk, and the police broke it up by arresting him and eight others, including three agitators suspected of being Communists. By the time the seven o'clock whistle blew the pickets had thinned out to a handful.

* * *

Harold Taylor was an easygoing, rather footloose young man who had managed to get along without ever holding a real job, and who enjoyed excitement. He lived in a third-class hotel in Hartford's north end. As secretary of the Building Trades Alliance, he took a keen interest in the Colt strike and was deeply upset by the likelihood of its imminent collapse. He talked things over with his friends — Edward Raffo, one of the strikers; Charles Carron, a former supernumerary policeman who had done picket duty; and Carron's brother-in-law, Thomas Raymond who worked in construction. None of them had been in trouble before.

The strike leaders seemed to have given up the fight. Francis Fenton had taken a group of fifteen pickets to Washington in a last ditch effort for mediation by the Secretaries of Labor and War. In Taylor's view, it was high time to bring the issues to a head in his own way.

Dynamite — that would wake people up! Raymond was detailed to steal eighteen sticks of high explosive from a building site. Carron would hide them in his home. Raffo would provide the automobile. The target: the Colt factory. But such a plot was impossible to keep entirely secret. An informer tipped off the State's Attorney's office that something might happen there, and as a precaution a heavy police guard was stationed around the premises day and night. Carron's house on Maple Avenue was placed under surveillance. On Sunday evening May 27th, the seventy-sixth day of the strike, the conspirators headed for the factory. They found it too well guarded and abandoned the attempt. Taylor, however, too keyed up to be put off without some action, directed Raffo to drive to President Stone's home in West Hartford. The gang parked near the house, while Taylor planted the dynamite on the front porch. The fuse failed to ignite. He retrieved the sticks, ran back to the car, and told Raffo to beat it. A half hour later they returned with another fuse, but were scared away by the sight of a police cruiser.

The next night, shortly before ten o'clock, they made a third try. With a gun in his pocket, Taylor and a very nervous Carron alighted from Raffo's sedan, ran up to Stone's modest home and tossed the bomb onto the porch. Mr. Stone was reading in his living-room, having just returned from Washington and a meeting with the Secretary of War. A tremendous explosion blew in the front door and shattered all the windows facing the street. He rushed to the hallway and found himself enveloped in smoke. In their nightclothes, his neighbors hurried to the scene. The blast was heard for miles. The damage, however, was minimal, and Stone was unhurt.

Word of the explosion spread quickly throughout the city, while the gang dispersed according to plans made beforehand in case they needed alibis. Taylor, less cautious than he should have been and consumed with curiosity, hunted up Dan Hurley. "I can't believe it," said the Irishman. "Some bastards are doing their damnedest to kill the strike. it must be those god-damn commies who've been hanging around town. C'mon Taylor, I'm going out to see Stone." Taylor had no choice but to accompany Hurley, who apologized to the president for the "terrible outrage" and asserted it was inconceivable that any Colt strikers were involved.

On Tuesday morning, State's Attorney Hugh M. Alcorn was able to locate the four suspects and place them under arrest. Barely a week later three of them pleaded guilty in Superior Court; Raymond's case was nolled because of his willingness to turn state's witness, but the rest drew jail terms. In the meantime, the spirit of the strikers had been broken by the plot. For the first time there was no booing or singing on the picket line; they walked in downcast silence. Sixty more returned to work. Fenton and Hurley called another meeting. Four hundred attended. The press was kept outside. Feelings ran high and were sharply divided. One group pressed for a change of leadership. Fenton was overheard saying that "we've exhausted every possible remedy there is in this country. I will not stand in the way of any decent settlement." Finally, the strike committee was directed to seek the help of the new State Board of Mediation and Arbitration, which Governor Cross had just appointed.

While only a few pickets paraded, and 1,100 were working again, the two sides were brought together in Robinson's office. All talk of representation and wage rates was forgotten. There was only one matter to resolve — the re-employment of the remaining 300 strikers, and the company stuck to its original position of refusing to take back any one guilty of violence. After a four-hour closed meeting, the joint council gave in, and the strike ended on June 3rd.

* * *

Actually the 13-week Colt strike had, in terms of its objectives, ended the day it began. From the union's standpoint, the real culprit was the weakness of Section 7-A. It had given them false hopes and severely damaged their cause — perhaps irreparably. Ironically, the Supreme Court ruled unconstitutional the entire National Recovery Act only the week before the settlement, while Congress was considering a new labor bill that would eliminate the ambiguities of Section 7-A. The historic Wagner Act, giving the NLRB enforcement powers and the unions secret ballot elections and exclusive representation, if a majority voted in favor, became law on July 5th.

President Stone was chuckling over the newspaper when an associate entered his office one morning. "You remember that student I tangled with on the picket line. Well, it turns out that he has been studying the classics at Yale for the past seven years — after graduating, mind you. And his father says here that his arrest was the best thing in the world that could happen to him! 'Mr. Clendenin described his son as super-educated and hipped on the sorrows of the forgotten man.' "

He turned serious. "It has been a costly thing — for them and for us, but I don't think they'll forget, or be forgotten. It's a new world. My time has gone. I'm no longer the boss who can walk around the factory and call most everybody by his first name, and the employees no longer look to me as the one to give them a square deal. We'll have a union, no question, and probably the leaders will be a lot worse to handle than Fenton or Hurley."

CHAPTER X

THE BENEFACTORS

During the Colt strike another calamity occurred across the river in South Manchester that, like the coming of collective bargaining, was a milestone in the history of Connecticut industry. The *Courant* headline read: "Cheney Brothers Petition to Reorganize." Below, the news article explained that the famous silk company was voluntarily declaring bankruptcy under Section 77B of the Federal Bankruptcy Act in a last ditch effort to meet its trade obligations and still continue in business.

Sam Stone could not believe what he read. It meant not only the fall of a great company that had existed longer than Colt's, but also the termination of a way of industrial life that New England would never see again. The president of Colt's was in a reflective mood as he settled back in his chair, lit his biggest pipe, and reminisced with his visitor. "I'll always remember the Philadelphia Centennial Exposition in 1876 — the greatest display of machinery and industrial progress the world had ever seen — even though I was only a little boy then. What marvelous sights! The Japanese Pavilion with its graceful roofs...rich carving...and the screens and bronzes. The giant steam engine in Machinery Hall and the electric telegraphs of Edison and Bell. There were all kinds of machine tools and hardware and cutlery. For a nickel you could ride a little train around the grounds and see all the buildings. There were thousands of exhibitors, most of them from foreign countries. But let me tell you: the American exhibits were the eye-openers. Colt's showed off its early revolvers, Civil War rifles, and the Gatling machine gun. Mrs. Colt attended along with Sam and Livy Clemens, the Battersons, and thousands of others from Hartford.

"Cheney Brothers had a magnificent display of their silks. It woke up the holier-than-thou English to the fact that America could now out-produce them. It was the same year, I think, that Frank Woodbridge Cheney became the boss of the Cheney Mills. It isn't enough to say Frank Cheney, because there were so many of them...eight brothers originally who started spinning silk about a hundred years ago. Frank was the son of one. I remember a story about his youth. He was sent to Brown, but never finished. He was expelled for going to hear Jenny Lind, the Swedish Nightingale, sing on the Sabbath. You just weren't supposed to do that sort of thing in those days.

"Like all the Cheney boys, he went into the mill. The ambition of every one I knew was to go into the mill, start as an apprentice during the summer, then join the fire company, then get to the firemen's picnic, and — best of all — to play on the ball team.

"Before he was thirty, his father and uncles sent him off to the Far East to see if he could buy raw silk. He almost got killed by pirates in China. He was one of the first American businessmen to enter Japan, and he found their silk first-rate. Then he came home and joined the Army. That was during the Civil War. He was wounded, discharged, and married Horace Bushnell's daughter — you know, the preacher.

"The Cheneys and Colt's have much in common. Louis Cheney was a Colt director for years. The Cheney clan lived right next to the red brick mills in the middle of a great park with broad lawns and giant oaks. There were no fences to keep the people out. There must have been twenty houses, big clapboard affairs — they had lots of children and servants — with endless gables,

The Colt exhibit at the Philadelphia Exposition in 1876.

dormers and ells. The houses were all heated by the power plant at the mill, with the steam piped underground.

"Frank W. was a wonderful host. Mark Twain and Charles Dudley Warner used to come for meetings of the Monday Club. He entertained a constant stream of foreign businessmen, veterans, editors, lecturers, and clergymen. Once a Frenchman came who claimed he had been hired by Barnum to bleach his elephant white under secrecy for $10,000. And twice a year Mr. Cheney had the dentist come and spend a week to take care of his children's teeth.

"There was no question about who was the patriarch of that clan and who ran the mill. He not only made Cheney tops in the silk industry but developed South Manchester into a model mill town that got him national attention."

* * *

The mill towns that flourished in New England during the last century were generally pictured as industrial fiefdoms, ugly brick factories and smoking black chimneys, surrounded by squalid cottages or rows of tenements, exploiting hundreds of unschooled children ten or twelve hours a day amid wretched working conditions. In the heyday of Victorian technology the natural environment seemed boundless, which no amount of abuse could destroy. But social critics were worried about what was happening to human beings. A clergyman in one village wrote: "I have stood where I could see the rustling throng issue from a mill as the bell rang and the gates were thrown open; and what I saw were no longer manly men, but men of stooping forms and hopeless faces; women dispirited, slovenly and aimless; and children, whose eyes were dull and whose cheeks were pale — the whole crowd a sorry spectacle of over-tasked, exhausted and despondent humanity." Humanity was cheap in those days, men the helpless slaves of their machines.

In Connecticut and Massachusetts there were exceptions, of course, where mill workers, though poor, lived in tidy respectable communities, and where employers took a sympathetic interest in their welfare. Early in the 19th century, idealists like David Humphreys and Francis Cabot Lowell had pioneered the creation of economic utopias. Their efforts did not prevent the evils of Birmingham and Manchester from being perpetuated in American cotton and woolen mills, but they did offer a more humane alternative which others would emulate. It was paternalism at its best. Even the average mill town, bad as we might regard it now, would have fulfilled the dream of any pioneer philanthropist in England during the first half of the 19th century.

The Cheney brothers, as their silk mills grew into the largest enterprise of its kind in the United States, did not consciously set out to create a model village nor to undertake a social experiment. Rather, they wanted to live close to their business amid surroundings that would be as salubrious for themselves as the people they employed. South Manchester had none of the usual attributes of a manufacturing town. Instead of tenements, they built cottages for the workmen, with running water and gas. The average rent paid was about eight dollars a month. For the unmarried there were two boardinghouses. In the early days girls were hired to skein the silk. As they toiled away from dawn to dusk, it was customary for one of them to relieve the monotony by reading aloud from the *Hartford Courant* or such books as *Uncle Tom's Cabin.*

At their peak, the Cheneys employed nearly five thousand. The mills covered thirty-six acres of floor space. When the tide of immigration began after 1870, first the Irish, then the Swedes and Germans ran the power looms alongside of native-born Yankees. Dress silks, satins, velvets, organzines, chiffons, costly draperies, crepes, pongees, twills, ties, ribbons, flags, and waterproof foulards were all produced. They carried in stock over 800 different fabrics.

In making silk, the Cheneys devised a method for using both raw silk from the original cocoon of the silkworm that could be reeled, and spun or waste silk from pierced cocoons that could not be unwound. The latter was soaked in boiling soap and water and then carded just like cotton or wool fibers. A great artesian well and four reservoirs provided the pure water needed. Some silk was yarn dyed, some piece dyed, and some printed in colors, one at a time. Weaving silk involved first warping or reeling the length-wise threads. The ends of the warp were mounted on a wooden frame containing a series of wires. Actual weaving began when the warp harness was placed in the loom. A shuttle, with a bobbin of thread unwinding as it moved back and forth through the warp, supplied the cross threads or filling. The lifting of different wires or shafts produced the desired weave. When finished, the cloth was machine printed with as many as eleven different colors by means of designs engraved on copper cylinders, then steamed to set the colors and washed. Silk goods were finished in various ways in order to stiffen, soften, smooth, stretch, or waterproof. In many cases, they had to be handled 150 times before being ready for marketing. The Cheneys not only manufactured the most versatile line of silks but had also the only integrated operation of its kind.

The spinning and weaving mills were very noisy. The rhythmic roar of the looms, with their spools rotating and the bobbins flashing back and forth, sounded like music to the ears of the owners in their nearby homes. Combing the washed raw silk was something like pulling burrs from hair, the material being thrown over giant spiked wheels to pull out the bits of cocoon. Jacquard designs were laid out on cardboard squares, reminding one of an immense roll for a pianola. Before electricity, seven steam engines, with an aggregate of 2,400 horsepower, drove the machinery with its thousands of spindles.

The intricacies of the silk business accounted for a large part of the education of the younger Cheneys. The daily table talk was often filled with discussion of the latest fashions, new equipment, labor relations, and the tariff that protected their sales. From the beginning, the Cheneys shared an artistic tradition that influenced their silk designs. Two of the original brothers, John and Seth, had been noted engravers. Almost every Cheney dabbled in painting, and they all had the ability to judge color. Whenever a new material was under development, swatches were brought home to the ladies for scrutiny. Whether a sheer printed chiffon or heavy upholstery, they tested it for durability, texture, and non-fading.

The Cheneys devoted a great deal of time and money to making South Manchester an ideal place to live. Cheney Hall, built in 1869, was a center for reading, entertainment, lectures, and exhibitions. On hot summer nights German waltzes, Polish polkas, and Irish jigs filled the air. The same year they completed a two-mile railroad to connect with the main line, the shortest steam railroad ever owned by one family, carrying nearly 100,000 passengers every year at a fare of four cents. In addition, they supported a school; operated a 700-acre farm, store, and grist mill; financed a volunteer fire department; formed a light, power, and horse tramway company; provided sewers and garbage collection; and maintained all the streets in the mill district. No liquor was permitted to be sold. A benefit association took care of workers who became ill or injured and provided pensions and death benefits.

A Cheney descendant confided what it was like to grow up amid this peaceful setting: "It was more like a park than an estate. No walls, no gates, hedges, or boundaries separated one family from another, nor cut off the streets. An unending sweep of lawn undulated and wound about the houses, with clumps of laurel, rhododendron, or other shrubs bordering the winding driveways and acting as a screen between the houses. The lawns and the oaks were the families' special love. On the long June evenings our elders were wont to stroll across the lawn, my grandfather and grandmother always dressed in sparkling white from head to foot, the aunts in flowered and pastel silk prints from the mill. The oaks were our playhouses and many times the setting for a wedding reception.

"Around the fire we would hear tales of the underground railroad and the Spanish-American War. Uncles and aunts read the Arabian Nights and Baron Munchausen to their nephews and nieces. There were a couple of winters when the Horace Cheneys and Howell Cheneys had a joint Bible class. Sunday walks and Sunday sports were great family joys.

"The family was very active in civic affairs. Cousin Louis was mayor of Hartford. Aunt Peggy worked to prevent child labor as a state representative. Cousin Will spent years on prison reform. Uncle Dave studied reservoirs and water conservation. Uncle Howell spent sixty years of continuous effort to improve the public schools. My father wrote "The Story of Silk." The twin aunts kept, mostly without help, the big formal garden next to the tennis court.

"I can't say this was *noblesse oblige*. It was our way of life. Loyalty was the cardinal virtue of this close-living clan. Let anyone from the outside betray a member, and the whole group came to the defense of their own. How so many and diverse and strong-minded personalities survived collectively, sharing work and property and their rivalries, is a miracle!"

Frank W. Cheney's penetrating blue eyes — a Cheney characteristic — snow white beard and white hair, gold-headed cane and watch chain, and immaculate dress all enhanced the image of a patriarch feared and respected by family and employees alike. His granddaughter said: "When he sat at the head of the table on Thanksgiving Day, surrounded by his twelve children, their families, cousins and aunts, over seventy by count, he was the focus of all attention."

Although he shunned the limelight, he did venture twice into politics, without success. In 1892, he ran for lieutenant governor on the Republican ticket. Two years later, confident the party would, this time, give him the gubernatorial nomination by acclamation, he became embroiled in a bitter fight at the state convention and again lost. The next day he ruefully commented: "I paid for a room at the Allyn House, for a box of cigars and for a good deal of experience and took a bath and washed the politics off from myself."

Until his death Frank ruled the mill, town, and family. His toughest job, he once told his daughter, was preventing the family from becoming too rich, and he met this challenge by liberal subsidies to every important community need. At the age of eighty, in 1902, he encountered a challenge from his mill subjects. They struck over his insistence that each hand run two looms, in order to meet English competition. One evening the strikers marched toward his homely, red-painted mansion, chanting "Two looms! Two looms!" To the family sitting outside the sound was ominous, becoming louder as they came nearer. One of the leaders carried a stick. The old man rose and started walking slowly down the lawn to meet them. The marchers stopped. No one moved or said a word. Frank Cheney fixed his sharp blue eyes on the assemblage. In a few minutes, they turned away and dispersed. Frank W. Cheney was still boss.

* * *

The Cheneys' Victorian paradise followed Colonel Colt's model community in Hartford by some twenty years. In the middle 1850s, the Colonel built behind the Armory fifty tenements in rows for his employees and their families, laid out several streets, dug a reservoir to supply water, and erected gas works. Rev. William Jarvis regarded his son-in-law's activity with amazement: "He is all the while putting up dwelling houses for his workmen, and at the rate he is going on, in a few years his land within the Dyke will be a densely populated city." As the Cheneys would do later, he erected a hall seating a thousand people where the workers could read, dance, or listen to lectures and concerts. Charter Oak Hall was dedicated in May, 1856.

His willow trees atop the dike grew so well that quite by chance they became the resource for a new business. In the southeast corner of the meadows, Colt built a small brick furniture factory. His father-in-law, who never tired of boasting about the Colonel's successes without ever admitting his excesses, said the willows "are used very extensively in the manufacture of baskets, children's cradles, wagons, and chairs... Probably a hundred persons, mostly Germans, will be employed constantly." Because of their coolness and lightness, the products sold well in Cuba and South America. To attract the kind of skilled help he needed, he brought over from Potsdam forty German master craftsmen and their families, for whom he erected chalets modeled after their native abodes and, to make them feel right at home, provided a beer-and-coffee garden and the musical instruments to form a brightly-uniformed band. Nine of these Swiss-style houses are still extant.

By the end of 1859, the Rev. Jarvis claimed that "the Colonel will derive a profit of $10,000 this year, with a great increase yearly for years to come... Colt was harvesting thirty tons of willows annually and expected to double the amount. Early in 1860 he considered employing Leopold B. Simon, whom Colt called a Jew "but an honest one," as head of the willow ware factory. Instead, he made Richard Jarvis, his wife's brother, president and treasurer.

Every winter when the earth had frozen, the well-rooted and fast-growing osiers on the dike were cut back to the ground. The sticks were tied in bundles, then peeled by a steam-powered machine invented by Colt engineers, and dried. At this point, the skilled German woodworkers took over and finished the pieces by hand with tools similar to those used by cobblers. Veranda seats were a popular item, mahogany in color and often decorated. After work, the Germans repaired to their saloon run by a Mr. Burcoltz. They loved to celebrate birthdays. Everyone's anniversary was an excuse for a raucous party of flowing beer and strange cheeses. Upon entering the basement saloon for the first time, an apprentice named Dwight Lyman was repelled by the peculiar odor. He asked his boss: "John, what stinks so?" The German sniffed and shook his head: "I nothing smells already." Lyman persisted that there was something rotten in the room. Finally, the woodworker smiled broadly: "Oh, I see dos is der limburger, da not smell bad, dos is good, chust try him!" In a few years rattan furniture became a formidable competitor, and when a fire wiped out the little factory in 1873, it was never rebuilt.

The Colonel's other major side interest was his greenhouse, half-a-mile in length, with over 2,000 fruit trees under glass. Exclaimed his father-in-law: "Such a profusion of rare flowers I have seldom seen; and there are pineapples, strawberries nearly ripe, figs, peaches, nectarines, grapes, oranges, and lemons. But the most singular sight was that of cucumbers, hanging down from the vines which were trained up to the roof, by hundreds." Between the greenhouse and the Armory the Colonel created a magnificent vista that included a deer park, artificial lake, orchards, and

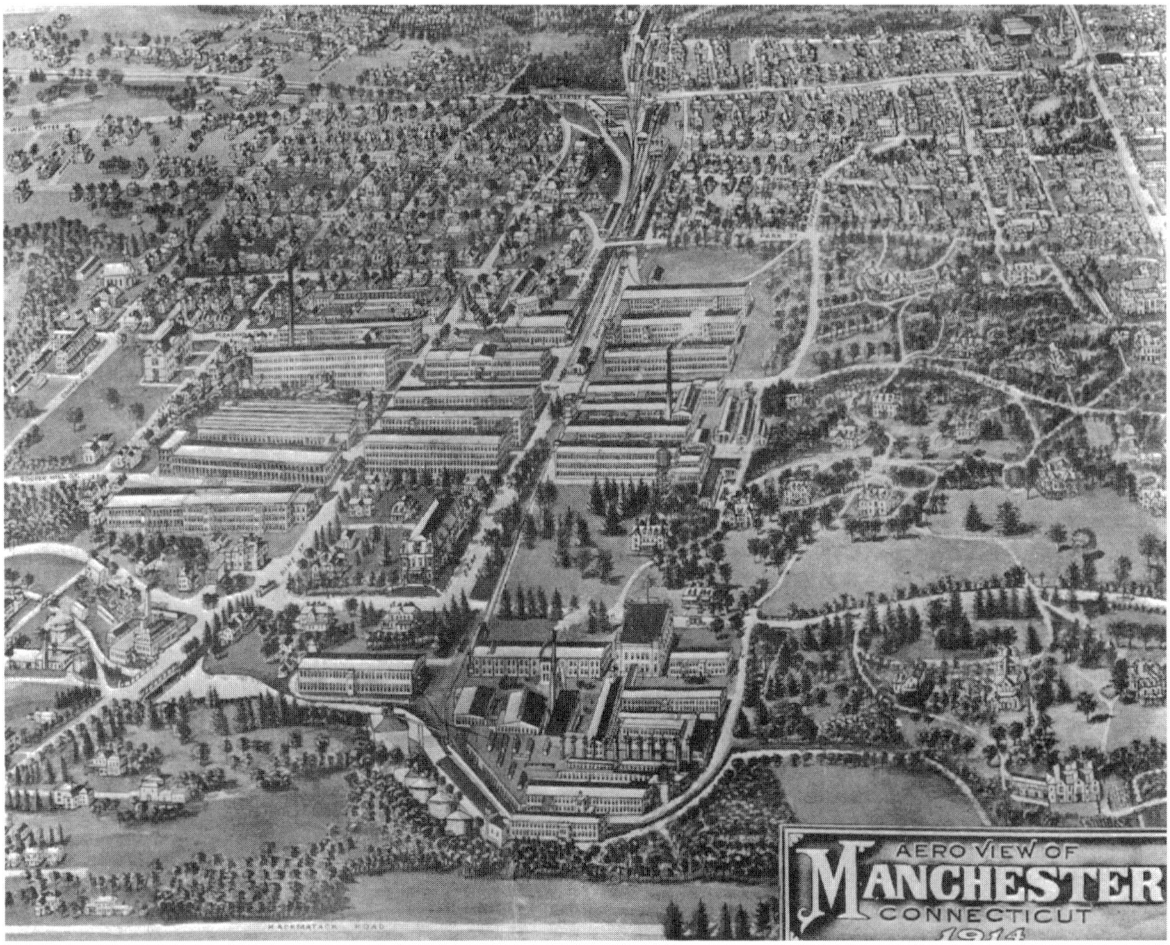

AERO VIEW OF
MANCHESTER
CONNECTICUT

Cheney Silk Mills and The Cheney Homes in Manchester. (Courtesy Connecticut Historical Society)

The Potsdam Village and Willow Ware Factory. (from *Armsmear*)

meadows stretching eastward toward the river.

Upon completion of all his improvements, Sam Colt's investment in the South meadows ran close to $2 million — a gigantic redevelopment project for that time, and one he accomplished without borrowing a dollar from the local bankers he so roundly detested. Neither did he receive help from the city fathers. Though he paid nearly one-tenth of Hartford's entire property taxes, the mayor and the council saw fit to contribute only three gas street lamps to his development. And when Sam started a private ferry from the Armory across the river to East Hartford to convey mechanics who could not be accommodated in company housing, the *Courant* accused him of trying to "dodge the rights of the Hartford Bridge Company." They were all Republicans, and the Colonel was a brash Democrat who paddled his own canoe. So enraged did he become over such niggardly and hostile treatment that he made a major change in his will, depriving Hartford of what might have been a great engineering college rivaling M.I.T. or Rensselaer. He had planned to leave a quarter of his estate for "founding a school for the education of practical mechanics and engineers." The famous educator Henry Barnard bemoaned the loss of what he called "the first people's college in the world."

For at least half a century the Colt Armory had a major impact on the economic and social growth of Hartford. Not only were several of its mechanically-trained "graduates" successful in founding manufacturing firms like Pratt & Whitney, Billings & Spencer, and Hartford Machine Screw, but Colt's techniques of mass production were adapted to making bicycles, machine tools, typewriters, and other durable goods. The housing which Colonel Colt erected for his employees on his vast estate inspired Colonel Pope in the 1890s to develop a residential area south of Capitol Avenue and to donate land for a park nearby. Many years later, when Pratt & Whitney moved to Charter Oak Park in West Hartford, that company promoted the building of single-family homes along the surrounding streets. Until World War II, the Armory's location dictated to a large extent the living patterns of the various ethnic groups comprising its work force, creating neighborhoods of Irish, Italians, and Poles which still have some cohesiveness today despite the flight of the second generation of immigrants to the suburbs under the impetus of the GI Bill of Rights.

* * *

During the 1920s the American silk industry reigned as the queen of textiles, cocksure that its enormous production and profit were as permanent as the economic boom itself. Cheney's annual sales had more than quadrupled since the turn of the century to $23,000,000. Its silks were accorded the honor of being the first American products to be exhibited at the Louvre in Paris. There were now twenty-nine mills containing 100,000 looms spread over nearly 1,300 acres, as well as 271 company-owned houses. The company, with properties assessed at $11 million, paid one-quarter of the town's total budget. Each manufacturing division was headed by a Cheney; altogether, twenty members of the family occupied executive positions, and all twelve directors were Cheneys.

But a new technology and the Great Depression changed everything. Just as the silkmen rode the crest of their growth, rayon appeared, the first of the man-made fibers. Rayon rapidly supplanted silk in the weaving mills. It was a cheaper and more consistent raw material, enabling a weaver to run a hundred looms instead of twelve with silk. During 1929, the Cheneys had to write down $6 million in raw material inventories; unsold goods glutted the storerooms in each division; their surplus of many years vanished. By 1931, sales had shrunk to less than half their best year and they reported a loss of $2.5 million. Raw silk, which had been selling for twenty dollars a pound in 1923, now could be had for only a dollar.

To stay afloat, the family began to liquidate the non-manufacturing appendages in their domain. They sold the gas and electric companies, the water and sewer services, their schools and recreation buildings, and the private railroad. Eleven Cheneys resigned as directors, leaving only Ward Cheney, the president, who brought in four outsiders for the first time since the company's founding in 1838. In desperation, Ward was compelled also to cut salaries and retire, without pay, eight executives, including two uncles and three cousins. A voting trust was set up for the family stockholders who owned eighty percent of all the stock.

It was too late. Operating losses continued to mount. Although the work week was decreased, wage costs rose at the same time that the earnings of Italian and Japanese weavers actually declined, owing to currency devaluation. Horace Cheney fought vainly to retain the industry's protective tariff. Despite all their benefits the employees became restless and turned to the United Textile Workers union for security. In 1934, the company borrowed $1,300,000 from the Reconstruction Finance Corporation. Then, unable to pay off the interest on his company's debts and retain sufficient working capital, Ward Cheney threw in the sponge and submitted to voluntary bankruptcy.

Afterwards, Cheney Brothers struggled vainly to get back on their feet. They managed to survive for another twenty years, but the dynasty was moribund, and the last vestige of paternalism soon disappeared when the federal government ordered the disposal of the company's housing. The auction attracted a large crowd who followed the auctioneers from house to house. Sixty-one tenants were able to buy their homes. Many sold for less than $4,000. Matthew M. Moriarity ended up with thirty-three. Thankful for the Cheney generosity to his family when he was growing up, he continued their policy of low rents and encouragement to purchase. Altogether, the transactions were reported as the largest turnover of property that ever took place in New England.

Some observers concluded that outside influences conspired to crush the Cheney silk empire. But it seemed clear that, more than anything else, the family way of life that created it also destroyed it. Nepotism and smugness had overtaken the fourth generation of managers. They refused to give up silk and substitute rayon. When bad times struck, their manufacturing integration — with several businesses combined into one — became a dreadful liability because of the large overhead required to support it. True to their heritage, they chose to remain in South Manchester and fight an uphill battle, rather than move to the South in quest of cheap labor, as many New England textile firms had already done. This was highly commendable, but foolhardy.

The Cheneys allowed human considerations and civic obligations to outweigh economic ones when the chips were down. In 1908, the famous inventor Christopher Spencer had written Horace B. Cheney a heartfelt tribute to the family:

"The highest sense of honor, conscientiousness and sympathetic action always pervaded dealings with Cheney Brothers. It was not in their nature to do wrong. They were always ready to contribute to any organization or society whose aim was to improve the condition of the people. The distribution of benefits was impartial. Precepts of right living were advocated. Their home and youth must have been of the most harmonious environment to produce a brotherhood so united."

It took the Cheneys eight decades to build the greatest silk firm in the United States, to make their silks the best in the world, to establish a harmony with labor rarely equaled anywhere, and to develop around their mills a community with a soul. In less than ten years their empire crumbled, the victim of management inflexibility and unregeneration. Their bankruptcy held two lessons for the business historian. The first was that companies, like human beings and even civilizations, are subject to the same life cycle. Secondly, the era of paternalism had come to an end in America. A new day was dawning.

CHAPTER XI

TOO MUCH WATER AND WIND

A protracted strike like Colt's is a divisive and embittering experience. It takes time for hostilities to cool and for production to return to a normal rhythm. Some never forget or forgive. But a natural disaster unites people and challenges their higher instincts; out of the hardships and losses shared by all concerned arises a spirit of working together for a common end. Such was the case during the Great Flood of 1936.

On Wednesday, March 11th a warm rain poured down on the snow-laden valley. Far upstream in Vermont and New Hampshire the heavy snow blanket began to melt fast into the tributaries of the Connecticut River. As the swollen streams churned into the river itself, the flood gauge rose by six inches every hour. Near Windsor, where the Farmington and Connecticut rivers join, a tremendous ice jam had formed, twenty feet high and three miles long. About three o'clock on Friday afternoon it broke up and with an ominous rumble moved downstream toward Hartford. Although the water level climbed to twenty-four feet, it appeared on Sunday that the flood had reached its crest, and it actually receded a few feet during the next two days. But there occurred more torrential rain and unseasonably warm weather; by midnight, Wednesday the 18th, the river had risen to twenty-five feet. Meteorologists would call it a 500-year or even a 1,000-year flood. The worst was yet to come.

The Red Cross announced its readiness for any emergency. The YMCA and YWCA offered their buildings as refuge centers if necessary. Several Coast Guard cutters stood by to dash the length of the river. Merchants on the east side of the city frantically began moving goods onto their top shelves or up to second stories. Inch by inch, sewers started backing up into cellars near the river's banks.

Before dawn the next day the tossing and turbulent river had leapt five feet, higher than ever before. The old record had supposedly been set in 1927, but it was not as memorable an event in Hartford history as the rain-caused flood of May 1, 1854. That one rose over thirty feet in front of Colt's and tested the strength of the unfinished dike which Colonel Colt, at his own expense and despite the ridicule of the Hartford Council, was building around his property. Extending nearly two miles, this earthen embankment with willows planted on top ranged in width from forty to one hundred feet, and in height up to thirty-two feet. Not only did it mean an investment of $125,000, but the Colonel offered to put up a thousand dollars as a guarantee of its soundness. The dike held, saving the new Armory which was then under construction, although a number of laborers who lived in shanties in the South Meadows had to be removed by boat. Unable to sail because the coal yards were under water, the steamer "City of Hartford" used her lifeboats to rescue stranded families. The rest of the city looked like an inland sea.

Pleased with his foresight and the mayor's belated recognition of it, the colonel boldly announced that "if the city will relieve my property from taxation, I will bind myself to exclude the river from the South Meadows; and, more than all that, if the city will pay for it, I will agree to dyke the Connecticut River from end to end so that nothing less than Noah's flood can reach the houses which are now inundated." The Council spurned his offer but did extend the dike upriver toward the covered bridge and in 1929 expended a million dollars for another extension southward to Wethersfield.

For eighty years, then, the Colt dike had protected both the Armory and its environs. Now, on Friday, it appeared that Noah's flood indeed threatened the city. Water was flowing at the rate of 300,000 cubic feet per second — sixty times more than normal. Would it hold once more? The bridge to East Hartford was closed at noon. In the meadows the electric light plant was cut off from land; the crew inside did their best to hold back the water from the boilers. Step-by-step they were forced to retreat up the stairs, praying that the red-hot condensers, now half submerged, would not blow up. At the same time hundreds were being evacuated from the East Side, as the streets in that low area became a new bottom for the river. Water-soaked rats scurried for land.

Three hundred American Legion volunteers, assisted by Boy Scouts, WPA workers, and the Governor's Foot Guard, rowed or paddled boats through the swirling eddies of the newly-formed canals around the tenements. Young and old, clutching bundles and suitcases, waited on second floor verandas to be rescued, the women and children weeping, their men folk shouting hoarsely for help. Some irrepressible souls however, turned the calamity into a frolic. Like Venetian gondoliers, Italians in canoes floated down Front Street carrying jugs of wine and playing mandolins.

Seeing a chance to make a quick profit, a few rascals launched homemade craft and ferried anyone willing to pay two dollars a head, until the police put a stop to the racket. Policemen also patrolled the area in outboards to prevent looting. With the arrival of the Coast Guard whaleboats, the evacuation process speeded up. Seeing two large gasoline tanks floating free, the crew of one cutter headed them off into Wethersfield Cove. After touring the downtown district, Mayor Thomas Spellacy announced that his office would be open around the clock for the duration of the emergency.

At Red Cross headquarters, wild confusion reigned as frenzied people sought help to locate relatives or to have them removed to safety. Lost children wailed for their parents. There was clamor for food and clothing. In the meantime the water slowly spread westward, up the Park River toward the hotels, office buildings, banks, and insurance companies. It soaked the generators of the transit company's power house, causing all trolley cars to stall in their tracks. At St. Anthony's Church water sloshed down one side of the nave, while on the other the huddled worshippers celebrated mass. Later, a body was found floating in the vestibule. Fear-maddened pets in the zoo at Colt Park were shot as an act of mercy.

Thursday night found the center of the city in darkness and the river up four more feet. Candle vendors appeared, hawking three puny tapers worth a nickel for 25¢. The Colt dike now became the focus of greatest concern. All day city engineers and a crew of hundreds had labored to raise it with sandbags. Around eleven, however, the raging, muddy water surged over its top, raced across the meadows toward the Armory, tore the huge tanks of an oil depot from their foundations, and threatened the power station. Within minutes the entire first floor of the Colt factory was under water, and two feet of the second floor. Quarter-ton molds were upended, and sheets of steel thrown around like tissue paper.

Three hours later, a twenty-foot wall of water roared through Hartford's squatter village south of the Armory, smashing the shacks into bits and pieces. The screaming inhabitants found themselves instantly engulfed by water and debris. In the pitch dark they battered down doors, pried up roofs, and struggled to escape, dragging their children behind. As they waded forth in every direction, the demolished dwellings swirled past them, knocking them down again and again. Luckily, rescue craft were nearby to haul them away from the water.

Several of the victims were Polish families living around the Armory. One man said:

"I've lived here ten years and never saw water look like that, just like the ocean, carrying along parts of houses, gasoline tanks and driftwood. I thought the Colt dike would protect us. By six o'clock at night, the water started coming in my store. I sat up and watched it get stronger and stronger. At nine the lights went out. I could hear the women and kids crying for help up and down the street, but no boat came until four."

Walter Sidor, a scoutmaster, managed to reach his home during the middle of the night, only to find his first floor flooded. He climbed a tree and entered a window; three hours later he left by boat from the same window, the water having risen eight feet. A mother trembled when she recounted her experience in broken English: "I was told the water wouldn't come any further, so I went to bed and was asleep when I heard people shouting. There was a boat outside. I got my seven children dressed; the baby was crying, my girl wanted to take her cat, but he scratched so hard I told her to leave him. I had food in the cellar, twenty-two bushels of potatoes, and lots of rabbits in the barn. But there wasn't time to take anything. The boat could only take three of us — they all wanted to go together, they were scared. And everything was black water."

The third day, Friday, was the longest. All the utilities except gas were crippled. Fifty thousand tons of coal had been swept downstream. A Stygian gloom descended on the city, intensified by more rain and the roar of the river. Telephones were out of order, the radio stations operated by battery, National Guard soldiers as well as policemen patrolled the streets. Hordes jammed the city, gaping at the stricken areas. Parking spaces downtown were immersed; some automobiles had disappeared; passengers arriving at the Hartford station had to exit by rowboat while guests entering one hotel were rowed to the desk to register. A bellhop netted three goldfish in the lobby. At eight o'clock Saturday morning the river crested at 37.56 feet — six feet above the previous record. One-fifth of the entire city was inundated, making it almost an island. Ten thousand refugees crowded schools and other relief centers or were cared for by relatives and friends. In one Polish parochial school near Colt's, the Red Cross was feeding several hundred three times a day.

Fearful of looting and vandalism by those who had no business in the city, police and military officials barred all sightseeing automobiles from the downtown area, issued passes to those engaged in relief work, and declared a midnight curfew. Taverns and liquor stores were forced to close early. Relief workers and refugees received the first of 25,000 typhoid shots. Those working along the flood front were required to wash their hands in Lysol when coming off duty. Many factories suspended work. Governor Cross formed a committee to coordinate the relief and cleanup programs.

By Sunday night the river had retreated two feet, and electric service had been restored, thanks to linemen who worked all night to erect temporary sub-stations. Telephones again rang. Mayor Spellacy met with his department heads to plan a massive clean-up program. The rain stopped, and the cold March winds took over. The curfew remained in effect.

Early Monday morning, three thousand workers began the dismal process of bringing the flood zone back to life. A flying squad inspected the shoreline and found most of the structures safe for re-occupancy. The Board of Aldermen voted an emergency appropriation of $500,000 for relief and rehabilitation. The Fire Department worried about the thousands of gallons of gasoline which had leaked into the river from the dislodged oil tanks. People were cautioned against fallen live wires on the streets and waterlogged insulation inside the buildings. Armed with shovels, axes, and mops, men from out-of-town Civilian Conservation Corps camps pitched into digging out cellars and disinfecting homes with chlorinated lime. The mud was knee deep, oil coated the sides of buildings, and everything standing dripped and stank. A burden of flotsam concealed the streets and sidewalks; underneath, the pavement had been peeled back in hundreds of places and curbstones stood almost on end. One man stepped into one of the deep pits and immediately drowned.

The Italian and Jewish shopkeepers returning to their East Side stores were greeted by a jumbled mass of soaked, battered, and buried litter. The racing currents had forced windows and doors, overturning counters and showcases, scattering their merchandise everywhere, both inside and outside along the street. It was impossible to distinguish clothing, furniture, or foodstuffs. The woodwork was swollen and warped. Cleanup crews shoveled the mess from shop to curb, where it formed a six-foot high mound. These merchants, everything they owned tied up in their little businesses, faced ruin.

At Colt's the water level was marked at 38.5 feet, six feet above the demolished dike. No one could get inside until Sunday, March 22nd. Twenty feet of water still surrounded the plant. To fill a rush order for 200 automatic pistols, shipping clerks carried the boxes to the window sills on the second story, from where they were loaded into motorboats. James Kinnarney, who lived nearby on Huyshope Avenue, had never seen anything like it in his nearly fifty years of working at Colt's. His father, an Irish immigrant, had been one of Colonel Colt's earliest hands, and Kinnarney himself had started working at the age of seventeen. His brother and sister were also Colt employees. The inside of his house and all his furniture ruined, Kinnarney set out to salvage what he could from his office. The only way he could reach it was to commandeer a skiff with an outboard, and with a couple of helpers he chugged along the second floor, skirting in and out of the machinery. He managed to retrieve a few papers. Robert Courtney had better luck; he saved the shipping ledgers, dating back to the 1860s, by moving them to an upper floor.

A quick survey revealed that every machine would have to be dismantled and cleaned, as well as the overhead belts and pulleys, and every motor dried or rewound. Tons of silt covered the machinery and walls of the ground floor; the aisles were sand dunes two feet deep. Getting back to normal was a costly and time-consuming task; the yard became a giant outdoor laundry, with blueprints, books, clothing, and all kinds of equipment drying in the sun. In the office, to the horror of one girl, a snake slithered past her, heading for its natural habitat.

Governor Cross, after a tour of the Valley, said the hardest hit area was in the vicinity of the Colt dike. The bleak houses behind the Armory were submerged or abandoned, except for wandering cats. Colt Park had become a lake; through the shattered leaded glass of Mrs. Colt's Church of the Good Shepherd one could see prayer books and hymnals floating. Men in boats, returning distressed owners to their homes or possessions, plied back and forth. Along the railroad spur between the Armory and the river, freight cars lay on their sides, the tracks twisted and torn. Yawning holes marked what had been sidewalks. Refuse hung from poles and wires. A crude doll sat forlornly on top of a wire fence. Chugging steam pumps sucked water back into the Park River. And from the fetid water rose a stench that no one quite forgot.

In the thirty-five town area, covering a hundred square miles flooded by the Connecticut River, the total physical damage was estimated at almost eleven million dollars, of which two-thirds was in Hartford alone. Amazingly enough, only three persons lost their lives. Colt's bill for damaged machinery and equipment and loss of inventory came to $747,000. Three buildings had to be razed, which were replaced by a new structure containing a much-needed cafeteria and recreation room. Despite the setback, the company managed to earn more than it did in the previous strike-bound year and to pay a ten percent bonus to all employees.

* * *

By June of 1936, the Great Flood had become for most people a collection of photographs or reminiscences to pass on to any one who would look or listen. Hartford had returned to its normal ways, the debris cleaned up, houses repaired, factories and stores reopened. The WPA allocated the state three million dollars for rehabilitation projects. The governors of New England talked about a compact for erecting dams on the upper tributaries of the river to control future flooding.

This was the year and month of Hartford's tercentenary. It came and went with hardly a ripple in the daily life of the city. There was a pageant of 400 school children in Bushnell Park near replicas of Thomas Hooker's home and the first meeting house, both of which had been submerged by the flood. There were services at the Congregational Center Church and Old Burying Ground attended by the governor, mayor, and some forty patriotic organizations. And the Metropolitan Opera star, Anna Kaskas, a native of Hartford, sang at a Bushnell Memorial birthday party. These events were enjoyed by those who took part, but the rank and file paid scant attention. After all, it was three hundred years since the Rev. Mr. Hooker led his band of a hundred followers through the wilderness from Cambridge to found the city — the first adventurers, incidentally, into the frontier of this country. And the fact that a few years later he inspired these self-reliant, God-fearing settlers to adopt the first written document that became the foundation of our constitutional government was equally remote. Most of the 164,000 residents in 1935 had more pressing concerns — such as making a living.

The previous fall, however, a remarkable industrial exhibition had filled the State Armory. It represented the culmination of Connecticut's development as a manufacturing state. Over three hundred manufacturers proudly displayed their products and skills. In one great hall could be seen the entire spectrum of material progress in one small state since the Revolution, and especially during the past seventy-five years. Here were the achievements of those resourceful inventors and clever machinists who had given Connecticut top rank in number of patents per capita, a world-wide acclaim for its metal-working skills, and a deserved reputation for being the "arsenal of the nation" in every war America had fought.

Spread over the floor were clocks, hardware, hats, machine tools, paper goods, silverware, springs, textiles, tires, tools, toys, and typewriters. At least half of the show was in motion, machines humming, deft hands assembling or spinning. The most colorful was the textile section, especially the Cheney girls unwinding silk cocoons, feeding them into automatic winders and weaving silk on power looms. Even the lowly silkworm, provider of the raw material, was busy munching mulberry leaves.

Outside, the firearms display hung a tribute to the inventive genius of Eli Whitney and Simeon North with the caption "Interchangeability of Parts." Besides Colt's, the firearms industry was represented by Lyman Gun Sight, Marlin, Mossberg, Remington Arms, and Winchester. A modern rifling machine contrasted with a colonial gunmaker's bench. The machinery exhibit had Whitney's pioneering milling machine, which he invented in 1818 — the forerunner of all the machine tools that made mass production possible.

Upon entering the hall, one's eye was immediately attracted to the replica of the grist mill and its splashing waterwheel which John Winthrop erected in New London in 1650. At the edge of the millstream stood the harnessed cart of the Yankee

Building up the dike to protect the armory.

The armory under water in 1936.

(Courtesy Connecticut Historical Society)

Colt office under water in the flood of 1936.

Peddler loaded with wares for the long journey to the frontiers of a growing America. The village mill and the peddler's cart — nothing could better show how it all began. Around the walls were murals depicting the step-by-step advancement of Connecticut industry, beginning with Eli Whitney's invention of the cotton gin and his musket, and culminating with the airplane and submarine. What a panorama: making paper, powder, and silk; forming hats; blowing glass; weaving wool; assembling clocks; rolling brass; hammering bolts; cutting nails; forging axes; shaping tin; beating leather; vulcanizing rubber; and building ships! There was almost nothing this little state, without any natural resources except brains, guts, and muscles, did not produce in quantity to improve the life of the average American.

Connecticut's preeminence as a manufacturing center dated back only to the Civil War period, although the growth of industry began about the same time as the birth of our country. For its first two centuries of settlement, the state, in common with the rest of New England, thrived mainly on farming and to a lesser extent on a spirited maritime trade. As soon as political freedom had been achieved, Connecticut Yankees were compelled, because the land could no longer support its population and the sea no longer was an open highway for commerce, to seek a new basis for economic independence. Merchants with surplus capital invested in woolen and cotton mills, quickly adopting the production techniques introduced in England and secretly brought here by men like Samuel Slater. Within a twenty-year period, led by Eli Whitney and Simeon North, they conceived and pioneered a factory system based upon the use of machinery run by waterpower, the standardization and interchangeability of parts, and the division of labor — all combined under one roof, often in a village especially created for the purpose. By 1860, Connecticut's output of manufactures on a per capita basis placed it second in the United States, next to Massachusetts, and more people worked in factories than on farms.

A large dinner before the opening of the exhibition also celebrated the twenty-fifth anniversary of the modern-day Manufacturers Association of Connecticut, which in turn had grown out of a trade association formed in Middletown as far back as 1815. Some five hundred gathered at the State Armory to hear Governor Cross and other officials. The governor, with perhaps a little hyperbole, boasted that Connecticut was the birthplace of American industry. E. Kent Hubbard, the leonine head of the Association since its beginning, blamed government tinkering and New Deal social experiments for the country's slow recovery from the worst depression in its history. He pleaded for a holiday from more lawmaking.

But Dr. Virgil Jordan, the erudite president of the National Industrial Conference Board, delivered a more devastating indictment of the New Deal to the delight of the mostly conservative businessmen. "I can see nothing in the experience of the past or of the present day in any country, nor any promise of the future, which justifies faith in governmental institutions or men in public office as the ultimate agency of economic and social welfare." He pointed out that America was still the world's most prosperous nation, despite the depression, because of the individual's desire for freedom to seek prosperity through his own efforts. Who will assume the responsibility for our well-being, government or private enterprise? "I see no reason to believe that government can do anything for us that we cannot do ourselves." The alternative, in his opinion, must be paid for by the decay of self-reliance and the loss of personal liberty. That choice, it seemed, had already been made: the majority of Americans, representing middle and lower income levels, had decided no longer to depend upon business alone. Henceforth America would have to accept and perfect a mixed system of capitalism and socialism.

Another highlight of the tercentenary celebration was the parade of 20,000 through the length and breadth of the city during the same month as the exhibition. Prizes were offered for the best floats. Significantly, a new generation of Yankees took top honors, an Italian for his re-creation of the first Thanksgiving dinner at Plymouth and a Swedish Society for its Viking ship. Hartford's foreign-born had quickly adapted to Yankee ways and absorbed much of the old Anglo-Saxon culture. One in four residents had been born somewhere in Europe and migrated here. Italians were two-thirds more numerous than the Irish or Polish, and in addition to these ethnic groups one could find Russians, Lithuanians, French Canadians, Germans, Armenians, and Greeks. Not too many years would pass before the original Yankee stock would be in the minority.

* * *

They say lightning is not supposed to strike the same place twice, but other natural forces can and did in Hartford within a thirty-month interval. The Big Blow of 1938 has been called New England's worst disaster in terms of lives lost and property destroyed, yet in the Connecticut Valley it caused less damage than the Flood of 1936. That summer had been unusually wet and muggy, a hothouse from Maine to Long Island, and on Saturday, September 17th, began a torrent of rain followed by flood warnings. The Weather Bureau reported on Sunday "a tropical disturbance of dangerous proportions" roaring across the Atlantic toward the Bahamas and Florida. The next day it abruptly turned north-eastward.

"On Monday I attended the Eastern States Exposition at Springfield. The rain was coming down in sheets and the grounds were thick with mud. The next morning I drove again from Hartford to Springfield through blinding torrential rains to assist in laying the cornerstone of the Connecticut Exposition Building... On my return to Hartford, again through heavy showers, I was troubled in mind by the rapid rise of the Connecticut River, which was spreading over meadows... I took preliminary steps towards dealing with another flood, should Connecticut again be visited by so terrible a disaster as in 1936. Nobody, I think, anticipated that a tropical hurricane in the West Indies might move far enough north to strike New England." So wrote Governor Wilbur Cross in his autobiography.

The weather forecast Wednesday morning was "cloudy, possibly rain." At that moment the storm was passing Cape Hatteras, spinning up the coast at fifty miles an hour, with whole gale winds. The barometer recorded a precipitous drop.

It was what the West Indians call *huracan* — the evil spirit. Not for 123 years had such a thing vented its fury on New England. The hurricane of 1815 had behaved the same way at almost the same time of year, beginning in the West Indies and speeding up the coastline in the wake of warm rains. There were fewer people then to lose their lives, and no railroad tracks to be washed out or utility lines to be blown down. On both occasions, however, the landscape was devastated.

Ironically, on Tuesday Mayor Spellacy called a conference of his Flood Control Commission and the Army engineers to expedite the new dike for Hartford's North Meadows, part of the city's extensive flood protection program. The new Clark dike, extending south from the old Colt section along the airport as far as Wethersfield, was nearing completion. Present at this meeting was Congressman Herman P. Koppleman, the East Sider who had taken a strong position against the New

Cave-in in front of office.

Sandbagging in the hurricane of 1938.

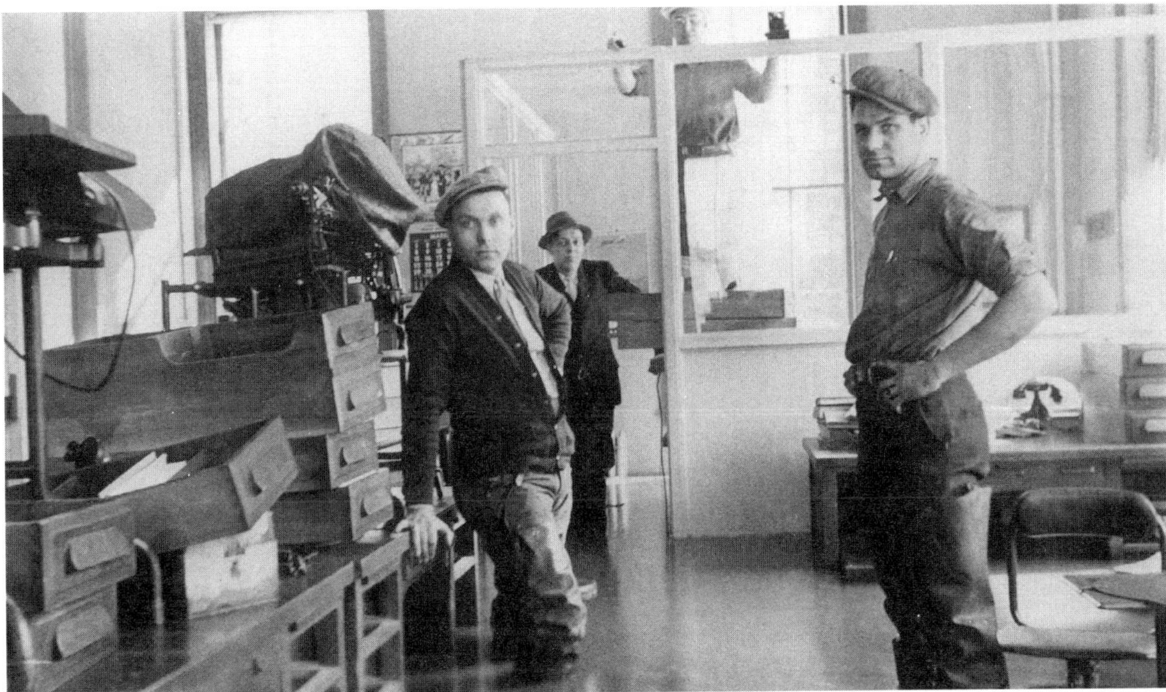

Cleanup crew surveys the damage in the accounting office.

England flood control compact proposed by the governor. As a liberal New Dealer, he believed that it played into the hands of the private power interests and instead favored a federally-funded TVA for the region. In the next few days, the congressman would be severely criticized for blocking the construction of upriver dams and reservoirs to contain flood waters, and his stand would defeat his bid for re-election. After ten inches of rain, the Connecticut River reached flood stage, sixteen feet, the level of the steamer dock at the foot of State Street. The Weather Bureau now predicted that the storm, more violent than ever, would hit the Virginia Capes.

It came in two malevolent rounds. The first, rotating counter-clockwise from the east, swept across Long Island in mid-afternoon Wednesday. Forty minutes later there was an ominous pause as the eye passed, then the sky darkened again, the wind shifted to the south, and the second round roared through with gusts reaching 100 miles an hour. Across Long Island the center headed for the Connecticut shoreline, leaving behind a shambles of summer cottages, a battered New Haven, smoking ruins in New London, the fishing fleet wiped out in Stonington, and a hundred yachts sunk in Essex. In Hartford the clock on top of the Old State House stopped at 4:10 p.m.

As elsewhere from New York to Vermont, the gale toppled buildings, uprooted giant trees, tore off roofs, and knocked down utility poles. The grounds of the State Capitol were virtually denuded. Around the venerable 17-foot statue atop the dome, known as the "Genius of Connecticut," there was scaffolding in place in preparation for inspecting its condition, but it survived intact. The scene in Bushnell Park was awesome, as first one, then another of the beautiful elms slowly and majestically fell to the ground. Pigeons were smashed against windshields. Fences floated in the air like paper. The river became an ocean of grayish white rollers sweeping upstream and casting spray hundreds of yards. By dusk the storm had abated. Five persons were dead.

On the land the greatest devastation was the Valley's tobacco crop and the leveling of so many trees. The streets were cleared soon enough, but there was still the swollen river to contend with, rising four inches an hour toward the 25-foot mark. As in 1936, families once more were being evacuated from the East Side. Many resisted, not believing it could happen a second time. The Red Cross set up disaster headquarters at the Old State House and began the process of finding temporary refuge for 4,000 homeless men, women, and children. But the biggest drama was about to be staged in front of the Colt Armory.

Except for part of the roof ripped off the oldest section, the Armory itself was secure. Eyeing the river Thursday, President Stone decided to close the plant in the afternoon and start moving machinery and goods from the first floor. Soon a delegation arrived, including the head of the local office of the Public Works Administration and the city engineer, Robert Ross. Quickly, they told him of their fear about the dike and their plans for a massive emergency defense effort. "If your dike goes," Ross said, "you know the whole southeast section of Hartford will suffer damage comparable to 1936. And I'll tell you something more in the strictest confidence: the Mayor has decided that if the Colt dike doesn't hold we'll have to dynamite the new Clark dike in order to relieve the pressure here and save the power plant and tank farm as well as your factory from complete destruction."

To organize the tense battle that ensued, Stone agreed to the use of the office downstairs as a command post. Men began arriving in trucks — WPA workers, veterans, Trinity College students, and National Guardsmen — who fanned out to order families in the South End to move. Those living on second floors or higher scorned them. Immediately, the sandbag operation got underway (sandbag is not the right word, since loam was used as a filler, trucked from the airfield a mile away). Initially, a single line two bags high was laid, and as the water level crept up, the line was raised and widened. The houses that fronted the river were made into barriers.

By nightfall, under the hiss of flares, over a thousand men were heaving fifty-pound sacks into place along two thousand yards of the Colt dike. Engineers raced up and down the street in cars. Dodging between red lanterns, a continuous stream of trucks brought more and more bags and hundreds of shovels. "Place 'em right, pack 'em careful!" yelled the foremen. Some of the workers were lucky to have boots, but many were barefoot. The advancing enemy had a sullen color — brown and oily but not turbulent. Twenty feet out in the river stood a white post, the top of which indicated the 35-foot level. Every one kept watching it with bated breath as the water touched the 33-foot mark. "What do you think?" an army engineer was asked. "It's a fifty-fifty chance," he replied.

Around eleven, water seeped through the sandbagging and gurgled across the street. The defenders quickened their pace. A brawny black, his eyes gleaming, wiped the sweat from his brow: "Boy, just like working on the Mississippi levees." Oddly enough, except for the shouting of orders, there was almost no talking — just back-breaking work. Off in the distance stood a dark mass of spectators. At midnight the water lapped just a few inches below the top of the sandbags. Robert Ross was undismayed: "We're keeping ahead!"

All night the little army defended the dike. Hundreds of new recruits tramped up to the office porch to be assigned to work gangs and to relieve those haggard from exhaustion. For eighteen hours the battle waged. Not until early Friday morning did they gain on the river, and then only one sandbag in height ahead. At 5:30 that afternoon the flood topped at 35 feet, two and one-half feet below the record set in 1936. A thousand or so heroes, blistered, sore, and limp, had won. To make sure, however, the engineers continued to reinforce the dike through Friday night until the water started to recede. A total of 400,000 sandbags had been used. Although the WPA expected to pay for the manpower, some 500 volunteers never bothered to collect. Such was the spirit of men united by a common calamity and determined to overcome the worst that Mother Nature in her fury could unleash upon them!

The Flood of 1936 and the Hurricane of 1938 wreaked more than temporary havoc on the city. It changed its face for good. A flood commission was established and $10 million appropriated to erect a new dike 45-feet high. The Park River, which emptied near the Armory, was buried in a tunnel with a highway on top. Four new bridges eventually spanned the Connecticut River, connected by an intricate network of highways in every direction, both of which obscured the river view. Downtown along the waterfront, a vibrant way of urban living was eliminated to make way for boulevards and office buildings. Thus were the people of Hartford separated from their greatest natural resource, making them forget the very existence of the sometimes terrible but always beautiful river.

CHAPTER XII

WAR AGAIN

On Pearl Harbor Day Colt's was still the largest private munitions maker in the United States and the only one turning out machine guns. Its backlog soared to $40 million; two shifts worked sixty hours or more a week; hundreds were being hired every month. Employment doubled to 5,600 in April, 1941, then to 6,000 in May and 6,800 in June. Besides machine guns, the company continued to supply the dependable .45 cal. automatic pistol; 1,800,000 were delivered during the War, all but 400,000 coming from sub-contractors. Unable to contain so many in the Van Dyke facility — which just a few years ago had ample unused space — management was forced to lease the six floors of the old U.S. Rubber plant on Park Street for making the 37mm air cannon, as well as three buildings of Pratt & Whitney Machine Tool's original complex on Flower Street for machine gun production. The Electrical Division also moved into the Rubber Works. A new office containing 42,000 square feet was built to consolidate various administrative functions.

Two other property transactions were historically, if not militarily, significant. Sam Colt's dock from which he had shipped revolvers directly by steamboat was sold to the city for $50,000 as part of the new dike under construction. And the state acquired fifty-four acres of the South Meadows for approaches to the new Charter Oak Bridge across the Connecticut River. The sale of this land eliminated the Armory's testing range, and it was moved further south along the river in Wethersfield.

Colt's response to President Roosevelt's call to arms after the "day of infamy" was a three-shift, seven-days-a-week outpouring of energy, as in most other war plants. Some two million dollars, half of which was contributed by the government, were quickly spent on new machinery. The guards around the Armory were strengthened; everyone, from President Stone down, wore an identification badge at all times. There were foolish rumors about aliens and spies. Over ninety percent signed up to buy War Bonds through payroll deduction. Eleven hundred were inducted into the armed services.

Colt old-timers searched their memories for stories of what the Armory was like in previous wars. A tireless inspector, Charles Miller, recalled he had drilled barrels for the old Gatling machine gun as a fourteen-year-old boy back in 1887; Bill Quish boasted *he* had started work at age twelve and become a *foreman* two years later — the same year Miller was hired. John Thuer, celebrating his 80th birthday, could count sixty-three years of service in "Old Colonel Sam's place"; his father had also been a Coltman and had obtained a patent for a breech loading revolver in 1868. He remembered his father telling him that during the Civil War, Sam Colt had bought $150,000 worth of Government bonds.

The left-wing United Electrical, Radio and Machine Workers of America, CIO, finally organized Colt in the spring of 1941 — an event Stone had long anticipated and the demise of a company-tolerated association that had long been irresponsible and unrepresentative. After a week of general unrest, periodic work stoppages, and a four-hour futile conference with a fourteen-man committee selected by the various divisions, thousands began to walk out of the Armory, many of whom headed for a mass meeting at the Polish National Home. They were not unanimous in their feelings by any means; heated arguments broke out in the streets over the wisdom of striking a defense contractor as essential as Colt's. They well knew that production of 37mm automatic cannon for both the U.S. and British governments, as well as sidearms and machine guns, would be lost. Robert Mintz, field organizer for the union, denied responsibility for the strike, claiming it had resulted from the company's "unenlightened labor policy." True or not, the strike served to release the pent-up emotions of a work force under siege for several months by both AFL and CIO affiliates, and to clear the ground of opposition for Mintz. It lasted only two days. It cost the company a wage increase of seven cents an hour and its consent for an NLRB election to determine a collective bargaining agent for all hourly employees. The vote on August 7th was an anticlimax. The union easily defeated the Independent Armscraft and became the second largest local in New England.

Unionism was anathema to managers who had grown up in the hard-bitten school of "every man for himself," and who were used to running things their own way without their authority ever being challenged. Now they had to contend with overeager, bumptious stewards who knew as little as they did about working together for the good of the organization. Actually, very little worthwhile research had as yet been done into what made people function effectively; the Western Electric studies by Harvard Business School were one exception. During the War, however, "human relations" seemed to be discovered all of a sudden. The term implied a ready-made solution for every management headache involving people. Personnel departments were deluged with literally hundreds of ways and means for winning attendance, loyalty, cooperation, and maximum output. Conferences and textbooks proliferated. Training programs came in neat packages. Companies large and small were sold on poster campaigns, incentive systems, suggestion boxes, and "music to make you work." Very few of these gimmicks had a lasting effect. The more thoughtful personnel experts realized that the ultimate challenge for their new profession was not merely to get along with organized labor, but to inspire individuals to reach their fullest potential, to make them understand company objectives, to give them feelings of security, recognition, and belonging; in short, to create an environment, based upon participation, in which productivity and job satisfaction would be inseparable.

At Colt's these were distant, if not impossible, goals, for the Armory had become an amorphous, unassimilated, almost unmanageable conglomeration which peaked at 16,000 men and women. It could never be a family as Stone had known it. The applicants who lined up in front of the employment office hailed from all over the east — French Canadians, Maine potato farmers, drifters, all ages and conditions, some with mill or factory experience but most unable to read a blueprint or a micrometer. As Herb Walker wryly remarked, "If they're warm, we take them." Four out of every ten hired were women. The handicapped — the lame, the deaf, even the blind — turned into the steadiest workers of all. The majority came by car, jamming the parking lots, and many commuted to work forty to seventy miles every day.

A story was told about a man called Bill Hale. Small, well-built, and handsome, with a jaunty air, he looked much younger than the 72 years written on his application.

"Where are you from, Bill?"

"Vermont."

"How did you happen to come to Colt's?"

"Well, I want to do my bit for the war, so I packed my things and walked down here from Rutland."

"You walked all the way from Vermont?"

"Yes, sir."

Bill had a fascinating background — Spanish War veteran, circus acrobat, hobo, and machine operator. Told he would have to work nights, he had no objection. Still doubtful he would pass the physical examination, the interviewer sent him off to Dr. Biram in the plant dispensary. An hour or so later, Dr. Biram reported that he had never seen a man his age so physically fit.

Hale became the pet of the second shift drilling department. His exaggerated tales of a misspent life kept the operators enthralled. As a joke, he was once asked how old a man must be to lose his desire for sex. "I don't know," Bill pondered. "When I go home the next time, I'll ask my father. He's ninety-one!"

Having so many foreign-born Italians and Polish created a language barrier. Another tale concerned a woman named Tekla who came into the dispensary one morning complaining of stomach pains. "Are you menstruating?" inquired the nurse. "No," said Tekla, "I run a drill press." Some plants offered evening classes in reading and writing English with positive results.

In spite of many handicaps, Colt's did its best to practice good industrial relations. It scored a first in September of 1942 when religious services were offered inside the plant for those working Sundays. Masses were said at six-thirty in the morning; Protestants and Jews prayed for peace in the Colt clubroom. About 300 attended.

The most challenging employment problem

New Colt office building, 1941.

had to do with blacks. Mr. Stone was fond of the waiters in the Hartford Club and a friend of Frank Simpson, a social worker in the North End who fought hard all his life for equal opportunity for his fellow negroes. Stone saw no reason why they shouldn't be hired, even though at the time there were few in the entire Armory. Gradually, with Simpson's help, more were taken on as laborers and handlers and later placed in higher skilled jobs.

At other plants in the city, doors were likewise being opened. At a nearby factory there was little reaction until, in the process of expanding its heat treating department, several blacks were assigned simultaneously. An uproar resulted. The union chief steward threatened a walkout unless they were fired. "All those niggers have syphilis and the men won't use the same toilet." Nearly blind with rage, the employment manager called the whole department together. After explaining the company's hiring policy, he said: "It has been reported to me that you think the new men have venereal disease. I want you to know that I have checked this out with the doctor, and it is absolutely untrue. On the contrary, I also learned that two of you now in this room have a history of such a disease, which is under proper medical treatment. Fellows, you can do one of two things: you can have your prejudice or your paycheck, but not both." Henceforward blacks were accepted without question. By the end of the war they accounted for nearly one out of ten employees in most local factories.

The same company had a desperate need for office space. The area around the Armory consisted mainly of saloons, Polish markets, and ramshackle tenements, many still lacking indoor toilets and running water. A number of them were owned by the Bailey family, prominent in Democrat politics in the city. Mother Bailey was a wizened old lady in rumpled clothes who once a week scurried from building to building to collect her rents. The company persuaded her to lease the first floor of one of her larger tenements. Cleaned and painted it seemed suitable for female clerks to work in, but soon there were complaints about cockroaches. The solution was to evacuate the tenants over a weekend and fumigate the entire premises. On Monday morning an irate hotel manager called to protest about the "guests" he had been sent and the little creatures they had left behind.

Early in 1942, War Production Board Chairman Donald Nelson proposed that joint labor-management committees be formed to help relieve the critical labor shortage. As in most companies, Colt's began with a plant-wide rally, slogan contests, and poster displays, but later settled down to the serious task of finding how to accelerate the delivery of guns. Subcommittees were formed to deal with such problems as transportation, health and safety, plant protection, scrap, and employee suggestions. The union stewards welcomed the meetings as an opportunity to sit down with management in a friendly atmosphere and freely communicate their ideas. Progress was made in reducing accidents and machine downtime; hundreds of suggestion awards were handed out; numerous war bond and charity drives sponsored. "The Coltman" kept those drafted into the armed services in touch. Mr. Stone, who usually detested committees of any kind, was quite pleased with their efforts: "If the union can learn to appreciate management's problems, and vice versa, it may be the saving of our system. Who knows?"

Given its head start on gearing up for the defense effort as early as 1939, it was not surprising that Colt's would be chosen one of the first plants in the country to receive the Army-Navy "E" for outstanding production. Coming as it did in 1942 amid the ferment of expansion, the announcement rekindled the spirits of the entire work force. On the afternoon of November 18th, operations ceased for a few hours to permit all employees to witness the presentation to President Stone of the "E" flag at the State Armory on Broad Street by the commanding general of the Aberdeen Proving Ground. Praising the teamwork between management and employees, General Harris told the throng: "For many years we have asked your organization to do many things, and in all cases you have done well. The products of this company have been the weapons of our armies in five wars: the Mexican War of 1846, the Civil War of 1861, the Spanish War of 1898, the World War of 1917, and World War II. The word 'Colt' has almost always been synonymous with the words 'pistol' and 'revolver'. When I was a boy fifty years ago in Texas, a man carried a 'Colt'; he did not carry a revolver. It was no uncommon event in my boyhood days to have a private argument settled with a 'Colt'. And in national conflicts the arguments have been settled largely through the use of Colts."

As master of ceremonies, Mayor Spellacy's eloquence brought a loud round of applause:

"You have received a coveted and not easily won award. Hartford is proud of you. That award is not alone the flag that will fly over your plants or the lapel insignia each of you will be privileged to wear — rather it is the consciousness of duty well done.

"You are a Hartford institution. The great flood of 1854, the fire that destroyed the East Armory during the Civil War, the flood of 1936 that nearly ruined your plant, or the flood and hurricane of 1938 — none of these catastrophes influenced any change in your location; you built anew, and in this war when it was necessary for you to expand, you still remained in Hartford.

"Here in Hartford democracy was conceived, born and nurtured. Here in Hartford are made the weapons that shall preserve it, both in war and peace."

The "E" award will be remembered as the high point of Colt's role in World War II.

* * *

On the surface it appeared as though Colt's production goals were being met in spite of the tremendous expansion of the work force, its inexperience and volatility, the lack of capable foremen, and shortages of various kinds. In 1943 eight instructors carried on an in-plant training program called T.W.I., a crash effort to make inspectors and machine operators out of greenhorns. Some 1,500 participated. In May, the inefficient third shift was abandoned. Since Pearl Harbor the Armory had been working three shifts of seven and one-half hours each, with every eighth day off, a schedule that was bound to result in fatigue and excessive absenteeism as well as an intolerable rate of rejected parts. Two long shifts on a six-day basis proved a better arrangement. In August, the personnel department staged a Victory Day celebration in Colt Park that drew 24,000 employees and their families, and a white star was added to the Army-Navy "E" for continued excellence in production.

At that very moment, however, Colt's was in the incipient stage of its eventual downfall, a regression impossible to halt once begun. For the past three years, from 1940 on, its net earnings had ranged from $1,368,000 to $2,561,000; 1943 also ended in the black, despite price reductions and government re-negotiation of so-called excess profits. But starting in July of that year Colt's showed a loss every month, which accumulated to $3.5 million a year later. The Electrical Division was sold to Federal Electric in mid-1944, while in January the Army cut back its orders for .50 cal. aircraft machine guns by forty percent. Layoffs were inevitable. In eighteen months Colt's surplus plummeted from $8.3 million to $4.9 million. Overburdened, top heavy, and unwieldy, the Armory had become a rudderless ship.

President Graham Anthony examines the Colt .45 revolver which he personally presented to President Truman.

The root of the trouble lay as much as anything in the organization's inability to adopt modern manufacturing techniques. The company originally hailed as the pacesetter for mass production had failed in its task of applying the principles it had developed to manufacturing the weapons of World War II, whilst elsewhere vastly more complex products such as aircraft engines and entire planes were being turned out by the thousands. Its past successes extending over nine decades had induced a state of smugness, a false sense of euphoria, a resistance to radical change. Sentiments like "we've always done it that way" or "change that and quality will suffer" prevailed. To hidebound department heads who had some up through the ranks, gunmaking was still and always must be a craft requiring the highest manual dexterity in the finishing operations. This was partially true, especially with regard to handguns, but other armories were nevertheless demonstrating an ability to meet both government specifications and delivery dates through the use of faster equipment and more sophisticated production scheduling.

Although nearly $5 million had been invested in the gun division since 1938, Colt's floors teemed with antiquated machinery, some of which dated back to the time of the Colonel and Elisha Root. Equally obsolete were the petrified attitudes of key supervisors who controlled the flow of production; government inspectors were astonished to learn that in many cases, instead of essential manufacturing data being recorded on blueprints or operation sheets, the knowledge reposed in the minds and memories of aging foremen and craftsmen. Such informality might be good enough for a thousand-man shop but not for a production line many times that size. Related to and compounding the inadequacies of equipment and supervision was the chaotic incentive system for pieceworkers. For years it had been allowed to develop haphazardly without regard for method improvements. In manufacturing it is customary, when a new machine or process is introduced, to increase the minimum production standard required of the operator in order to take advantage of the gain in productivity. Colt's never adjusted its rates as methods were improved, allowing pieceworkers to earn inordinately high wages and creating hostility between them and the more numerous day workers who filled their work bins, maintained their machines, and repaired their tools.

For failing to keep up with the times, Colt's was now paying the price in pitifully low output, excessively high costs, and internecine strife among the work force. Upstart competitors like High Standard in New Haven were showing up Colt's weaknesses, and the government was rapidly losing confidence in its management. To those in the know, Colt's acted like an old man verging on senility. Samuel Stone himself personified Colt's plight. He, too, was an old man.

At 75, full of Yankee integrity but ingenuous to a fault, Stone no longer could cope with the Armory's deep-seated problems and the intrigue surrounding him. Some of his directors pressured him hard for a change in management. Two of his close friends — "Charlie" Cook, the head of Royal Typewriter, and Lucious Robinson, Colt's counsel for many years — stuck by him to the end. Stone rued the fact that he had outlived his four ablest subordinates, Walter H. Penfield, Fred Moore, Harold Fairweather, and Leslie Goodrich, any one of whom might have been qualified to succeed him. None of his managers, he felt, was strong enough to handle his job, but one director was, if only he could be persuaded to give up his present position as head of Veeder-Root. Graham H. Anthony, a highly personable, impressively tall, ambitious Southerner and a graduate of North Carolina State College, had migrated to Connecticut in 1915. He first worked for the W.L. Gilbert Clock Company in Winsted and then spent ten years with Allen Manufacturing, the hex socket screw pioneer, as secretary and factory manager. Allen's factory was located on Sheldon Street only a short distance from Colt's. In 1932 Anthony became president of Veeder-Root, a prosperous maker of counting devices. He was considered one of the ablest manufacturing executives in Hartford. To the surprise of many, he accepted Stone's offer, agreeing to run the company for five years. He took over on April 6, 1944. The old man was given the title of chairman and shunted off to a corner office. It was abundantly clear that he was no longer wanted, and in July Stone walked out for good. Despite his age and a colostomy operation, he remained a director; moreover, until his death in 1959 at the age of 90, he continued twelve other directorships.*

Years later, Anthony recalled how he had saved the Armory from disaster: "They called me there in 1944 — there was a war on, or I wouldn't have gone. I suppose you could say it was in a mess. My first month we did $6 million worth of business and managed to lose $225,000 — something was dreadfully wrong. It's a long story of management and labor relations. I checked and found fantastic payrolls. More than 1,000 men were earning $500 a month or more. I recall one man whose only duty was to swab out machine gun barrels with a greasy rag, once the guns had been test-fired. He did nothing else. On piecework, in the year 1943, he made $13,600."

Colt's deteriorated fortunes were reflected in the turmoil which permeated the union. There was constant infighting among the weak leadership of Local #270. It, too, was paying a price — in factionalism and disunity — for Colt's unbalanced wage structure. The company attempted to set matters right through the re-negotiation of both day and piecework rates; unable after eight months to reach agreement with the union, the company referred the dispute to the Regional War Labor Board in Boston in March of 1943. A year later the arbitrator, Douglass V. Brown of M.I.T., upheld the proposed revision, which included an unprecedented reduction of 46¢ an hour or 25 percent in piecework rates.

On his very first day of work, President Anthony was confronted by Brown and the union leaders. The professor insisted that all the 16,000 employees would be idle the next day unless Anthony made an immediate decision on various grievances. "Professor Brown," Anthony inquired in his still pronounced North Carolinian drawl, "do you mean to say that after being Colt's president for five minutes, I must decide this right now or the men will walk out?" Brown replied in the affirmative. "Then tell 'em to go to hell," and he left the plant for the day. Brown's favorable ruling, however, did result in 2,500 workers walking out in protest, despite the no-strike pledge in the contract and without the sanction of union officials. That same month the union chose a new

* His grandson, Samuel Stone II, is an electronics wizard and small entrepreneur who, from his New Jersey home, operates what *Fortune* magazine (July 31, 1978) says "may be the world's first cottage conglomerate." "Little operations like Stone's," comments *Fortune*, "play an important, if largely invisible, role in American industry by supplying items that major manufacturers don't often bother with."

business agent, Patrick J. Ward, a Hartford alderman and Democratic politician from the East Side.

All that Ward and the union could do was to appeal the arbitrator's award, contending that it failed to correct "gross inequities." For its part, management insisted the Brown award was final and binding since both parties had agreed to accept it. Rumor that the Board had again ruled against the union perpetrated another work stoppage early in May; some 500 left their jobs in the Van Dyke and Flower Street plants. The WLB immediately refused to resume consideration of the union petition until they returned. At the same time Julius Emspak, general secretary and treasurer of the United Electrical, Radio & Machine Workers, wired president James J. Connors of Local #270 a stinging rebuke:

"The small faction that is provoking this undisciplined action is harming the welfare of thousands of Colt workers...the interruption of production in the face of the coming invasion cannot be tolerated and violates this international union's no-strike policy."

Meanwhile, the company informed the union of its intention to dismiss some 100 employees who had curtailed their production since the implementation of the Brown award. President Anthony revealed that in the four weeks ending April 23rd, Colt's had suffered a loss of $729,000, making a total loss of $1,135,000 for the year to date. "The situation," he added, "is the most serious in the history of the company and comes at a time when our country is fighting for its existence." Saul Wallen, chairman of the Regional WLB, directed Colt's to stay any disciplinary action pending the board's decision on the union's appeal. At the same time, he wired Connors:

"It is officially reported to me that the level of production at the Colt plant has declined to such an extent that coupled with huge production losses during the two strikes of the past two months procurement of vital war materials for the armed services is being seriously, if not disastrously, delayed.

"With the invasion of Europe at hand, and the drastic need for the type of weapons produced at Colt's recognized by all, no single moment in this nation's history could have been more inappropriate for such a situation than the present. It is imperative that production be lifted immediately."

On May 20th, Professor Brown completed his review of the case and courageously left standing the revision of the incentive system but restored $2 million, or five percent, of the reductions he had previously ordered in the straight-time payroll. Four days later, the company laid off 643 employees and discharged 130 obstructionists. Union dissidents clamored for the resignations of the entire executive board. Business agent Ward predicted that "Colt workers face the grim future of further layoffs unless our house is set in order." In October he was thrown out of office, losing by a vote of 1266-1261 to President Connors. Ward demanded a recount of the ballots to no avail. Thereafter, the turmoil in the union ranks subsided.

* * *

During the Fourth of July week, as Colt's was preparing to lay off 300 more employees out of a total of 3,000, the Ringling Brothers, Barnum & Bailey Circus arrived in the city and set up its tent on Barbour Street for its annual spectacular. Thursday, July 6th was a warm summer afternoon with a brisk southwesterly breeze. Under the oil-impregnated canvas, 6,000 circus fans applauded the animal act. Just as the lions were herded back into the runway cages and the Flying Wallendas ascended to the high wire, it happened. Fifty feet from the main entrance was a four-sided canvas screen for the men's toilet. Some one inside carelessly tossed his cigarette butt onto the ground. In seconds a flame crept up one side of the partition and licked at the guy ropes. One of the Wallendas pointed to the blaze from his perch above and cried: "The tent's on fire!"

Ushers ran to the fast-spreading flames with buckets of water, but they were already beyond control. For a few moments there was quiet and a few exhortations to keep calm and move slowly. Then, as the band continued playing as loudly as they could, someone screamed, panic erupted and the crowd stampeded toward the exits. Flaming pieces of canvas fell into the multitude and ignited their hair and clothes. Ropes burned through and dropped heavy trapeze equipment into the center of the arena. The big tent poles crashed. At one exit a circus attendant inexplicably held back the pressing mob. Scores of others, unable to climb over the steel animal runways, were knocked down and trampled to death, their bodies discovered later when the firemen were wetting down the ruins.

Many fought their way to the top tier of seats, where they leapt fifteen feet to the ground or slid down the poles and ropes. Police Commissioner Edward J. Hickey, shepherding his nine nieces and nephews, was one who tossed his charges to safety. Those who dashed from the grandstand to the arena floor, desperately pushing chairs aside, soon realized there was no escape through the jammed exits, turned back, and climbed to the top. Meanwhile, an animal trainer had the presence of mind to grab a whip and drive two lions still in the runway cage back to their wagon. The strong wind swept the fire across the top of the tent.

In ten minutes, 139 died and 225 were seriously burned or injured on that sultry afternoon in 1944.

In the field outside milled the terrified, disheveled survivors, mothers and fathers running to and fro looking for lost children, shocked rescuers carrying blackened little bodies, some still alive, and some not. Emergency aid was quickly mobilized. Several of the larger war plants sent equipment and personnel. Colt's despatched four ambulances, four doctors, eight nurses, and twenty guards. Soon the hospitals were full of victims, and the State Armory was hastily converted into a morgue. Frantic relatives, a dozen at a time, were led by a nurse and policeman past the row of cots. By five o'clock all that remained of the circus on the Barbour Street lot were acres of ashes from seventeen tons of flammable canvas and the ruins of the grandstand that a few hours earlier had seated so many Hartford-area families looking forward to an afternoon of fun in the most critical year of the War.

* * *

Reaction to the two surrenders in World War II was far calmer than in 1918, perhaps because each time its imminence had been discounted and communication was so much faster with a radio in every home and shop. At President Truman's request the nation hardly paused in its war effort on V-E Day, May 8th, 1945. At Colt's the employees observed a minute of silence, shouted a few "hoorays," shook hands all around, and then went on with their work. "We'll celebrate when the war with Japan is over," many said. In the downtown churches chimes rang at noon, the schools got a half-holiday, the liquor stores were closed as a precaution, and some confetti fluttered down from office windows. The most dramatic response, however, was that at dusk the lights outside the theaters, stores, and restaurants came alive. For the first time in three years, the clock face on the Old State House was illuminated.

Before V-J Day, the tension mounted over the weekend of August 10th when the Japanese made peace overtures. On Tuesday, when surrender became official, a large and noisy celebration in the city blocked traffic for awhile but it was still orderly and somewhat somber. People already seemed concerned about how contract cancellations, reconversion, and returning veterans would affect their jobs. The White House announcement brought forth spontaneous cheers from the war workers, who — as planned ahead of time — shut off their machines and filed out. The end of the War also meant the end of gas rationing, and the liberated workers wasted no time getting their cars out and congesting the streets and highways.

As many feared, the well-earned holiday ended in a nightmare for thousands who found themselves out of work. United Aircraft temporarily released their total force of 28,000 in East Hartford and satellite plants around the state. Marlin Firearms and Winchester announced they would soon be fully reconverted to making sporting arms. It so happened that Colt employees were on vacation during the week in which V-J Day fell, and they returned only to find that almost everybody had been laid off. All of its government contracts were canceled overnight. The Arms Division shut down tight. In fact, the Armory ceased forever the production of machine guns; tools and gauges were greased and wrapped in wax paper, while the machinery was either stored or sold. Although the dishwasher and plastics divisions continued to operate, Colt's — unlike its competitors in New Haven — was unprepared for peace.

CHAPTER XIII

THE TAKEOVER

For some fifteen years after World War II, Connecticut held onto its position as the second most highly industrialized state in the nation. Its research and development capability made great strides, ranking third in the number of patents granted and in the number of research laboratories on a per capita basis. It was also still third in the volume of defense contracts — behind only California and New York, but first in relation to size — mainly due to its dominance in aircraft engines and submarines.

Hartford could count over 1,200 firms, big and small, engaged in some kind of manufacturing. But a radical change in its economy was imminent. While at its peak, manufacturing provided six out of ten jobs. After 1952 industrial employment ceased to grow, except in the mammoth aircraft engine facility across the river from the Armory. The total fluctuated around 90,000 as the city began to shift inexorably toward a post-industrial society with the emphasis on services rather than production. By 1960, for the first time, more persons would be working in finance, insurance, government, and other service-type jobs. The hundred year era of Connecticut's manufacturing supremacy was passing into history.

Colt's itself, alone among Hartford manufacturers, was critically ill, though few in management would have admitted it at the time. Despite frequent changes in top management and drastic efficiency measures it would never recover from the severe losses, both in money and reputation, suffered toward the end of the War. In 1946, it showed a loss of $753,895. President Anthony, still deeply involved in the affairs of Veeder-Root and Holo-Krome Screw as chairman of both, interpreted his role as more a management consultant than a chief executive and delegated operating responsibilities to B. Franklin "Ben" Conner, who was elevated to executive vice-president in 1946.

Conner had come to Colt's in 1920 when his family's plastics business, Conner & Lattin of Newark, was acquired. Since that time, he had been primarily concerned with running the Plastics Division. Under Anthony's guidance he tackled the job of "industrial rehabilitation," as they called it, relocating and modernizing all three divisions — dishwasher, gun, and plastics. As executive vice-president, virtually in command of the entire plant, Conner wielded his new authority with a heavy and, in several eyes, unscrupulous hand. Intolerant of subordinates who refused to "yes" him, he seized upon the flimsiest excuses to get rid of them. One who felt his wrath was Dwight G. Phelps, a veteran of forty-four years who, ironically, had been instrumental in Conner's coming to Colt's. Phelps, a native of Hartford, had earned his spurs selling firearms, rising to a sales manager in 1921, heading the electrical division until its spin-off in 1944, and finally becoming a vice-president and director. Tall and handsome with a genial, enthusiastic air, he was well-liked by everybody and active in numerous civic activities, such as Junior Achievement, the Community Council, and Hillyer Junior College. As head of manufacturing he was too strong a personality to be pushed around, but Conner undermined him behind his back to the point where Phelps sadly handed in his resignation.

The year 1947 marked the 100th anniversary of Sam Colt's Walker Model revolver, which he had made for the Army at Eli Whitney Jr.'s armory in Whitneyville. There were no celebrations because his successors had long ago decided to date the company's founding back to 1836 when Sam started the Paterson, New Jersey plant. Since that operation failed, it might seem more logical to designate 1847 as the real beginning of the successful Colt Patent Firearms Manufacturing Company, when the founder set up his own plant first on Pearl Street and then on Grove Street in Hartford. One incident that occurred in June signaled the end of an era: the original, H-shaped West Armory built by the Colonel in 1861 was torn down; it took two weeks and cost $80,000.

Despite a drop in sales in all divisions and a loss on firearms, Colt's managed, during 1947, to show its first overall profit in four years — a modest one of $149,186. President Anthony reassured the stockholders that the year had been one of substantial progress and that "the corner has now been turned" in the gun division. For the first twelve weeks of 1948 he reported a profit of $64,099. Gun production, entirely civilian in nature, was now running at the rate of 2,000 per week, double the amount of the previous year. Furthermore, as a result of Congress's renewed interest in preparedness, he expected that Colt's would soon be in line for a large Army contract.

The favorable news, however, did not prevent a spirited attack on President Anthony at the annual meeting. A group of speculators, encouraged by a few Colt directors, had picked up at bargain prices (about $28 a share) over the past two years one-third of the outstanding shares. Spokesmen for the group were David A. Goodkind, a New York CPA, and Paul H. Hershey, head of his own metal products company in Ansonia, Connecticut. Severely criticizing management's performance and the longevity of the majority of directors, they nominated themselves and four others for places on the eleven-man board. After eight hours of contention, the attempt to seize control was repulsed by a vote of 94,000 shares for the present management to 62,000 for the opposition. Afterwards, Anthony remarked: "I didn't know I was such a tough guy."

Undaunted, the dissidents continued banging on Colt's door and gained entry the next year. Facing turmoil both outside and inside the company, mindful too of the reputation which he had carefully nurtured over a 30-year career, Graham Anthony was glad he had reached the end of his five-year agreement — as it seemed now, a nearly fruitless effort to revive the ailing Armory. Goodkind and his associates won three seats on the board. Conner succeeded Anthony as president, who remained as chairman for two more years. Francis W. Cole, chairman of Travelers Insurance Company, and Charlie Cook, now retired from Royal Typewriter, resigned as directors. In addition to Goodkind, the outsiders elected were William T. Golden of Washington, an investor in several mining companies, and Sylvan C. Coleman, general manager of E.F. Hutton & Company in New York.

Besides Anthony and Conner, the other directors, all friendly to Anthony, insured that the control of Colt's would remain in Hartford, for the time being anyway. They were: John H. Chaplin, president of Veeder-Root; William A. Purtell, president of its subsidiary Holo-Krome; H. Struve Hensel, a New York lawyer; Ostrom Enders, president of Hartford National Bank & Trust Company; James Lee Loomis, former head of Connecticut Mutual Life Insurance Company; and Lucius F. Robinson Jr., senior partner in one of Hartford's top law firms.

Hartford's newspapers gave front page treatment to these changes. They were greatly relieved that an accommodation had been made with the New York interlopers. The *Courant*, in an editorial headed "Colt's Stays In Business," said "Liquidation of Colt's merely to assure a sizable profit to those holding its stock would have been a melancholy disservice to the whole community." The *Times* gave Anthony credit for achieving a large degree of progress in the past year, improving relations with both the Ordnance Department in Washington and the Colt's union. The victory for the local interests also indicated that the cohesiveness that had been paramount among Hartford businessmen since the Civil War still flourished. A handful of men, no more than thirty, constituted the power structure of the city bankers, insurance executives, and manufacturers. Morgan B. Brainard, president of Aetna Life Insurance Company, was generally regarded as the godfather, inheriting the prestige of his uncle Morgan Bulkeley a generation earlier. Chaplin, Cole, Cook, Enders, Purtell, and Robinson — as well as Anthony — belonged to this economic oligarchy, the members of which operated quietly but effectively through holding stock and directorships in one another's companies.

The atmosphere of harmony inside Colt's, however, soon evaporated. The outsiders had no interest in what Anthony and Conner had done to rehabilitate the company. Looking only for a quick profit from their investment, they pressed the new management to explore merger possibilities. At the annual meeting in April, 1949, a smaller return of around $100,000 was reported for the previous fiscal year, and the backlog of orders amounted to $3 million. As the months dragged by during this period of national recession and no buyers could be found, the New York investors demanded a bailout. The board agreed to retire all stock tendered during the month of April, 1950, at $52 a share, a price more than twelve dollars above the market, in exchange for a commitment that the three outside directors would resign. There were then 195,000 shares outstanding with a total value of $13.4 million or $68 per share. One hundred and twenty-seven thousand shares were tendered, consuming $6.6 million of Colt's surplus. It was a crippling blow that could not have come at a worse time.

The Korean War, from 1950-52, infused new life into the Armory but not enough, as events proved, for a permanent recovery. The government's confidence had never been fully restored since its production failures toward the end of World War II, even though the company boasted a backlog of $9.2 million in defense orders in early 1952. Sales during this three-year period totaled $37 million and profits $2,278,000, a six percent net return.

Still hell bent on cutting costs and improving efficiency, Anthony and Conner sought out more expertise in management — in May, 1951, bringing aboard as executive vice-president Walter P. Jacob, president of Hartford Electric Steel and a Yale engineering graduate. That same month Graham Anthony stepped down as chairman, confiding to one friend that he had lost twenty pounds fighting the Wall Street wolves during the past three years. Dividend payments of four dollars a share, plus a dollar extra, were resumed, the stock sold for around $70, and the surplus — despite the losses from 1943 through 1946 and the treasury raid in 1948 — stood at $8 million: a book value of $100 per share. Thirty-five percent of the stock was owned by Connecticut residents, while New Yorkers held slightly over one-third. Altogether, there were 1,488 stockholders. The financial community had every reason to believe Colt's had returned to good health.

The first year of the Eisenhower administration was also salubrious. Sales jumped a third to $21,306,111, while net earnings rose slightly to $703,770. The military backlog increased to $17.7 million. At the annual meeting the directors declared a stock split of four for one, and two prominent Hartford business men joined the board: Wilbur C. Stauble, president of Holo-Krome, who succeeded John Chaplin; and Erle Martin, vice-president of United Aircraft and general manager of its Hamilton Standard Division. Two new weapons were in production — the Colt Officer's Model match revolver and the Aircrewman handgun, lightest and most efficient for its size and adopted by the Air Force as regulation equipment for all airborne personnel.

Colt's still called itself the number one manufacturer of small arms, both revolvers and automatic pistols. Recognizing the need for more aggressive sales techniques and stronger supervision, the management added new people to the sales, advertising, and manufacturing staffs. It was no longer a seller's market, and competition was keener than ever. The Armory also beefed up its other three divisions. The line of Autosan commercial dishwashers, which had been produced since 1919, was expanded; models for every size of installation were being made, up to a giant combination washer, sanitizer, and dryer able to handle the dishes and tableware used by 2,500 persons in one meal. The Plastics Division struggled to keep pace with competitors in this mushrooming industry by making articles such as containers and closures for the drug and cosmetic trade, translucent streetlight globes, and inexpensive lampshades. The fourth division was new. In 1951, Colt's acquired the Rite-Size Box Machine Company for $50,000 in cash and 8,927 shares in stock, in an effort to tap the market for machinery to fabricate shipping cartons in various sizes.

But the truce in Korea and the resultant cutback in military orders were beginning, in 1954, to expose the underlying weaknesses of the Armory. The backlog of defense-related work dropped $7 million, and in July the Ordnance Department terminated substantially all of Colt's contracts. Sales fell to $16.7 million from $21.3 million the year before, and profits slumped to a paltry $246,670. The work force was cut from 1,864 to 750 employees. Late in October the company made two important announcements, the first of which hit Hartford like a bombshell while the second reflected a renewed state of turmoil within the management.

For months the directors had been debating the fate of the Armory, and now they decided to forsake it. It had become too big, too expensive, too obsolete for the company's needs. They voted to purchase 117 acres of farmland in Windsor Locks near the Bradley International Airport at a cost of $260,000. "We need a modern one-story building," President Conner said. "The land in Windsor Locks is ideal; it is flat and has an adequate railroad siding. Rising labor costs have made handling of manufactured goods between the plant

President Conner *(right)* tries his skill on the firing range with David M. Williams, inventor of the M-1 carbine.

Chairman Graham Anthony chats with President Ben Conner on his last full day at Colt's — May 20, 1951.

and railroad cars almost prohibitive at the present site." Conner and the directors were especially enthusiastic over the detailed layout for a new plant developed by Philip W. Schwartz, then vice-president of manufacturing, who made a model that showed the old blue dome in a prominent position. No date was set for the move.

The Hartford *Courant* voiced greater concern over the possibility of losing the "Moorish dome" atop the ancient Armory than in having the gunmaker leave town and take several hundred jobs with it. "An incongruous cupola that annually commands the attention of the occupants of 18,500,000 cars crossing the Charter Oak Bridge...it stands today as a symbol of the founder's rugged individuality, a by-product of his desire to be different, and direct...prospective customers to him and his revolvers."

The other announcement climaxed another shift of power that had been germinating for several months. Burton W. Bartlett, treasurer of Bartlett & Brainard, a leading local contracting and construction firm, and Chester Bland, a Hartford entrepreneur who headed several small manufacturing companies, had been quietly buying Colt stock. A respecter of tradition, Bartlett believed it would be far better to retain ownership locally rather than to let it pass by default to another group of out-of-towners who, on the second try, would be likely to take what remained of Colt's out of Connecticut entirely. Anthony invited him into his circle of compatible directors. Now, on this autumn Thursday, Burt Bartlett astonished the board by proclaiming that he and Mr. Bland now controlled a majority of the stock. In businesslike fashion Bartlett was elected chairman, while Anthony agreed to step down to the titular position of chairman of the executive committee. The operating vice-presidents were assigned new duties: Richard S. Havourd, Autosan Division; Philip W. Schwartz, Arms Division; John M. McNally, plant services and ordnance; Alton K. Marsters, Packaging Machinery Division; and Charles W. Bentley, Plastics Division.

Early in February, 1955, the company appealed to the government for more defense business in order to survive. At a private luncheon in Washington, officials and union leaders joined in laying out Colt's plight to Connecticut's congressional delegation. Representative Thomas A. Dodd of West Hartford pledged his support: "I'm going to ask the administration to see to it that Colt's is preserved... Colt's is an old and highly skilled industry. The government is spending a lot of money to keep defense plants and machinery in readiness for a possible emergency, and it's just as important to keep skilled hands in business. The government has got to give them work." Congressman Albert W. Cretella of North Haven, on the other hand, pointed out that Winchester Arms in his district was having no difficulties because it had been able to diversify to a greater extent.

Chairman Bartlett, in the meantime, consolidated his hold by first bringing his associate Bland onto the board and then — at the end of March — making him president, forcing the retirement of Ben Conner. Like an industrial Captain Bligh, the aggressive new chief executive concentrated on bailing out the sinking ship by resorting to every drastic measure he could think of. Some were picayune. Refusing to occupy the venerable office of the president, he ensconced himself in the directors' room, where he demanded to see and approve every purchase requisition — from paper clips to raw material. For hours he could be heard calling the company's suppliers and with shylockian tenacity haggling over their prices, or placing orders with various small "bucket shops" in which he had a financial interest. For tax purposes, the inventory of finished goods was doctored; old machines were dumped right and left. Strangers walked through the plant for unexplained reasons. Heretofore, steady customers hesitated to make new purchases. No one knew what would happen next, and morale sank to zero.

Yet, the blue dome and the old Armory were destined to stay in place for at least another 25 years, as tumultuous as that year of 1955 was for Colt's. Despairing of ever being able to combine profitably the manufacture of handguns with totally unrelated products, Bland and Bartlett soon agreed that the ultimate solution for the company and their combined investment was to seek a suitable corporate marriage. The stock had tumbled to $13 a share and the 85¢ dividend had been eliminated.

Spread over more than sixteen acres, the Armory's twenty buildings looked almost deserted, even though nine firms rented space. The main office was leased to Pratt & Whitney Aircraft. There was no more talk about building a new one-floor plant in Windsor Locks. But their search for a savior failed to find anyone interested in buying Colt's unless all the operations could be moved out of Connecticut. Somehow the directors, desperate as they were, could not bring themselves to break faith with the tradition that had kept the Armory in Hartford for a century.

Throughout the year, as each month showed once more a mounting deficit, Colt officials closely watched the events taking place a few miles

Curator Charles Coles

west at Pratt & Whitney Machine Tool Company, which had become stodgy at the top, unwilling to spend money on developing new products, and had been smugly hoarding its surplus cash — a condition to be found in the 1950s in many other fine old New England enterprises that had grown weary with age and were slowly deteriorating. Pratt & Whitney's profitability came almost entirely from its jealously independent Chandler-Evans Division. Its stock was so widely dispersed and the management controlled so little of it that Pratt & Whitney were easy prey for the corporate wolves prowling the country in peacetime.

One such came in the shape of a short, pudgy, broad-shouldered financier in his early fifties whom the news magazines dubbed a "corporate fisherman," but who preferred the title of "professor of sick companies." The son of middle-class German-Jewish parents, Leopold D. Silberstein had displayed a knack for finding gold in distress situations where most saw only dross, as a member of the Berlin stock exchange and an investment manager in a Berlin bank. "I follow the philosophy of old Mr. Rothschild. When people want to sell something badly, I oblige them. When they want to buy badly I also oblige." Fleeing from the Nazis in 1933, first to Holland and then to England, Silberstein landed in New York after the war, bringing with him about $150,000 for bargain hunting. In four years his fancy footwork enabled him to pick up a dozen companies worth $50 million for only one million in down payments, which he melded into a holding company called Penn-Texas. His empire now included coal and gas properties, a warehouse terminal, a wire and cable firm, and manufacturers of heavy earth-moving and materials handling equipment.

Here was a new breed of entrepreneur, as aggressive and as brash as Colonel Colt himself had been a century earlier, but whose route to becoming a manufacturing tycoon was the lightning one of financial wizardry rather than the old-fashioned evolutionary process of inventing, making, and selling a better product. Silberstein enjoyed the game of capitalizing on the efforts of others, but oddly enough his objective was not personal wealth. As the owner of less than one percent of Penn-Texas stock, he once remarked: "You have to make up your mind what you want, money or power." In his meteoric rise, observed *Fortune* magazine, he has "aroused more passionate controversy than any other new arrival on the business scene since World War II."

Now the German "professor" sought his biggest prize yet. Pratt & Whitney was larger than all of Penn-Texas, and it would cost him $8 million in hard cash. In Washington, Congressman Dodd voiced concern about the spread of corporate pirating and proposed an investigation. The last three years had seen two of the state's oldest firms, Hendey Machine in Torrington and Peck, Stowe & Wilcox in Southington, snapped up and bled — with hundreds of employees thrown out of work. Representatives of Silberstein called on Dodd to assure him that if they won control of Pratt & Whitney "there will be no milking or liquidation." Relieved of his fears, Dodd said: "I know it will be good news to the employees, to the individual stockholders and generally to the citizens of the Hartford area."

Pratt & Whitney, however, put up a determined if belated fight. At stake was operating control of a $44 million business. Up for election at the annual meeting in April were three different slates of directors — the fourteen present ones, four men supported by an anti-management stockholders' committee in New York, and ten new directors all beholden to Silberstein. For months, each group bombarded the stockholders with letters and advertisements seeking their proxies. Silberstein obtained a court order preventing management from placing a block of unissued stock into friendly

APR 12 1955

NUMBER 9209

SHARES -100-

COLT'S MANUFACTURING COMPANY

INCORPORATED UNDER THE LAWS OF THE STATE OF CONNECTICUT.

This is to Certify that -KIDDER, PEABODY & CO.- is the owner of -ONE HUNDRED- Shares of the capital Stock of Colt's Manufacturing Company, transferable only on the books of the Company by the holder hereof in person or by duly authorized Attorney upon surrender of this Certificate properly endorsed. This Certificate is not valid until countersigned by the Transfer Agent.

In Witness Whereof this Certificate has been prepared by the Directors, and the said corporation has caused the same to be signed by its duly authorized officers and to be sealed with the seal of the corporation the day of MAR 18 1955 A.D. 19

SHARES $10 EACH

COUNTERSIGNED: THE CONNECTICUT BANK AND TRUST COMPANY, HARTFORD, CONN. TRANSFER AGENT. AUTHORIZED SIGNATURE

COLT'S MANUFACTURING COMPANY HARTFORD, CT. U.S. AMERICA.

Dana W Hayward SECRETARY.

PRESIDENT.

AMERICAN BANK NOTE COMPANY.

Colt stock certificate. (Courtesy Connecticut Historical Society)

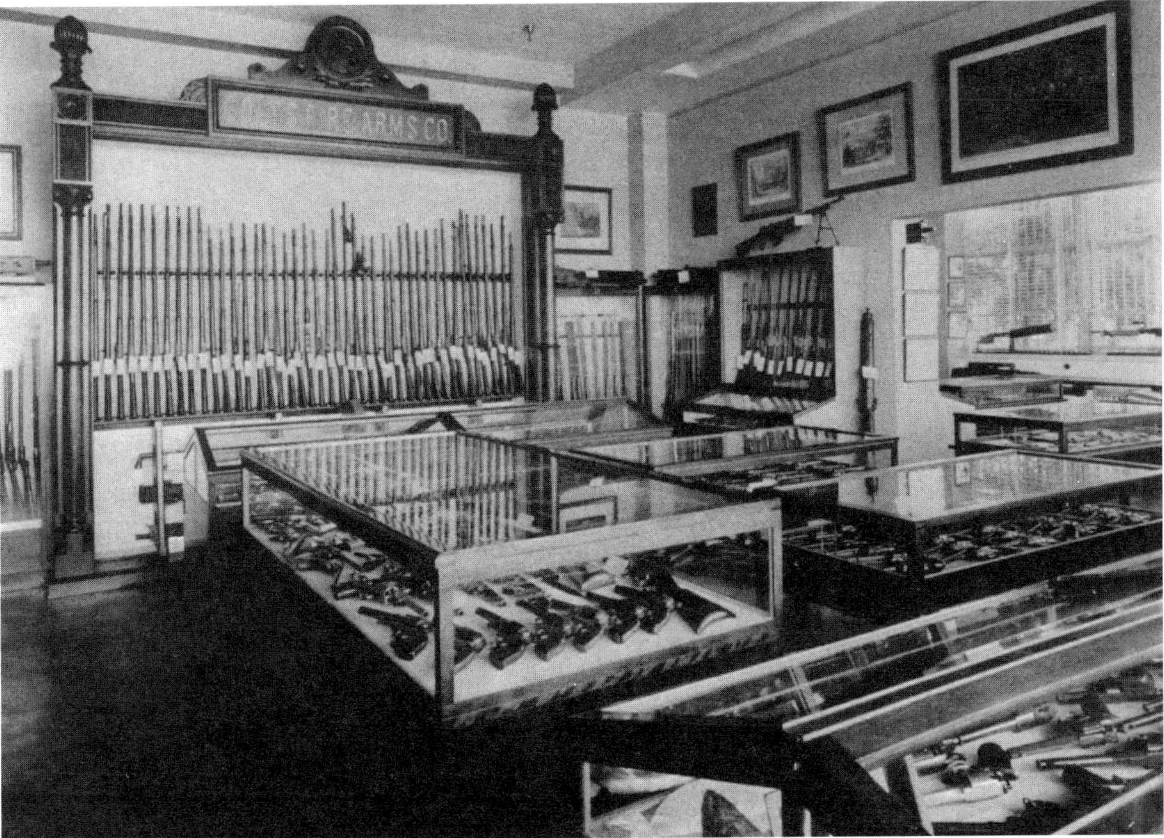

Colt museum set up by Samuel Stone around 1940.

hands. Three hundred were present when the meeting began at ten o'clock on a Wednesday morning. Some wanted to change their proxies; others challenged votes. A recess was called until the tellers could finish the count. Silberstein claimed he had no doubt of the outcome since he already had in his pocket 520,000 of the 868,000 shares. "I will retain everyone who has been loyal to the company, including the chairman." Lewis Gilbert, self-appointed champion of the small stockholder, questioned him closely on the conglomerate's past record and accounting methods. Although most of those Gilbert spoke for supported the management, Silberstein won on Saturday with sixty-one percent of the vote. At once he broke one of his promises, replacing the chairman with himself.

Nevertheless, to the beleaguered Colt directors Silberstein, devilish though he might be, looked like their bridegroom. At least he would keep the Armory where it was. Company assets had sunk below $9 million; but a cash balance of $1 million was a tempting morsel for a prospective buyer. Making a direct approach to Penn-Texas, they got an offer for an exchange of stock worth slightly more than $6 million. Word of the pending deal leaked to the brokerage houses, and Colt's stock rose to $17 a share. By the end of September the Armory joined Pratt & Whitney as a Penn-Texas subsidiary, exactly 100 years after its incorporation by Sam Colt.

There were the usual glowing predictions of "no liquidation," "complete rejuvenation," "higher employment," and "a bright future." The soothing financier promised to make the Hartford area one of the most important gun-making centers in the world. He hinted that the Armory might be moved to the West Hartford location of Pratt & Whitney, which had several acres of unused land. At a special meeting of the stockholders in November to ratify the sale to Penn-Texas another champion of the small stockholder, James Fuller of Coral Gables, Florida, enlivened the occasion by asking a number of embarrassing financial questions that had Bartlett, Bland, and the treasurer frantically thumbing through past annual reports for answers. "Why is it," Fuller demanded, "that Colt's has always come in second?"

It is a truism of corporate takeovers that nothing stays the same for very long, no matter how many promises are made and assurances given. The following month, Silberstein put in a new slate of officers and directors. Charles T. Lanham, a retired major general and vice-president of Penn-Texas, became chairman, and Sidney A. Stewart, vice-president and general manager of the lucrative Chandler-Evans Division of Pratt & Whitney, succeeded Bland as president. Silberstein's son was made a vice-president. Dana Hayward, Colt's secretary, was demoted to assistant secretary. Bland was given Anthony's meaningless post as chairman of the executive committee, and of the eight directors only he survived from the former board. In other actions, the company's name was changed back to its original form for the purpose, Silberstein said, of undertaking a broad firearms expansion program. "Plans are already underway to have European companies enter into agreement with Colt's to have foreign guns made in Hartford." It was also decided not to move the Armory, but instead to repair and modernize the present site.

A highly capable executive who still continued his duties at Chandler-Evans, Stewart saw himself as a transition president with the particular assignment of trying to straighten out the mess left by his two immediate predecessors. He was aghast at its condition. "From an operating standpoint it was little more than a great name plus a conglomeration of obsolete machinery. If old machines were as valuable as old cars, ours would have been a priceless collection." Production was in a shambles. Semi-finished parts were being moved from floor to floor and building to building, up and down, back and forth. There was no production control and almost no sales department.

Even though Colt's name was still alive, the Armory no longer could call its soul its own. The crowning indignity was Silberstein's decision to give away the Colt collection of firearms. It seemed like desecrating a grave, an opportunistic disregard for the achievements of Sam Colt, Sam Stone, and the thousands of Colt workers. In 1940, at Stone's insistence, a museum had been set up in the main office to display a model of nearly every handgun, long-arm, and machine gun manufactured since 1855. The collection of 2,000 firearms*, letters, and other memorabilia had a value of close to a million dollars. Charles Coles, Colt old-timer of sixty-two years, was its proud curator. Silberstein made the donation to the State Li-

* The three most valuable were a .44 cal. Dragoon model made in 1853 worth $35,000; a belt pistol having a bust of Abraham Lincoln on the handle, worth $25,000; and a .31 cal. pocket model worth $20,000, all elaborately engraved and gold-inlaid.

Coles receives a plaque from President Fred Roff on the occasion of his 69th Anniversary as a Colt employee in 1969.

brary look like a magnanimous act: "The collection properly belongs to the people of this state to be enjoyed by them in perpetuity as part of their heritage," he wrote the governor. Perhaps he was right, but no one stopped to think that his real motivation was to take advantage of a hefty tax deduction.

Back in his plush New York headquarters, Silberstein worried more about cash than anything else. Profit-wise, Penn-Texas was doing well; on Wall Street the stock had doubled in value. But playing his kind of game required a lot of clubs — notes, options, and stock issues. On one day alone the directors voted to issue 60,000 shares which devalued the stockholders' equity by fifteen percent. From Colt's he squeezed out nearly $4 million, half by selling and leasing back its plant, the rest by disposing of both the dishwashing and plastics lines in 1957 and taking advantage of the tax savings from previous losses. The Plastics Division was moved to North Grosvenordale, Connecticut. Penn-Texas sales in 1956 rose to $125 million, more than half of which came through its latest acquisitions. Pratt & Whitney contributed all of the profit. Silbertsein decided the time was right to stage his biggest coup — one that would double the size of Penn-Texas and put it among the 150 largest corporations in America. His quarry: the venerable, family-run Fairbanks Morse Company of Chicago, manufacturers of diesel engines, pumps, and scales. To raise a war chest, he increased Penn-Texas' short-term borrowing from $11 to $23 million and from sales and lease-backs of subsidiaries netted another $10 million. By January 31, 1957, he held 550,000 shares of Fairbanks Morse at a cost of $25 million, a near majority of the stock.

President Robert H. Morse Jr., however, proved an indomitable foe. For the Morse family, the company was a way of life. The seventeen-month bitter proxy fight that ensued caused reverberations in Congress, the SEC, Swiss banking circles, and the courts. At least a million dollars was spent. Silberstein's first maneuver, which had worked so well with Pratt & Whitney, failed. A Federal judge, seeing no reason why Morse could not swap a sizable chunk of treasury stock with a friendly company, admonished the financier severely: "Penn-Texas looks like a conspiracy of some type to raid the stock market; this kind of slugging operation has no place in a court of equity."

Twice Silberstein tried to take control, but was rebuffed each time. Then Morse mounted a counter-attack, backing a pugnacious Washington attorney named Alfons Landa, who formed a Penn-Texas Stockholders Protective Committee and filed two lawsuits charging Silberstein with milking his acquisitions. In Landa's view, the financier's forays had left behind a "wreckage of improvident ventures." Still owing $18 million for his Fairbanks Morse holdings and locked into an untenable position, Silberstein finally capitulated in May of 1957. The eleven-man board was divided between his associates and the Morse family, while the decisive vote was given to an unallied outsider, president of a Chicago investment firm. Silberstein agreed to sell back 300,000 shares and make no further effort to gain control.

By the end of the year, the Penn-Texas empire was crumbling. Silberstein had to sell off six of his subsidiaries to pay his debts. The stock dropped from $22 to $4 a share. No dividends had been paid since June. In the meantime Landa won two seats on the Penn-Texas board, and now three former allies of Silberstein joined the revolt and, in turn, forced the election of three "neutral" directors. In March, 1958, as he sat in silence, the financier was stripped of his command. From the debacle there arose Fairbanks Whitney, a holding company, that included all that remained of Penn-Texas, plus the heretofore reluctant Fairbanks Morse. On December 9, 1959, the same day that former Colt's President Samuel Stone died, Fairbanks Whitney re-acquired the huge Pratt & Whitney property in West Hartford, declaring the Penn-Texas lease-back "a fraudulent conspiracy" costing a million dollars annually. It was the fifth time in four years the real estate had changed hands. But downtown at Colt's, the extinguishing of the lights atop the blue dome, plunging that old landmark into darkness, was like lowering the flag, a sign of mourning for the fate of the once great Armory.

CHAPTER XIV

RECOVERY

The mostly law-abiding citizens of the United States are ambivalent about owning firearms. On the one hand is the undying tradition handed down from colonial times of the right of freemen to bear arms, as stated in the Second Amendment to the Constitution. To some extent the persistence of this tradition may be a nostalgic residue of our pioneering spirit, when the earliest hunters and settlers struggled west seeking their own paradise and relying on guns for food and protection.

On the other hand, Americans are basically peace-loving. Not only are they still wary of foreign entanglements and military adventures, despite our enormous power and world-imposed role as defender of freedom, they deplore the crime and violence which seem endemic in our society and which often involve the use of guns. To anti-gun adherents, very much in the minority, a firearm of any kind, whether used for hunting, target practice, or self-defense, is as great an anathema as the munitions industry was to the isolationists of the 1920s and 1930s.

Should handguns be banned? That has been a burning issue off and on since the end of the Civil War, when large surplus stocks of military weapons were sold. The adoption of the Sullivan Law by New York State in 1911 established the pattern for restricting handgun ownership to those able to obtain police permits. Distrust of the foreign-born, especially New York's Italian immigrants, was the underlying motivation for the Sullivan Law, and similarly headlined incidents, involving blacks, radicals, and labor agitators, resulted in certain other states and municipalities following suit. Until its defeat, the most progressive and humane opinion leaders embraced Prohibition as the ultimate solution for ending crime and violence. Its dismal failure turned them, in the early days of Roosevelt's New Deal, toward seeking national legislation prohibiting handguns. Gun owners, millions of generally non-vocal people, felt their liberties threatened. The National Rifle Association, heretofore a tiny, elite group of marksmen, ballooned into a massive organization with more than 1,300,000 members.

Surprisingly, the relatively insignificant small arms industry (whose sales have never exceeded .03 percent of all manufacturing) have favored some federal firearms restrictions. For decades it urged the banning of mail-order sales and imports of military surplus guns, as enacted in the Gun Control Act of 1968. That same year, in concert with anti-gun lobbies, Smith & Wesson and six other manufacturers endorsed, for a limited time, a national system of mandatory licensing for handgun owners. Even so, such legislation never garnered majority support, and in recent years the number of anti-gun advocates has dwindled steadily. While nine states passed gun restriction laws before 1934, only Puerto Rico has done so since that time. The main reason seems to be not the clout which pro-gun lobbies wield in legislatures but the incontrovertible fact that the states banning handguns have equivalent or higher levels of violent crimes than those allowing them. Today at least one gun can be found in nearly half of all American households. Prominent liberals are increasingly defending the pro-gun cause. The late Senator Hubert Humphrey eloquently summed up the matter: "The right of citizens to bear arms is just one more guarantee against arbitrary government, one more safeguard against the tyranny which now appears remote in America, but which

Inspection and final assembly of revolvers.

Assembling Colt M-16 guns at the Pratt & Whitney division of Colt Industries in West Hartford.

historically has proved to be always possible." In the foreword to a recent treatise entitled *Restricting Handguns — The Liberal Skeptics Speak Out*, Senator Frank Church wrote: "Activists for minority rights, women's rights, rights for the poor — all human rights — are coming to understand that gun controls work against their interests. In the inner cities, where the police cannot offer adequate protection, the people will provide their own."

Leaving the die-hard activists to battle futilely against private ownership of firearms, most gun-haters now seem to be directing their fire at military weaponry and the Pentagon budget. Following the debacle in Vietnam, companies supplying arms to the government were cowed into lowering their profile; some of the largest (like United Technologies) extensively diversified, not only to become less dependent on Pentagon contracts, but also to shrink arms-making to a fraction of their total sales. In peacetime, the arms manufacturer finds the going painful and profit-poor; government work is seldom a road to riches. Yet, most Americans agree that their country, for the sake of their own survival as well as that of the non-Communist world, must always maintain the strongest defense posture possible, requiring the expenditure of billions annually for research and development and for military hardware. As a percentage of the federal budget defense spending has declined alarmingly, while outlays for social services have soared. In fiscal 1980 about $130 billion will go for defense, less than a quarter of the total U.S. budget. By contrast, the Soviets during the past decade have devoted twice as much of their gross product for military purposes.

Connecticut, as we have seen, has always played a key role in keeping America strong. Even today it is estimated that about a quarter of its factory employees are involved with defense-oriented production, the highest percentage of any state. In 1978 Connecticut received $5 billion in prime contracts, 16 percent of its gross product, which includes both manufacturing and non-manufacturing output. This happened to be a bonanza year for defense companies, and the bulk of the contracts went to a pair of giants — Electric Boat in Groton and United Technologies in East Hartford. By comparison, defense work during the Korean War accounted for a third of the state's gross output and at the height of the Vietnam War, 16.5 percent. In most years, it averages well under 10 percent.

* * *

During the turbulent 1960s and 1970s, the Colt Firearms Division, considerably shrunken from the eminence of its happier days, continued to occupy under lease some of the buildings which had formed the Armory complex. Ownership of the entire property changed three times after the Penn-Texas takeover, its assessed value declining steadily from $6 million to $2.25 million. For several years, annual gun sales amounted to only $6 million. Dealers and customers grumbled about parts service, shipping delays, broken promises, and the management itself. Some dealers dropped the line and turned to competitors like Smith & Wesson.

Then, as the conflict in Southeast Asia intensified, Colt's luck took a sharp turn for the better. In November, 1963, the Army Weapons Command at Rock Island, Illinois awarded the company a fixed-price contract of $13,297,000 for 104,000 rifles and repair parts. Rifles, not revolvers or machine guns — the brand new fully automatic, low-recoil M-16 which was soon to become the standard Army and Air Force weapon. How the demoralized Armory rose to this challenge is a classic case study in the development and mass production of a weapons system. One must begin with its predecessors. In World War II the G.I.'s protector was the Garand semi-automatic M-1, which had been standardized as early as 1936. General George C. Marshall acknowledged its military success: "Our superiority in infantry firepower, stemming from the use of the semi-automatic rifle, was never overcome." The Germans were never able to duplicate it. Nevertheless, it had several shortcomings, principally a magazine capacity of only eight rounds, not fully automatic, and a weight of nearly ten pounds.

During World War II, steps were taken to correct these disadvantages. Magazine capacities were increased to twenty rounds, firing was made fully automatic, and recoil was decreased with a muzzle brake. The end of the war came, however, before the improved weapons could be produced in quantity. In 1953 the NATO nations adopted the 7.62mm (or .308 cal.) cartridge, about one-half inch shorter than the .30-06, as standard. Meanwhile, the U.S. Army concentrated on developing a new rifle that would incorporate all these improvements and provide, as well, greater firepower, simpler operation, and easier maintenance. The objective was to replace both the M-l and the Browning Automatic Rifle (BAR). In May, 1957, the Secretary of the Army announced the adoption of a new weapons system comprising the M-60 machine gun and the M-l4 automatic rifle. Responsible for both was the Springfield Armory, which prepared a "production package" of M-l4 manufacturing drawings for contractors, the first two being the Winchester Division of Olin Corporation in New Haven and Harrington & Richardson in Worcester. In World War II, the former had turned out more than 500,000 M-1's; the latter firm nearly attained that output during the Korean War.

Both experienced such difficulties and delays on the M-14 that Congress and the press grumbled that it was a Jonah which couldn't be made and wasn't worth making anyway. Even Defense Secretary Robert McNamara termed the program "a national disgrace." Springfield Armory and the two commercial contractors, which by the end of 1960 had orders for 268,000 rifles, still felt confident they could achieve mass-production. Brigadier General Elmer J. Gibson, head of the Ordnance Weapons Command, on hearing that entirely new production processes might be successfully applied to gun manufacture, decided to hold a competition for a third M-14 contractor. In October, 1961, out of forty-two bidders, he chose Thompson Ramo Wooldridge of Cleveland. The contract called for 100,000 rifles at a cost of $8.5 million, plus $6.5 million for new equipment. A year later TRW received a second contract for nearly 220,000 more at a price of $79.45 per rifle, lowest of any contractor. Although a leading supplier of automotive and jet engine components, this company had never before engaged in gunmaking. Corporate eyebrows were raised. But TRW regarded the M-14 as just another precision device that could be mass produced if radically different techniques were used, and it was prepared to lose money on the first contract as its "entrance fee" into the arcane world of firearms.

Specifically, what TRW's Ordnance Works initiated were precision forging, in which parts are forged in dies to closer tolerances than customary, and chain broaching, which cuts steel to final dimensions with high accuracy and speed. But no less important than these new methods was the manager of the Ordnance Division who conceived of and dared to apply them. William H. Goldbach, then 42, had practically grown up with TRW, starting as a machinist trainee in 1941 and rising to chief industrial engineer. He captained the team which worked on the company's bid for the M-14 contract. Combining the brashness of a tireless gambler with the thoroughness of a craftsman, Goldbach put together a production team, selected eleven critical parts out of the total of 121 to make in-house, and sub-contracted the remainder (such as the walnut stock). The first 1,000 weapons, not one of which was rejected, were delivered weeks ahead of the November 30, 1962 target date, as Goldbach's crew geared up for a production rate of 24,000 monthly by the summer of 1963.

Back in Hartford, while TRW made gun history with its manufacturing achievements, Colt's was promoting another automatic weapon. In February, 1960, it had revealed that production had begun on a light-weight, low-recoil rifle designated the AR-15. The Hartford *Courant* predicted that the AR-15 might prove to be "the most famous Colt firearm since the Peacemaker." It had been invented by Eugene Stoner for the Armalite Division of the Fairchild Engine & Airplane Corporation, from whom Colt's acquired exclusive manufacturing and patent rights. It would soon be labeled "the world's deadliest weapon."

Combining the light weight of a submachine gun and the accuracy of a sniper's rifle with the firepower of a machine gun, the AR-15 fired over 700 rounds a minute, compared with 500-600 rounds for the BAR and 400-500 rounds for the Army .30 cal. machine gun. Its velocity caused severe damage to whatever it hit. Amazingly enough, it used only .223 cal. ammunition. Its power disproved the old concept that the bigger the bullet, the greater the killing effectiveness. Loaded, it weighed only seven pounds, compared to 19.4 pounds for the long-range BAR, 10 pounds for the M-1 and M-14 rifles, and 5.2 pounds for the .30 cal. M-1 Army carbine. President Fred A. Roff Jr. claimed that high echelon military officers of several nations who had witnessed demonstrations of the test models considered the gun "the best small arm turned out in the past 20 years." In his opinion, it was certain to "strengthen the bastions of freedom around the globe, since nuclear power will never completely replace the need for the foot soldier."

But to gain military acceptance was a long, uphill struggle. No new arm is accepted overnight by the ever cautious and critical ordnance experts, especially one created "out-of-house" by private firms. Even the "in-house" Springfield-developed M-14 took a decade to prove itself. The U.S. Air Force was the first to express interest, looking at the AR-15 as a possible replacement for the .30 cal. carbine carried by airborne troops in Vietnam. By the end of 1963, the Air Force had ordered more than 25,000. The Army, however, reluctant to abandon its commitment to the M-14 after years of sweating out its produceability, threw up a host of alleged objections: the rifle was prone to jamming, its accuracy was poor, it lacked killing power beyond close ranges, and the bullet was too small. No, the Army told Congress in the spring of 1962, it would stick with the M-14.

A year later, it reversed its position. Ordnance officials said they changed their minds because of modifications in the design. They now wanted the rifle for air assault and guerrilla fighters. Thus did Colt win its first major contract in nine years, and thus did the new M-16 begin to eclipse the M-14 as the official rifle for all U.S. armed forces.

This time, too, the Colt decision makers were determined not to boggle the job. A new top management team had been brought into Fairbanks-Whitney from International Telephone and Telegraph: George A. Strichman as chairman and president, and David I. Margolis as financial vice-president. In December, 1962, they in turn hired David C. Scott, a General Electric executive, as group vice-president in charge of Chandler-Evans, Pratt & Whitney, and Colt's. The next month Colt President Roff resigned for "personal reasons, and Scott assumed his duties temporarily. In anticipation of the AR-15 contract, he increased employment during 1963 from 600 to 850. A magazine article alerted him to the brilliant work being done in Cleveland by Bill Goldbach, whom he persuaded that at Colt's as great, if not a greater, challenge awaited him. In August Goldbach joined Colt's as vice-president of operations, replacing Philip Schwartz. Obviously, Scott hoped that Goldbach would be able to perform his production magic inside the Armory and elevate Colt's prestige to the top once more. Publicly, he said: "Colt's rising volume of military products and recently introduced commercial products have required changes in manufacturing processes and executive skills. Production of Colt's proprietary lightweight military rifle, the AR-15, made it necessary to obtain the services of a manufacturing man familiar with high-volume production of precision components." For president, Scott selected Paul A. Benke, 42, previously vice-president and general manager of H.K. Porter in Pittsburgh, who arrived in December to fill Roff's shoes.

The Army's acceptance of what now became the M-16 triggered a decision by Fairbanks-Whitney to move all of the Colt operations out of its antiquated, leased plant on Huyshope Avenue in Hartford to the huge machine tool complex in West Hartford occupied by Pratt & Whitney and Chandler Evans. David Scott said Pratt & Whitney had already helped Colt's in developing manufacturing processes for the new rifle. The big move to the 200,000 square feet of the Knudsen Building was set for the first quarter of 1965. It was hoped that the famous Colt dome could be moved, too, and set atop the company's new home. In addition, ground was broken for a new rifle range near the Knudsen Building.

In May of 1964 the parent company itself was reconstituted. The directors, seeking a new identity, consulted a public relations expert. His recommendation was a name known throughout the world, the one belonging to the smallest and previously most unprofitable unit of the holding company: Colt. And so Colt Industries was born. Strichman and Margolis set in motion a strategy to exorcise the corporate taint left by Penn-Texas and to make Colt Industries one of America's most prosperous international conglomerates. From a loss of nearly a million dollars in 1963, the company earned $3.6 million in 1964. Sales and profits continued upward at a fast pace for the next four years:

Year	Sales (in millions)	Profits (in millions)
1964	$171.7	$3.6
1965	199.2	8.5
1966	240	13.0
1967	642.5	22.0
1968	663.9	20.8

The high rate of net return on the Firearms Division's M-16 contracts contributed substantially to this turnabout during these years, though profits sagged in 1969 due to an $18 million write-off on a diesel engine program unrelated to the Firearms Division.

By 1979, with sales of over $2 billion, Colt Industries ranked 162 in *Fortune's* list of the 500 largest manufacturers. Chairman Strichman characterizes his firm as "a well-diversified specialty materials and industrial products company" which markets primarily to other capital goods producers. It has six operating divisions classified as industrial and power equipment (including Fairbanks Morse engines and Pratt & Whitney machine tools); fluid control systems (including Holley carburetors, Chandler Evans fuel pumps for gas turbines, and Fairbanks Morse pumps); materials (crucible alloys and stainless steel); industrial seals and components; shock mitigation systems; and overseas operations. The first three of these divisions account for more than three-quarters of its income. Guy C. Shafer, one of five group vice-presidents, oversees the operations of the three Hartford companies, having succeeded David Scott, who became president of Allis Chalmers. Conspicuous by its absence, however, was any reference to the Firearms Division in the 1978 annual report.

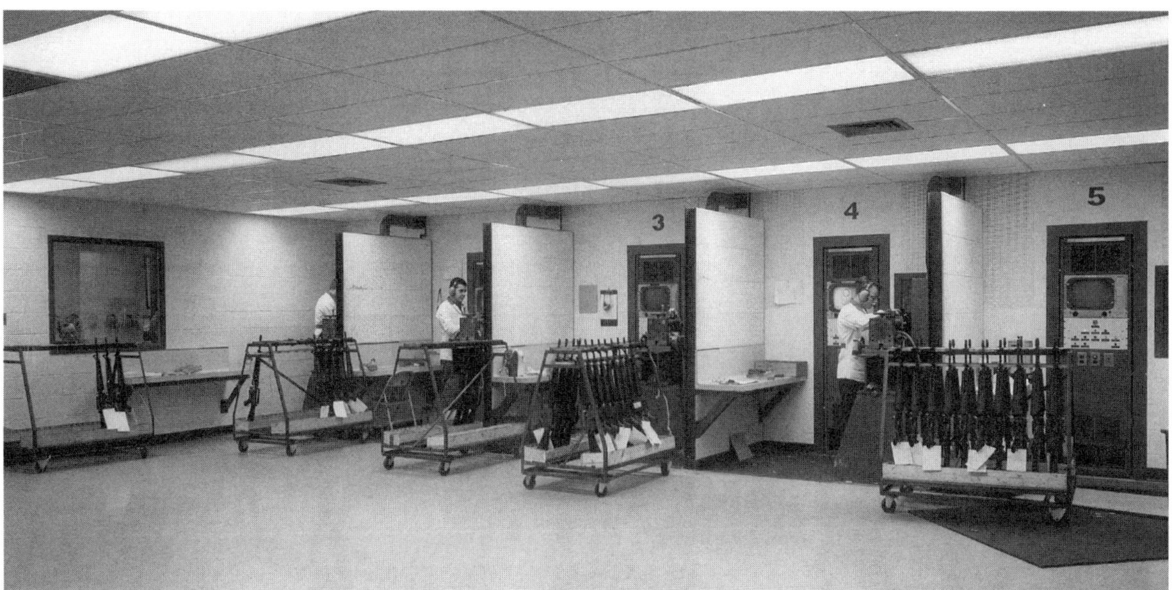

Firing range for M-16 located at Pratt & Whitney Division.

Colt's plant in Rocky Hill built after World War II. The only new facility since 1916 and vacated in the late 1970s.

During his nine-year tenure at Colt's, Bill Goldbach more than lived up to his reputation. Applying the same methods he had initiated in Cleveland, such as closed-die forging and extensive sub-contracting, he engineered a production peak of 50,000 M-16's a month, while sales climbed to $90 million annually. Over $3 million of new machine tools, such as Bridgeport profilers and custom-built De-Hoff gun drillers, were purchased. Goldbach's philosophy was to gear his machines to improve both output and quality control.

Two years after the first Army contract, General William C. Westmoreland urgently requested that all of his troops in Vietnam be equipped with the M-16. At the height of the futile struggle in Southeast Asia, in June, 1966, the Army ordered 403,905 more at a price of slightly above $110 apiece. Colt's employment then stood at 1,600 — 700 of whom were engaged on the M-16, with 400 more due to be hired before year's end. Space was made available by moving back into sections of the old plant that had been leased to outsiders; the archery, gun parts, and repair departments were relocated to the second floor of the 1867 Armory. In other military work, Colt's turned out 40mm grenade launchers for the M-l6, light-weight Commando sub-machine guns, and spare parts. Ironically, while the rejuvenated old company was acquiring new equipment as well as people, working three shifts, and adding new suppliers, the famous Springfield Armory was phasing out its military production altogether. In 1969, Colt Industries decided to separate the Firearms Division into military and small arms units; Goldbach was named president of the former — by far the larger of the two — while Benke became a corporate vice-president.

Yet, Colt's almost miraculous recovery between 1963 and 1969 was not without setbacks, both internally and externally. Significantly, the lights on the Colt dome were again ablaze, but the euphoria in Hartford was dampened by the usual public carping voiced over any new invention in proportion to its success. From Vietnam flew a rash of complaints about malfunctions due to jamming. The trouble was mainly the result of poor care by infantrymen fighting in a fetid, humid environment. Unbelievably, it was charged that insufficient cleaning rods had been passed around. There were ammunition problems, too, stemming from the use of ball powder. The Army, however, found no fault with the gun's basic design or quality: "the principal cause of the difficulty in Vietnam" it announced, "was inadequate maintenance," and it confirmed its full confidence by ordering 242,716 more (a $25.9 million contract) in September, 1967. By now, Colt's M-16 orders totaled almost a million. Commented the chairman of Colt Industries, George A. Strichman: "Our own continuing study indicates that it is the most effective and efficient military rifle produced anywhere in the world..." Nonetheless, Colt's saw fit to improve the design by chrome-plating the barrels and beefing up the buffer assemblies.

A five-week strike during the summer of 1967 held up M-16 deliveries. A dispute over wages, it coincided with the annual plant shutdown for vacations, so for the first two weeks production was not affected. Subsequently, the Army, completely dependent on Colt's, became increasingly nervous until the settlement in August. Always looking for a scapegoat, Congress now took the warpath. In October, a House Armed Services subcommittee criticized the Army's "unbelievable" management of the M-16 program and demanded an audit of Colt's profits. Noting that Colt's was the sole supplier, it called the Army to account for failing to negotiate a deal on manufacturing rights before the start of large-scale buying. To its credit Colt's had three years previously made four different offers to sell its rights, including an outright release free in exchange for a large contract. The Army refused to cooperate.

As for profits, the committee report charged:

A 10 percent profit rate was negotiated on all production contracts. The records and information made available by Colt's indicate that profits before taxes were 19.6 per cent for calendar year 1965; 16.8 per cent for calendar year 1966; and 13.4 per cent for the first four months of 1967, an average of 16.8 per cent.

The sub-committee considered "at least unethical" the employment by Colt Industries of Major General Nelson M. Lynde Jr. as a consultant immediately following his retirement as head of the Army Weapons Command. "It is actions such as these," the report went on to say, "that cause the American taxpayer to lose faith in the integrity of both military and civilian officials associated with the expenditure of millions of dollars yearly in the procurement of supplies and materials to meet our military requirements." Lynde replied that his duties had nothing to do with selling the M-16. Smarting from all this criticism, the Army got down to business, paid Colt's $4.5 million, and in 1968 the Rock Island Arsenal added the Hydramatic Division of General Motors and Harrington & Richardson in Worcester, Massachusetts as suppliers.

Several years later, in the fall of 1971, Colt's again came under attack. Based on affidavits from several Colt employees, the Connecticut Citizens Action Group accused the company of cheating on government quality control tests by hiding malfunctions and performing illegal repairs. As a result, the Justice Department ordered an FBI investigation of the allegations. One employee, an ex-Marine master sergeant, told federal agents that rejected M-l6's which were consistently off-target in firing tests were repaired by bending the barrels back into shape on I-beams in order to correct the sighting. He claimed that firing range employees, including himself, covered up malfunctions during endurance tests and covertly replaced worn parts while inspectors from the Defense Contract Administration Service were distracted.

It was a tempest in a teapot. Every gunmaker knows that no barrel can be drilled perfectly straight. At Thompson Ramo Wooldridge, Bill Goldbach used bending fixtures as a government-approved method for straightening barrels 10 or 20 thousandths of an inch. It required expert judgment to determine whether a barrel was crooked or not. Goldbach substituted a different type of fixture, and the investigation was quietly terminated. A properly-aligned barrel was only one of the critical inspection tests. The Army required that every M-16 meet a number of rigid reliability and accuracy specifications. In addition, from each production lot one rifle was selected to undergo a 6,000 round endurance test. Another involved the interchangeability of parts: ten rifles were picked at random, disassembled, the parts mixed together, and then reassembled.

Faced with the necessity of accelerating M-16 output in 1968, its floors crowded with some 2,300 employees, Colt's had to look around for more room. The decision made almost four and one-half years before, to move out of Hartford lock, stock, and barrel, had never been implemented. The old company stayed under the blue dome right through the 1970s. To relieve the congestion, however, it purchased twenty-four acres in Rocky Hill, south of Hartford, and constructed a one-story plant of 89,000 square feet, to which were transferred the Python .357 magnum and the Mark III J frame revolver operations. It also leased 40,000 additional square feet in the West Hartford complex, where all M-16's were assembled.

By the close of that year, Colt's had delivered over a million rifles. In fact, General Westmoreland, now Army chief-of-staff, personally examined the millionth arm at the U.S. Army Association show in Washington. The following July the Armory received a contract to cover production from May of 1970, when it expected to complete deliveries on all previous orders, through 1973. This new award, the result of competitive bidding, totaled $41.2 million for 458,435 guns, with options for 900,000 more in both 1972 and 1973.

Under Goldbach's leadership Colt's had learned a lot about efficient mass production since the fiasco of World War II. It had been able to steadily whittle down its original cost per gun from $122 until it reached a low of $82. By comparison, General Motors, which got an order for 229,217 concurrently, bid $103.76, which did not include government-paid-for equipment. From the start, Colt's used its own resources to equip the M-16 program. That same year Goldbach was called upon to build a "turn-key" plant in Singapore to produce up to 10,000 M-16's monthly, and in 1972 he masterminded a similar facility for Korea.

While over 500,000 Americans were vainly fighting far away in Vietnam, at home anti-war fever mounted to the crisis point. On October 15, 1969, the nation witnessed the biggest war protest yet. In Moratorium Day rallies, hundreds of thousands strong gathered on college campuses and elsewhere, urging the United States to pull out. Numerous senators and congressmen voiced their support for withdrawal. President Nixon was unmoved, saying he would not allow his efforts to make peace "to be swayed by those who demonstrate." In Hartford's Bushnell Park, 10,000 chanted, waved banners, and shouted "Peace, now!"

Meanwhile, Colt's was dealing with quite a different form of demonstration. A week earlier, Colt employees in West Hartford staged an illegal walkout protesting the bringing in of supervisors on Sundays to inspect M-16's at the testing facility. Two days later, UAW Local 376 voted to sanction the strike, and all work ceased. Management wired UAW President Walter Reuther that it would seek $500,000 a day in damages. Either the threat to sue or the contract language forbidding walkouts convinced Reuther, for he refused to back up the local, and the strike collapsed after a few more days. Nearly four years later, a more serious labor dispute occurred, lasting nineteen weeks, as the result of employee fears that Colt's was finally getting ready to move out of Hartford entirely. Management scoffed at the rumors, but severance pay was a major provision of the final settlement, on the basis of one week for every four years worked should Colt's be relocated.

In any munitions plant, security is of paramount concern. During the Vietnam War, Colt's expended hundreds of thousands of dollars every year to prevent the theft of guns. Yet smuggling did occur, especially in wintertime when parts could be concealed under heavy clothing. Colt's, from the very beginning, had maintained extensive records of every firearm produced and its serial number, but even these could not account for rifles or handguns, either parts or assemblies, stolen from production departments. From 1967 through 1971, court records reveal that at least sixty M-16's had been stolen. "If you want to get a gun out of there, you can do it," admitted one employee. "You can take it out piece-by-piece. Of course, the M-16 breaks down into two easy parts and each one can go under a pant leg." Another, more likely possibility for theft lay in the fact that M-16 parts were transported every day from the Armory for assembly in West Hartford. Some of the smuggled rifles were later found used in an underworld gang war and in an aborted invasion of Cuba.

Fourteen were recovered from the bottom of the Connecticut River by Middletown police searching for a missing .22 rifle. Others disappeared after being sold on the black market. Hartford police recorded more than 140 stolen Colt revolvers taken from suspects they had apprehended.

Federal agents accused management of subordinating security measures to production schedules. Colt's issued an emphatic denial: "We have an extensive security system, and we are constantly reevaluating it to find any possible flaws." Company officials pointed out that guards provided by a private security firm patrolled the three plant locations; daily inventories were taken of gun parts and assemblies; and such devices as metal detectors, electronic alarms, ultrasonic equipment, and closed-circuit TV cameras had been deployed.

Some of the culprits, most of them former Colt employees, were caught. One ingenious thief took advantage of his handicap. Each night he left the plant, his artificial leg tripped the metal detector, and after a while the guards paid him no attention, unaware that concealed in his hollow leg were gun parts. Edward T. McMurray, production control supervisor at Rocky Hill, was indicted for illegally selling some seventy-four revolvers and sporting rifles to other Colt employees and outsiders. He told police that security was so lax it would be difficult ever to trace smuggled arms. Yet, the total lost was still minute compared to the number produced.

The most brazen incident involved Colt's export manager, Walter S. Plowman, who was indicted for sending more than 2,000 Colt guns to a legitimate South African dealer between 1973 and 1975. Blameless herself, the dealer said that she had often done business with both Colt and Winchester officials. The U.S. Neutrality Act prohibited the sale of any firearms to South Africa in line with the embargo voted by the United Nations Security Council in 1963 in protest against South Africa's apartheid policy. However, Colt's had obtained licenses to export M-16's and other weapons to other countries not on the blacklist, although members of Congress and the media lifted disapproving eyebrows. One sale to Lebanon raised the possibility that U.S.-made guns would be picked up by Palestinian guerrillas on the open market, endangering the administration's official position of neutrality between the warring Christian and Moslem sects. Although Rep. Les Aspin of Wisconsin labeled the action "ill-timed and extremely irresponsible," the onus rested not on Colt's but on the State Department.

In Plowman's case, he was specifically charged with submitting false information on eight Colt applications to the State Department for export licenses, claiming the country of final destination as West Germany. In addition, Plowman ran a registered gun business openly from his home in Haddam, Connecticut with weapons purchased from Colt's but never paid for. In July, 1976, he was sentenced to two years in prison; as a first offender he was paroled after serving one year.

* * *

When Goldbach left Colt's in 1972 the Vietnam War and the M-16 program were fast coming to an end, and the shadows of internal dissension were again falling on the Armory. Group Vice-President Guy Shafer restructured the company into one division and chose David C. Eaton, then head of Chandler-Evans, as president. A plant-wide retooling was undertaken to produce more sporting arms. One small acquisition evoked memories of the other gunmaker in Hartford during Sam Colt's lifetime: in 1968 the Sharps Arms Company had been formed in Salt Lake City to create a modern version of the Borchardt rifle made famous by the original Sharps Rifle Company, and in 1970 Colt's business in sporting guns — rifles and revolvers — amounted to $17 million. The Sharps rifle, however, did not catch on; it was priced too high for the market, and only 500 were sold at $1,695 apiece.

Colt's had already lost to Smith & Wesson its long-dominant position as the supplier of law-enforcement weapons. The lessons learned in making the M-l6's had not been carried over to handguns, which — though of the same excellent quality — were being made essentially the same way as they had before 1900. But one still popular model was the 1911 .45 automatic pistol, the improved version of which was called the Mark IV. Since its introduction, nearly three million .45's have been sold. But *in toto* Colt's was selling only one out of every four domestic or imported revolvers (excluding the disreputable "Saturday Night Specials," a popular media term for cheaply-produced pocket revolvers better known to collectors as "Suicide Specials").

Then, as so often happened in Colt's history, a brand new market beckoned to a management hungry for business. It had been first discovered, but not exploited, in the early 1960s when gun collectors began to demand fancy replicas of famous Colt originals like the Navy 1851 or the Peacemaker. A two-day open house was held in 1961 to celebrate what the Armory called its 125th

Modern version of the Sharps rifle made by Colt's for a limited period.

M-16 rifle.

anniversary, thus perpetuating an error made by an earlier management which had incorrectly dated the Armory's origin back to 1836, the year that Sam Colt opened his ill-fated Paterson, New Jersey factory. Then-president Fred A. Roff Jr. had displayed a replica of the 1873 Single Action Peacemaker, gold inlaid with seven scenes from Colt's past. The engraving alone represented 900 hours of work, and it carried an appraisal value of $12,500. Actually, the first replica to be produced for the collector market was the Colt Derringer; 100,000 were made at a price of $27.50. Six other models followed that year. Some 400 "quick draw" clubs sprang up around the country, and in 1967 Robert Cherry and Wallace Beinfeld formed the Colt Commemorative Gun Collectors of America, which attracted several thousand members.* Only two engravers were then employed to turn out orders sporadically. Gradually it dawned on the Colt organization, as sales of police guns withered away, that custom-made guns might fill the vacuum. More and more collectors were clamoring for exotic designs, deluxe embellishments, differing barrel lengths, calibers, finishes, special serial numbers, and limited editions. Colt's has tried to satisfy this demand since with an annual series of commemorative issues.

Every since the Armory opened in 1855, ledgers of gun sales and serial numbers had been meticulously kept by generations of Colt clerks. As time passed, these records became invaluable for identifying and tracing various models, particularly for the 20,000 dealers and innumerable collectors spread around the world. After World War II, as many as 2,500 inquiries were received each year on the origins of antique weapons. Responsible for answering these requests was Ron Wagner as manager of the Parts & Research Department. Affectionately called "the voice of Colt," Wagner could boast of the second longest service record in Colt's history. In 1919 he had taken a job as a messenger at the suggestion of his father, already a Coltman. Upon Wagner's retirement at the age of 67 in June, 1972, Colt's new president David C. Eaton, remarked: "Ron Wagner's half century of service with Colt's may never again be equaled."

In 1976 the Custom Gun Shop was formally established, staffed by a dozen top-grade gunsmiths and five master craftsmen who perform elaborate scroll and inlay work and make their own tools. There are probably fewer than 50 firearms engravers currently active in the entire country, only a few of whom come close to matching the Colt engravers' skills. Steve Kamyk, who served his apprenticeship at Smith & Wesson, says that it takes a year just to learn how to sharpen engraving tools. From the Gun Shop came the magnificent "Bicentennial Dragoon" No. 1776-1976, the inspiration for which were the pistols — gold-inlaid, engraved, and cased — which Colonel Colt had presented to Czar Nicholas I of Russia and the Sultan of Turkey around 1854. The modern dragoon sold at auction for $55,000 and would have topped $100,000 had the sale been by voice bid instead of sealed bid.

In creating the Custom Gun Shop, President Ed Warner in effect revived a tradition which Colonel Colt himself had begun. The company's breathtaking color catalog, entitled *The Personal Touch*, observes that the inventor appreciated the promotional value of custom-made, decorated products, hired the leading engravers of his time, and personally presented heads of state, generals and other influential personages with "the finest handguns made in 19th century America." Some of these works of art can be seen in the Colt Collection at the Connecticut State Library (see Appendix I). In 1979, the Custom Gun Shop grossed over three million dollars. R.L. Wilson of Hadlyme, the noted gun historian, claims that Colt's is "the world's foremost producer of commemorative arms — not in quantity, but in quality, inspiration, and merit."

An innovative addition to the Colt line is the "Authentic Blackpowder Series" of classic revolvers originally issued between 1847 and 1873. These muzzle-loading cap-and-ball guns are being made to the same old designs and specifications but with the improved metallurgy and production techniques of modern times. They feature the lustrous blueing and case hardening of their famous forerunners, and each model bears serial numbers that follow those stamped on the originals. First in the series was the 1860 Army Single Action revolver with detachable shoulder stock; during the Civil War, 129,000 of them were delivered to U.S. troops, more than any other Colt model or any other make.

Others include the 1847 Colt Walker, the First Dragoon (1848), the 1851 Navy, and the 1862 Pocket Police and Navy — last of the muzzle loaders attributed to Colonel Colt. The Armory also supplies the accessories essential to firing muzzle loaders. These, too, were designed by the Colonel himself. His second patent, in 1838, covered flasks, molds, and combination tools. A London firm supplied his percussion caps, and Sam Colt

* Disbanded in 1979.

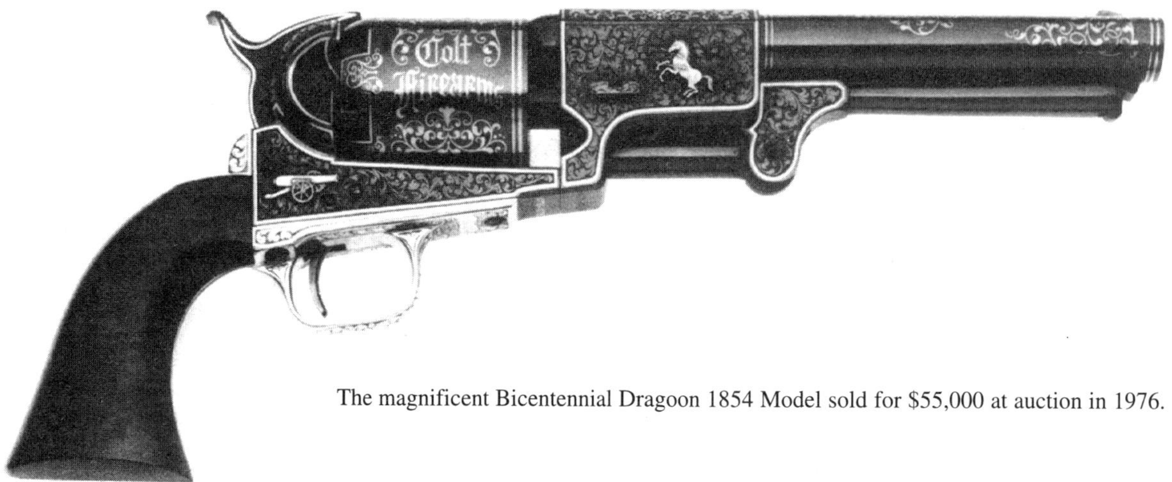

The magnificent Bicentennial Dragoon 1854 Model sold for $55,000 at auction in 1976.

selected the correctly calibrated conical balls. For Colt engineers, the introduction of the Blackpowder Series has been — in a sense — a giant step backwards, for these revolvers continue rather than reproduce the legacy of quality set by their inventor; but they met with instantaneous success in the gun collector and gun buff market.

Today, according to *Business Week* (November 27, 1978), the U.S. firearms industry suffers from a plethora of headaches, more so than during the Great Depression: "skyrocketing product liability costs, highly restricted export markets, burgeoning labor and material costs, an aging plant and skilled labor force, foreign gunrunning and scandals, the recurring threat of federal gun controls, diminishing hunting grounds and shorter hunting seasons, stiff competition from imports, and — recently — competition from foreign companies manufacturing firearms in the U.S." The total 1977 sales approximated $500 million for about two million handguns and three million long guns, while imports of all types exceeded one and a half million.

Yet, the industry continues to show an above average return compared to other manufacturers:

Company	1977 Sales (in mill.)	Profit (in mill.)	Return
Winchester (Olin Industries)	$289*	$25.5	8.5%
Remington (DuPont)	235	16.8	7.1%
Smith & Wesson (Bangor Punta)	84	18.4	21.8%
Colt Firearms Div. (Colt Industries)	77	11.0	14.3%
Marlin Firearms (independent)	34	?	?
	$719	$71.7	10.4%

* Includes ammunition

Return on investment, however, is much lower. And image-conscious giants like DuPont and Colt Industries dislike being tagged as dealers in death. *Business Week* speculated on whether, in view of the decline in firearms sales, Colt Industries would phase out the business altogether. It pointed out that the parent company "has one of the oldest plants in the firearms industry, and while it still produces a quality product, it has been shaving old lines and raising prices on new ones in a desperate effort to meet management's profit goals." One competitor declared Colt's had priced itself out of the market in many customer lines.

It is certainly true that the cessation of M-16 contracts substantially reduced profits for the Firearms Division in 1977, although at the end of that year Colt's obtained approval for selling 21,000 rifles to the Malaysian Army. Some 300 out of 1,400 employees had to be laid off. Furthermore, admitting its failure to compete, the company announced that production on the .38 cal. snub-nose revolver, long the favorite weapon of detectives, would be phased out. Later, it decided to keep the revolver in the line. It also announced the closing of the Rocky Hill facility in the spring of 1978 and most of the employees there were transferred to West Hartford.

Even Smith & Wesson's position as the biggest moneymaker of all munitions manufacturers is insecure, as their respective fortunes continue to change, both up and down. Sturm, Ruger in Southport, Connecticut is challenging Smith & Wesson's hold on the lucrative market for double-action police revolvers. Its president, William B. Ruger Sr., whom Larry Wilson calls the Sam Colt of the 20th century, declares that "we want to do the same to Smith & Wesson that it did to Colt." To complicate the competition further, two foreign firms have invaded Connecticut to do battle with the struggling American gunmakers. A subsidiary of Jucar, a Spanish outfit, has a plant in East Haddam for muzzle-loading kits; an Italian company, Pietro Beretta Fabbrica Armi, has set up a marketing operation for the handguns which it makes in Maryland. Moreover, Interarms, founded by the world's leading munitions dealer, Sam Cummings (a U.S. citizen residing in Monaco), recently opened a factory in Virginia to produce a line of single-action revolvers which in appearance resemble the venerable Colt Army gun.

The newest supplier of light machine guns to the U.S. Army, Belgium's Fabrique Nationale has apparently shed its image of being a staid, strike-ridden arms manufacturer whose name was often linked to the illegal weapons trade, according to an article in the October 13, 1980 issue of *Business Week*. Called the "Minimi", the new gun is 5.56 caliber, weighs 24.3 pounds and can fire up to 1,100 rounds per minute. It is intended to serve the function of the old Browning automatic rifle as a cover weapon for a rifle squad. Fabrique Nationale took over Browning in 1977, but its affiliation with that famous name dates back to 1897 when John Moses Browning granted Fabrique production and sales rights for all Browning arms outside the United States. The new machine gun may be produced in its new South Carolina plant.

* * *

As the Firearms Division accelerates its efforts to dominate the profitable gun collector market, the directors of Colt Industries seem to be having second thoughts about abandoning the gun business. Commemoratives, deluxe engraved handguns, sporting rifles, and muzzle loaders do not carry the stigma attached to such lethal items as automatic rifles and grenade launchers. Publication by Simon & Schuster of Wilson's *The Colt Heritage*, the definitive compendium of the long line of Colt firearms from 1836 on, has whetted the appetites of collectors even more. And there still exists a steady demand from police, security, military, and hunting clients for arms made by the one and only Colt concern.

However, the Firearms Division currently (as of January, 1982) occupies only a small portion of the once great Armory complex. All manufacturing has been moved to West Hartford, except for production of the M-l6 rifle, which is concentrated in the saw-toothed building at the southern end. The Custom Gun Department has also been recently moved into this space. In 1981, the company moved its offices from a building in the rear of the Armory facing Huyshope Avenue to new quarters in West Hartford. The remainder of the property, which is owned by an out-of-state limited partnership of real estate investors, has been leased to various small enterprises and government agencies, altogether a rather dowdy and disparate collection of structures. As dismal as the future of the old Armory may seem, the area around it has been undergoing redevelopment. The Colt-built tenements have been restored as housing for middle-income workers, the Church of the Good Shepherd in Colt Park has been refurbished, one nearby old factory has been converted into offices, and other projects have been planned or started.

From the interstate highway separating it from the Connecticut River, the traveler can catch a brief glimpse of the weathered brick structure in the center of the Armory and that remarkable bulbous blue dome, sixty feet in diameter, with the gilded colt on top still clutching the broken spear. The latter, of course, is an ancient symbol of the war horse in battle pursuit even after its master has fallen, and it also served as Colonel Colt's own trademark and family crest. Recently something new has been added to the dome: the stars that originally adorned it have been restored, the anonymous gift of a Colt antiquarian. It all resulted from a casual conversation between the donor and Larry Wilson. Hearing that the dome in Sam Colt's day sported about eighty gold-leafed stars, the gun fancier wrote to President Warner offering to underwrite the cost of a complete restoration. The letter was ignored. "You get a lot of crank mail," Warner admitted, "and we just kind of laughed this one off." Rebuffed, the benefactor went back to Wilson and urged him to vouch for his sincerity. The stars were fabricated from aluminum in the Armory and installed in September, 1976. To protect his anonymity, the mysterious donor was billed $8,000 through Wilson.* Now there is more reason than ever to preserve Hartford's most unique landmark.

The inside of the East Armory, built by General Franklin in 1867, is virtually empty since the removal of the Firearms Division's offices. But its floors and wooden beams are still sound, and in the center the upper portion of the impressive Franklin steam engine is still in place, a monument to the past that will remain as long as the building itself.

One can still wander through the aisles from floor to floor, imagining that he hears the throbbing of belt-driven machinery and sees workmen adjusting, inspecting, or scurrying to and fro. In the attic, junk of all kinds litters the floor: an old pistol grip, several bullet molds that must date back to the percussion days of the Civil War, a crucible for forging small frames.** They conjure up the image of Colonel Colt himself admonishing his hands to "wirk ten hours during the runing of the engine" or that of Sam Stone coaxing Polish mothers into the Armory during World War I. Sam Colt and Sam Stone: still here, in another form, as real as atoms and waves. Can human energy be destroyed any more than the energy in wood or metal? And are companies really any different from people? They, too, age, become senile, and die, but sometimes they revive or are reborn. Colt's, in a sense, is another manifestation of the giant old Charter Oak tree which finally toppled near the Armory just as the latter came into being; in common with all energy systems, organizations generally run down like unwound clocks — unless there is constant infusion of new blood and new energy. No doubt the world would forget the many individuals who had nurtured Colt's — Root, Franklin, Ehbets, Skinner, Stone, Browning, Moore, Goldbach, and nameless others, yet these walls after crumbling to dust, these spirits permeating them with their visions of mass production, they would live on as part of the cosmic web in which time and space are one. Colt's will exist always — somehow.

If the physical decline of the once great Armory depresses the visitor seeking the roots of the Colt legacy, he may find inspiration in the nearby Church of the Good Shepherd, the Caldwell Colt Memorial Parish House, Armsmear, or the Colt statue. A stirring reminder of the entrepreneurial tradition set by her husband and embraced ever since by American industrialists is the stained glass window which Mrs. Colt installed in the rear of the Episcopal church erected to his memory. The window shows the biblical Joseph with the unmistakable face of Colonel Colt gathering sheaves of wheat and carrying loaves of bread, symbolizing Egypt's seven years of plenty and Colt's lifelong ambition to create abundance for the common man. Colt believed that technology — the application of scientific principles to machines and metals — was the almost magical plowshare that would eliminate slavery and enable Americans at every level to reap a constantly enlarging harvest of material and social goods. Today technology is under attack by 20th century Luddites, yet in a world of shrinking resources, burgeoning populations, and almost insoluble international tensions it will be Western technology that provides the solutions, if anything can, for man's survival.

* His identity became known after his death in January, 1979. He was John B. Solley, III, an heir to the Lilly pharmaceutical fortune, who put together the finest private collection of American firearms in modern times.

** At one time, the attic was the repository of a king's ransom in historical relics, memorabilia, and records. The bulk of these items was given to the State of Connecticut in 1957. But over the years not a few treasures were lost to scrap drives, souvenir hunters, and the junk yard. Among the missing: Colonel Colt's saddle, his fancy desk, door handles and hinges in the shape of firearms, and Gatling guns.

CHAPTER XV

RESURRECTION

Had Colonel Samuel Colt been alive in the 1980s and 1990s he would have been appalled and distressed by the events that battered and bloodied the great armory that he created in Hartford, Connecticut. Red ink aplenty, mismanagement, obsolete products, loss of markets and contracts, defense cutbacks, a four-year strike, a buyout, and bankruptcy. The combination of destructive forces would have sent the inventor to his grave even sooner than his untimely death at the age of 47.

Today his armory towers over the west side of Interstate I-91 like an industrial dinosaur. A shabby derelict, it no longer contains any gun operations. Colt carbines and revolvers are now produced in the more modern facility next to the defunct Pratt & Whitney Machine Tool factory, another casualty of the steep decline and disappearance of metalworking in Connecticut. The only survivor of Colt Industries in Connecticut is Chandler-Evans, a manufacturer of aircraft fuel controls located behind the abandoned Pratt & Whitney. As for the Armory itself, it has become an inexpensive shelter for artists' studios and small businesses. The venerable blue Colt dome still crowns the main brick building, but the rampant colt on top has been removed and sold by the building's out-of-state owners, and the dome itself seems ready to collapse.

Colt's latest problems began in the late 1970s when the market for handguns changed course. Like other domestic producers, the company was caught off guard by gun enthusiasts' preference for the new breed of pistols with clips of bullets that could quickly be reloaded. With only one such model in its line, Colt's lost sales to foreign companies like Glock and Beretta. Declining orders forced the layoff of 530 workers during 1982, more than a third of the force. A strike was narrowly averted by the signing of a new contract that gave raises of 28 percent over a three-year period, bringing the average rate up to $9.76 an hour. The sole ray of sunlight was the Army's commitment of $13 million to buy 18,000 modified versions of the M-16 rifle for the new Bradley tank-like vehicle designed to carry a squad into battle. The next year saw the expiration of its M-16 patents, and in 1984, deciding to stick with its tried and true Colt .45, the company withdrew from a competition to furnish the Pentagon with a 9mm handgun.

Consisting of 23 buildings spread over 17 acres, now listed on the National Register of Historic Places, the Colt complex had been purchased in 1978 by Water+Way Properties, an out-of-state real estate partnership. The chief investor was Charles C. Holt III, a flamboyant multi-millionaire from Palm Beach with little concern for the Colt legacy. In the leased Saw-Tooth Building, Colt's was still making parts for M-16 rifles, while the interior of the center structure had been remodeled for studios and offices, a cheery contrast to the grimy exterior. Paying only two to four dollars a square foot, compared to the going rent of $17 downtown, the occupants included 26 artists, eight commercial photographers, a potter, and sign painter. On the third floor, where German craftsmen once painstakingly inlaid gold into the butts of revolvers, a public relations and advertising firm was ensconced.

Colt's Custom Shop, however, was still functioning, continuing the founder's tradition of engraving, scrolling and inlaying presentation guns. Wealthy personalities like Charlton Heston, Mel Torme and Chuck Yeager were eager to pay up to $5,000, in addition to the basic cost of $1,000, for these beauties. All the designs were hand-drawn under the supervision of Al DeJohn, a veteran of 42 years. Robert G. Morrison, vice-president of marketing, called De John's artisans "keepers of the flame."

Frequently, guns were donated for motion picture and TV productions on condition that the actors using them agreed to their being auctioned off afterward, with the proceeds going to a charity of their choice. The model most in demand was the Peacemaker. When Ronald Reagan left office, he was given a Peacemaker — like every other outgoing president. In celebration of Colt's 150th anniversary in 1986 — the length of time being arbitrarily based on Colt's disastrous venture in Paterson, New Jersey — the only handgun made for the occasion was bought by a collector at a Las Vegas auction for $150,000.

Modest profitability and rising labor disharmony were pushing Colt Industries, the parent of the Firearms Division, to shut down its operations in Hartford completely. In March 1985, the union rejected the final proposal for a new contract but voted to stay on the job out of fear that a move outside the city might be impending. City and state officials were also worried and offered $1.8 million for renovation of the Armory, but Colt's eventually turned the help down.

Manifestly unhappy, the employees objected to what they considered harsh discipline and refused to work overtime. A machine operator complained: It's like walking into a gas chamber every morning. You don't know whether you've got a job or you're fired." Union officials were convinced that Colt's wanted to destroy the union, and there was no doubt of management's hostility to the antagonistic attitude of Philip A. Wheeler, U.A.W. regional director. Colt's not only filed charges of unfair practices with the NLRB but sued the union for sabotage, harassment and arson.

Giving up all hope of a settlement, the members of Local #376, U.A.W. finally walked out on January 25, 1986. It was the beginning of the longest and most bitter strike in Connecticut's industrial history. Picket lines surrounded the entrances to both plants, demonstrations and clashes with the police were frequent, and several strikers were arrested. Management accused the strikers of setting fires, sabotaging machinery and acts of violence. One group even marched to the home of Guy C. Shafer, vice-president of Colt Industries in charge of both the Firearms Division and Chandler-Evans. The company remained open by hiring hundreds of untrained replacements, the effectiveness of whom was scoffed at by the union because of their high turnover rate and reports of poor inspection procedures and excessive scrap.

In September, the company reeled from a double blow. The state ruled that it had imposed a lockout, thus making the strikers eligible for unemployment compensation benefits, while the NLRB accused it of unfair labor practices. More blows were forthcoming. Early in 1987, the union urged the Legislature and Connecticut's congressional delegation to press for a cutoff of Colt's contracts. Since the end of the Vietnam War, Colt's had been the sole supplier of M-16s. A year later, in October, the Army pulled the plug, giving the Columbia, South Carolina subsidiary of Fabrique Nationale, S.A. of Belgium a $112 million contract for the M-16A2. The Army insisted its decision had nothing to do with the strike or quality, but was based solely on price — $420 per gun compared to Colt's $477.50. U.A.W.'s Wheeler commented: "We would rather see Colt out of business than have a factory full of scabs."

By April of 1989, Colt Industries had had enough and put the division up for sale. (The parent soon transformed into a private company called Coltec.) The lack of profitability was not the motive since analysts estimated that on sales of between $110 and $120 million, the Hartford plants were earning $15 to $20 million annually. The decision to sell sparked the formation of a coalition of private investors to keep Colt's in the state. Its leader was Anthony D. Autorino, a former president of Hamilton Standard Division of United Technologies. Though he had no background in firearms, in fact had never owned or shot a gun, he cited two reasons for his interest. As a boy on Wethersfield Avenue he used to play in Colt Park, and he felt strongly that Connecticut could not afford to lose more jobs in manufacturing, especially an enterprise as historic as the Armory.

"Colt's used to be the number one gunmaker in the world," he said. "The name is very powerful. It is the seventh most recognized name in the world. In Japan, it is number three; in China, number two… But Colt is not first right now. Marketwise, it's probably two or three, against the competition of Smith & Wesson, Ruger, Steyr, and Beretta." To restore Colt's superiority, Autorino conceived the idea of sharing ownership with management and labor. "The employees really care a lot about Colt's. Generations have worked there. It's a family. I think that family needs to be able to get some economic gain as we succeed. We have got to form an economic bond between what is typically called management and labor, so that everybody gains."

In the deal signed on March 22, 1990, an agreement that critics later termed flawed, the new owners paid around $75 million for the assets of the Firearms Division. But the use of the Colt name for purposes other than making guns was peddled to a different group of investors for $12 million. The new company was called Colt's Manufacturing. Besides management and the union, the investors included two foreign banks, Creditanstalt-Bankverein of Vienna and National Westminster Bank of London, and the State of Connecticut. In an unprecedented move to save 1,000 jobs, Treasurer Francisco L. Borges contributed $25 million from the state's pension fund for a 64 percent interest. Another former president of Hamilton Standard, Richard F. Gamble, was chosen president and Ronald E. Stilwell, Colt's vice-president for military sales, became executive vice-president. Autorino agreed to serve as chairman. Before the end of the year, Gamble resigned and was replaced by Stilwell.

As part of the deal, the company agreed to pay $13 million in back wages to the strikers because of its violation of labor laws, the largest settlement ever made in the history of the National Labor Relations Board. To the cheers of strikers crowded into the press conference at Borges' office, Autorino handed the first installment — a $10 million check — to Wheeler, who passed it on to Peter Hoffman, NLRB's regional director, for distribution. All 580 replacement workers were immediately laid off. The sale ended the government's case.

The former strikers returning to work the next month realized they were now part owners of the new company, having 16 percent of the stock and three seats on the new 11-member board of directors. Management received a stock option plan. Colt employees thus joined the fast-growing ranks of American workers with a direct financial stake in the success of their companies. Nationwide, more than 10 million own some part of 10,000 firms. President Gamble promised that management would treat the work force as a valuable resource. "We will get people together and ask what they think needs to be done, particularly as it relates to quality." Back on the job, the workers voiced optimism about the future. "They want to get in there and make some money for this company," said Russ See, president of UAW Local #376. "They care about it. They will turn the company around."

Unfortunately, his prediction was premature. Almost two years to the day after the rescue in 1990 had been joyfully announced, the cash-strapped company filed for bankruptcy, placing in jeopardy the future of 925 employees and the state's investment of $25 million. Despite a struggle to win back customers and boost sales, the company had failed to offer the right products at competitive prices. For weeks the major lenders and investors had been meeting frequently, even on weekends, to avoid the inevitable. Talks reached a climax when Creditanstalt, the principal lender, threatened to push for liquidation. Colt's showed liabilities of $82.5 million and assets of $91.5 million, while its holding company had liabilities of $8.3 million and assets of $7 million. Governor Lowell P. Weicker, Jr., saying "this is one crown jewel that doesn't leave Connecticut," committed the state to keeping the company alive. The Department of Economic Development, which had already loaned $500,000, came through with a $3 million line of credit, and Creditanstalt cooperated by at once advancing $7 million. President Stilwell was elated at having the breathing room to restructure. "It gives us $10 million for operations, product development and aggressive marketing projects that we had begun but which had been adversely affected by the lack of ready funds."

The bankruptcy of Colt's was the latest in a series of defeats for the Connecticut Valley's once-thriving firearms industry, already staggering through decades of decline caused by foreign competition, outdated factories, costly liability insurance, gun control laws, the worst recession since the Great Depression, defense cutbacks, and fewer hunters. High Standard of East Hartford failed in 1984. Besides Colt, the survivors in "Gun Valley" were Sturm, Ruger & Co. of Fairfield, Smith & Wesson of Springfield, U.S. Repeating Arms of New Haven, Marlin Firearms and O.F. Mossberg & Sons of North Haven, Remington Arms of Bridgeport, and Savage Industries of Westfield, Mass. From a World War II peak of over 20,000 to a Vietnam-high of nearly 10,000, the number of jobs in Connecticut had plunged to around 2,500 in mid-1991. Only a week before, the State had cobbled together a package of public and private incentives, valued at $10-20 million, to keep U.S. Repeating Arms, maker of the Winchester rifle, from pulling out of New Haven. Smith & Wesson turned to a United Kingdom holding company to help underwrite its comeback to the handgun sector, while Sturm, Ruger moved much of its production to lower-cost sites in New Hampshire and Arizona.

The big question was whether the badly battered and subsidized Colt could survive in the tumultuous business climate resulting from the end of the Cold War. The State's investment had depreciated to $10 million. There was another change of command at the top, Stilwell departing and Ronald C. Whitaker stepping into his shoes. He expressed confidence that the efforts to improve quality and cut costs would sell more guns to individuals, the U.S. military and foreign armies.

For two years in the federal bankruptcy court in Hartford, Colt's creditors and investors, supported by a host of lawyers (whose fees amounted to $6.4 million), fought over the terms of the settlement that would facilitate recovery. Unsecured creditors were owed $7 million. The claims and counter claims made the Chapter 11 proceedings one of the most complex and apparently irreconcilable ever heard. The first ray of hope for reorganization appeared in the fall of 1993, when a partnership headed by Greenwich multi-millionaire William R. Berkley made a cash offer of $12 million in tandem with the state's agreement to invest another $12 million. But in December the Berkley group backed out, partly because of the difficulty in reacquiring the rights to the Colt name. The collapse of the negotiations caused the loss of a $40 million sale of M-16s to the Dutch government. "We're damaged goods," bemoaned President Whitaker.

The spring of 1994 brought forth a new group of would-be buyers with stronger ties to Connecticut and a greater appreciation of the Colt legacy. Wooed by the Connecticut Development Authority, Zilkha & Co., New York merchant bankers, made a similar offer. The Zilkha family had made their fortune as commercial bankers in the late nineteenth century in the Near East; subsequently, they continued their banking enterprises in Europe and the United States and became industrialists. They were known as generous benefactors to Wesleyan University. Ezra, the father, was a 1947 graduate, trustee emeritus and also a director of CIGNA Corporation. His son, Donald, a 1973 graduate and present trustee, was Zilkha's president and founder. One of its partners, John Rigas, said, "We're interested because it looks like an opportunity to take a company that doesn't deserve to be in bankruptcy, out of it." CDA was determined to retrieve the Colt name and turn it over to the Zilkhas. Its loss had been partially responsible for the company's woes, since a royalty was being paid for every gun branded "Colt" at a cost of several million dollars a year. This time, the deal was consummated to the relief of all parties on September 28th. It provided for senior secured debt of $17.5 million, the recapture of the Colt name for $10 million and unsecured creditor claims of $3.6 million. The State gave up its common stock for $10 million in preferred shares. The union's ownership was reduced to 7.5 percent, which can grow to 10.5 percent over time, and the balance of the common stock is held by the investor group and management.

When Colt's was only two months into bankruptcy, Ron Whitaker was persuaded to take over as president and CEO. Since November of the preceding year he had been discussing the challenge held out to him and had walked around the plants. Despite his lack of a gunmaking background, he had a talent for knowing now to fix sick companies, and he quickly sized up the fact that Colt's had too many people and too much inventory. A Philadelphian, Whitaker had attended Wooster College in Ohio and obtained a graduate degree from Dartmouth. His entire career had been spent with larger corporations as a troubleshooter, turnaround artist and buyer and seller of divisions and subsidiaries. After a stint at Gould, Inc., he ran his own business for seven years, then in 1979, at the age of 32, joined FMC Corporation as general manager of its special products group, a collection of tiny, money-losing units. There, for eight years, he built a reputation for being a quick study of what should be fixed, sold or closed. In 1987, he moved on to Wheelabrator, which had been spun off from Allied Signal to the Henley Group of merchant bankers.

In tackling the Colt situation, Whitaker, as he had done elsewhere, asked for a grace period of 100 days to make things right. He saw himself not as a savior but as a savvy fixer who could show his subordinates what had to be done. His first step was to shrink the management hierarchy; within 75 days he had removed one quarter of the salaried force. Because Colt's had been run more like a hobby than a regular business, the manufacturing operations were out of control, and the market possibilities had been ignored. Gradually, he combined the two plants into one without losing capacity. "Mismanagement, not the union, was killing us," he observed. By the fall of 1992, he realized that any plan of reorganization would fail unless more equity was poured into the company. So he concentrated on making presentations, at least once a week, to potential investors. The coming aboard of the Zilkhas was a great blessing because of their international contacts. "They see the world as our market and appreciate that Colt's great name, the quality of its products and its hold on the finest military and law enforcement weapons will make us a global supplier."

COLT® SPORTER™ LIGHTWEIGHT RIFLES

R-6530 Semi-Automatic Sporter Rifle.

M-4 Carbine.

The new Colt 22 Target Pistol.

Under Whitaker's leadership, Colt's Manufacturing has concentrated on finding out what products customers want and delivering them. It introduced a .22-caliber target pistol, much in demand in the shooting world. The Sporter semi-automatic rifle was well received and accounts for about a third of its annual sales. Ironically, Connecticut's strongest proponent of restoring Colt's health, Governor Weicker, had signed into law a ban on the sale of 60 types of assault weapons, including the Sporter, at the same time that his administration was trying to find a buyer for the company. In Congress, the state's two senators barely averted the inclusion of the Sporter in the list of weapons outlawed under the new anti-crime bill. This year brought better news. In August, the Army awarded Colt's $11 million for 24,000 of the patented M-4A1 carbines, the successor to the M-16s. It was the largest contract in recent years. In October, General Wayne A. Downing, commander of the Army's special operations (including the Green Berets and Navy Seals), took personal delivery of what may become the next generation of standard rifles — before a cheering throng of workers. The new gun is about eight inches shorter and one and a half pounds lighter than the M-16. "It could be our largest product line down the road three or four years," a pleased President Whitaker commented.

In his frank, articulate, upbeat style, he details his proudest accomplishments that together have created a new culture. The first was the transformation from the staid, discrete hierarchy in effect for most of this century to what he calls "world-class manufacturing" for the 21st century. Instead of a pyramid-shaped organization he describes the new one as atomic in nature, made up of self-sufficient business "cells" with their own staff support that make all the day-to-day decisions and are measured monthly on their profitability.

The second achievement was the hammering out of a unique union agreement which he claims is even superior to the pioneering one negotiated by General Motors for its Saturn plant. "We had a lot of old baggage to discard, and this agreement has tremendous upside potential for both the union and management." As a starter, the number of job classifications was cut from 156 to 11. Now

THE BATTLE FOR NEW GUN CONTRACTS

In a time of heavy defense spending cuts, Colt's is in a head-to-head battle for the meagre handful of military purchases by the Pentagon. President Ron Whitaker says the company depends on about $20 million a year in government work to meet its financial goals. So far, it is falling far behind. Since 1990, Colt's has received orders for about $31.5 million from the Army, while its chief competitor, Fabrique Nationale in Columbia, South Carolina, won contracts for just under $71 million for the same period.

Attempting to preserve the industrial base for the manufacture of small arms, the Army is awarding contracts on an ad hoc basis, with Fabrique Nationale getting the bulk of the M-16 work, while Colt's supplies the smaller, lighter M-4 carbine. Colt's lobbyists in Washington emphasize the fact that Fabrique Nationale is a foreign-owned company subsidized by the French government as opposed to Colt's nearly 150-year history of being an independent American industry.

there are four levels of machine operator, from button pusher to a certified cell operator who is paid 50 cents more an hour for being totally responsible for his quality. Instead of being on piece-work, the worker is rewarded for his degree of competence. The company offers training on the job, the cost of which is shared. In addition, each cell, including both hourly and salaried members, has the opportunity to earn a bonus based on its profit each quarter and at year-end. Problems that arise on the factory floor have to be identified and solved by a team of three union and three management people from the business unit. In case of stalemate a problem is reviewed at two higher levels, ending with Whitaker and Wheeler, but so far everyone has been settled on the floor.

Colt's president has a well-thought out vision for the future that builds on the new products already available. One of his earliest discoveries when he met with the marketing staff was the lack of a .22 target pistol. The Woodsman had been discontinued in 1974, but other manufacturers were selling a million such pistols every year. Colt's new version uses a shortened M-16 barrel and magazine loading. "We can't make enough," he says. During the long strike, the .38 detective special was also dropped, even though 300,000 of this type are bought by law enforcement agencies annually. And the Sporter semi-automatic rifle continues to be a big seller.

Looking ahead, Whitaker ticks off four areas of growth:

- more platforms for law enforcement pistols and rifles;
- the introduction of high quality shotguns;
- upgrades to the M-16 through add-on systems — like grenade launchers and adapters for the M-203;
- and, long-term, head of the pack in "smart gun" technology — guns that will fire only for the owner or are less than lethal.

In May of 1994, when the last of the gun operations ended in the downtown Armory, the ghost of Samuel Colt may well have shed bitter tears. The departure marked *finis* to 147 years of gunmaking in Hartford, during which Colt's, Sharps, Pope Manufacturing, and Pratt & Whitney had lifted the state out of its agrarian past into an era of industrial power and prosperity. The complex's 180 tenants were probably oblivious of what was happening on that final day in the Saw-Tooth Building. Surrounded by a sea of idle machines destined for the scrap heap, a lone worker packed the remainder of the M-16 rifles into boxes for transportation to West Hartford, where the consolidation of production was expected to save as much as $4 million annually. As obsolete as the machines, were the Armory's floors were broken up by columns that were totally incompatible with modern assembly procedures. Already underway was a study of the potential future uses of the buildings by the Greater Hartford Architecture Conservancy, which worried about the extent of pollution from the testing of weapons and underground contamination by hydrocarbons. The possibility loomed that the entire Colt complex might be razed.

But in West Hartford, the Colt's Manufacturing Company is very much alive and looking forward with confidence and pride to celebrating its true 150th anniversary in 1997.

COLT'S LAST DESCENDANT

Harold Colt, who claimed to have been the illegitimate great-grandson of Samuel Colt, died in January of 1995. He had made his home in New Hartford, Connecticut, overlooking the Barkhamsted reservoir. Although proud of his Colt lineage, he had no interest in the legacy of the Armory or in firearms. Instead, he had the largest private collection of records in New England, some 50,000 to be exact, which he willed to the Boston Symphony.

All his bachelor life he had been involved in the study, appreciation and recording of music. "Actually, I don't consider myself a collector in the standard sense," he said. "My principal interest is a quest for new music and music that I haven't heard before." It is estimated that he owned 50 recordings of the Tchaikovsky "Pathetique" symphony alone. At various times, Colt had been a recording engineer, an FM radio personality and a violinist. He used to play professionally once a year at the May Festival in Prague. In his living room, he built a stereo system with massive speakers and behind his house he had a large satellite dish to make videotapes from concerts in England and Spain.

Appendix I

From the Hartford years of the late 1840s, the Colt's Patent Firearms Company earned an enviable reputation for its virtuosity in the manufacturing of high-quality products, marketed through aggressive advertising. The traditions Samuel Colt established in the 1850s continued beyond his early death in 1862 and the disastrous factory fire of 1864. These same traditions have helped to sustain Colt in its 130-year Hartford history, and the firm has a rightful claim to recognition for substantial contributions to American industrial achievements. The heavy demand for Colt firearms, the company's stress on high-quality production and a skilled work force led to an ever-increasing confidence in its product line. Over the years, Colt developed major innovations in armsmaking and in custom-made machinery. These machines were produced for Colt's own use as well as for other companies. The significance of Colt beyond armsmaking *per se* is one of the best kept secrets of American industrial history.

Colt's began to expand its scope of manufacturing in the 1850s, soon after the Colonel's purchase of Hartford's South Meadows floodplain. A two-mile dike protected the lands from periodic flooding by the Connecticut River, and soon afterwards, thousands of willow trees were planted to protect against erosion. Cuttings from the willows inspired the establishment of Colonel Colt's Willow Ware Works with a line of products ranging from chairs and sofas, to baby carriages and cradles. The Willow Ware Manufacturing Company was an early sideline of the Colt enterprise, however not the first diversification from gun-making.

In the late 1830s and early 1840s, Colt had begun experimenting not only with firearms — but also with the manufacturing of accessories for their use. By the mid-1850s, he had a separate building at South Meadows for making tinfoil cartridges, an invention which became the first of his products marked with a rampant colt trademark. All arms leaving the factory were easily identifiable with the COLT name, but ironically, during the Colonel's lifetime, this self-contained cartridge was the only product made with the rampant colt trademark as a standard feature.

The company prospered throughout the second half of the 19th Century with thousands of orders for arms as well as further contracts for machinery and other non-firearms products. These items varied from railway register punches to steam engines to printing presses to much, much more. Production of each was innovative and served as a stepping stone for diversification and plant expan-

Decorative device formerly used on Colt's shipping receipts.

Detail of lamp screen (entire screen is approximately four feet tall) made of carved ivory in a relief depicting various aspects of Colt's history. In the central panel is the rampant colt with the Charter Oak Tree behind it, as well as a view of the Colt factory. On the sides are crossed pistols and rifles, and at the top — the American eagle. This beautifully worked screen is secured in an elaborately-styled Charter Oak frame and raised by a small metal revolver handle. It is believed to have been manufactured at Colt's plant, which adds a new twist to its extreme rarity. Gun stockmakers were known for their exceptional skills with wood and ivory carving, and this screen, the ivory-handled cane, and the rampant colt atop the Colt dome are all attributed to Colt factory production. (Courtesy Wadsworth Atheneum)

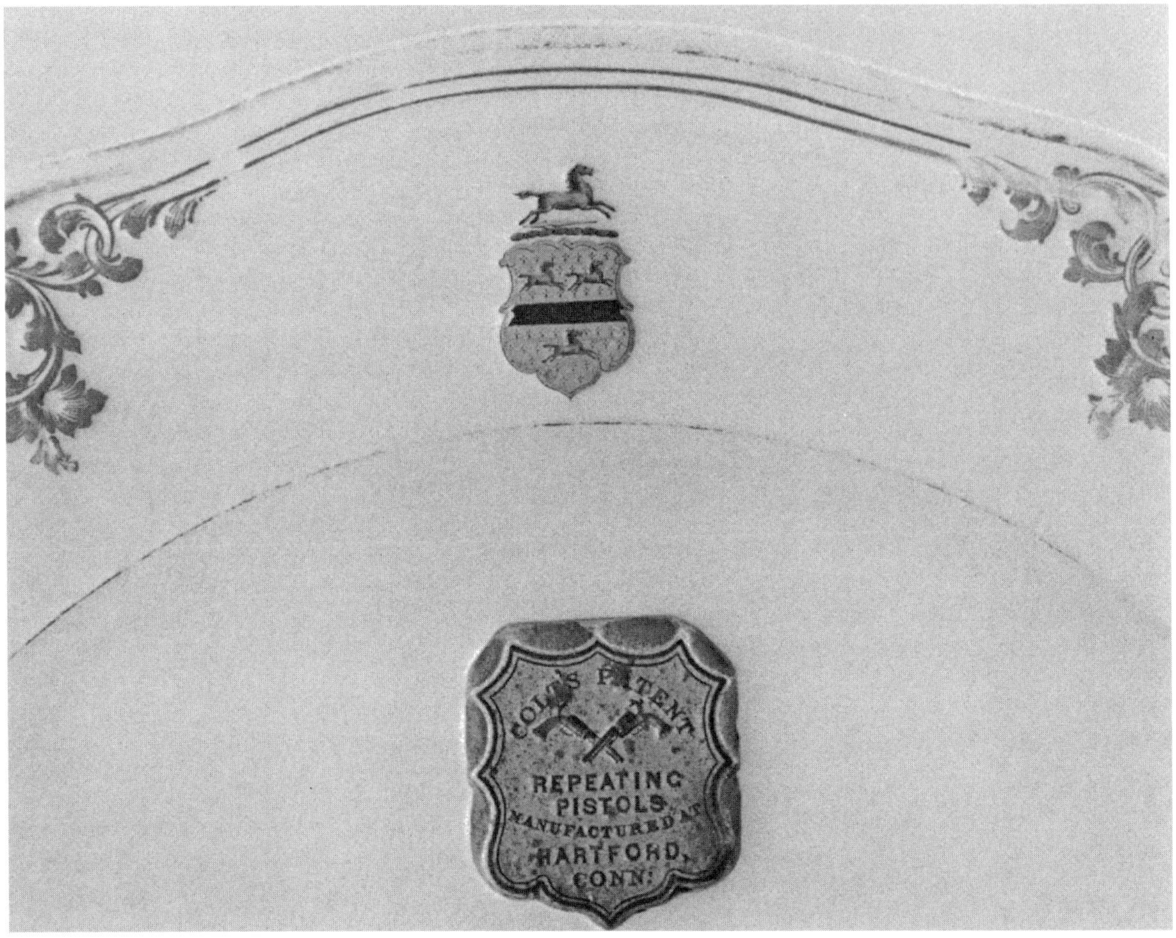

Detail of serving plate — only remaining piece from set of porcelain at Armsmear; showing Colt coat-of-arms, and decorated with borders of gilt scrollwork, also employing shield-like business card of the late 1840s-early 1850s. Possibly made in France.
(Photo by Sid Latham; courtesy of R.L. Wilson)

sion. Various firms and individuals sought to have their products made at Colt's Armory, and did so from a well-grounded faith in Colt's experience, know-how, and traditional quality. Colt's was heralded as a world leader in manufacturing. The company name and fame, exemplified by its increasingly recognized trademark, acted as catalysts toward diversification of the Colt product line.

Two styles of sewing machines were produced at the Colt plant. First of these was the Charter Oak Sewing Machine Company, which contracted Colt's to manufacture their Family model in 1874-5. In 1881, Thomas Morrison of Hartford had his patented design produced at Colt's. Neither model remained in production for long, nor has a single working model been located to date.

Successive Colt administrations continued, in their own style, the emphasis on advertising begun by Samuel Colt. Aggressive promotion was one reason the firm had been successful in an era when transgressions of patent rights were not uncommon. Throughout the late 1800s, most Colt brochures and catalogues displayed the popular rampant colt appearing sometimes on virtually every page. Variations of the trademark can be traced through these Colt publications as can the evolution of the company's advertising.

Colt's was continually a trend-setter in advertising and design, and catered to the concerns of the public. The company maintained its supply of arms to the U.S. Government for protection during wartime, and adjusted that ideal — with additional stress on household and family security for those at home. Colt's continued this appeal for public awareness and confidence throughout the 1920s and 30s, and soon, COLT became a household word. An advertisement for firearms of 1924-5 in *National Geographic Magazine* appeared on the same pages as display ads for home products like Campbell's and Heinz.

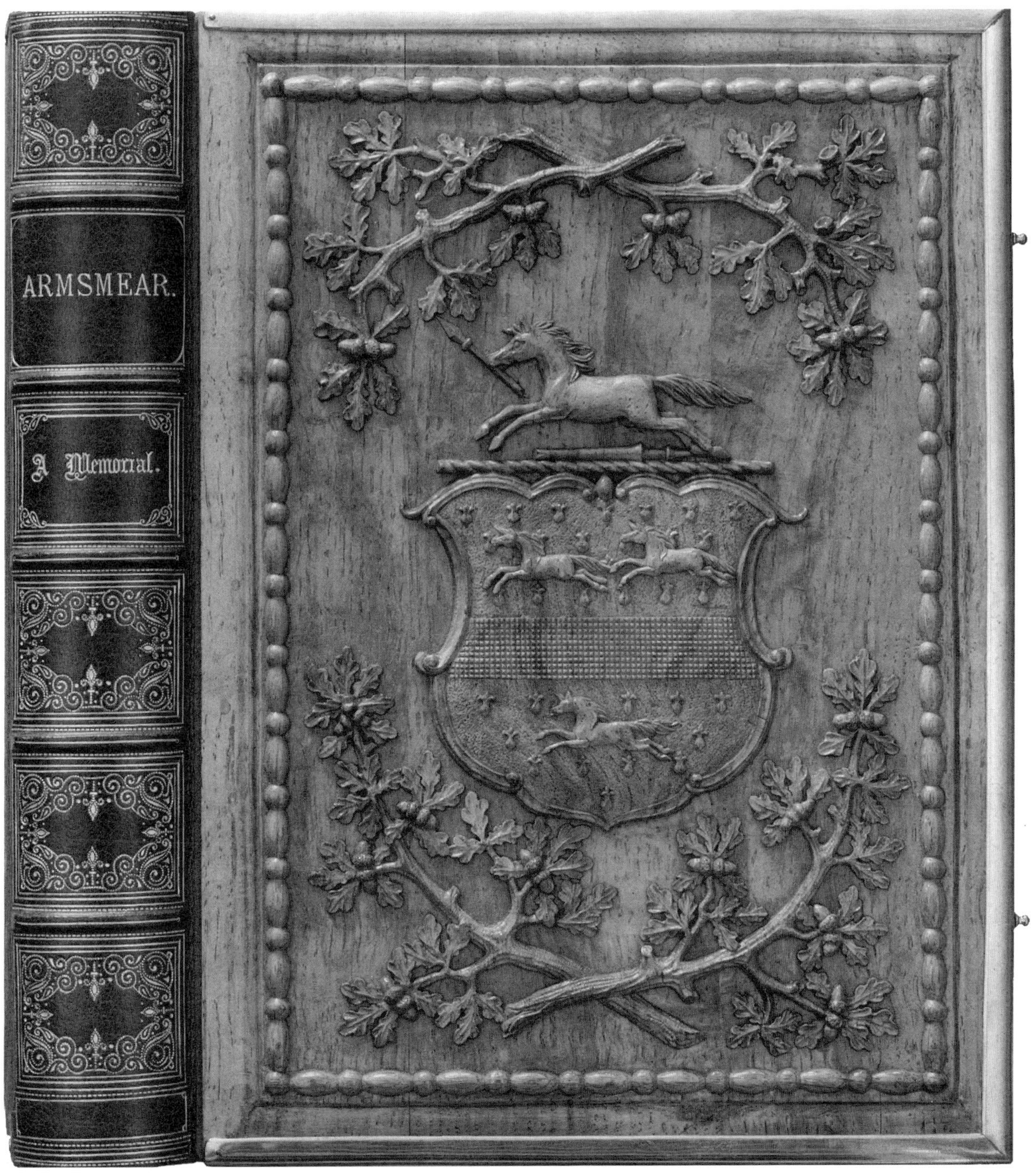

Deluxe edition of Armsmear, a memorial for Samuel Colt, was commissioned by his widow in 1866. This spectacular version is bound in Charter Oak and gilt calf, with a relief carving of the Colt coat-of-arms skillfully worked by Hartford craftsman John H. Most. The coat-of-arms was used excessively by both Samuel and Mrs. Colt on a wide variety of personal objects. It can be found on their sterling silverware, porcelain dinnerware, the Colonel's silver cigar stand, and became the standard cover design on each issue of *Armsmear.* (Courtesy Wadsworth Atheneum, Hartford)

A turn-of-the-century period of transition in production and in Colt advertising lasted well into the 20th Century. The demand for arms continued steadily and catalogues and advertisements appeared with greater frequency. Production remained the same until the onset of World War I, when orders increased substantially. Over 8,000 workers were employed in shifts around the clock. With the close of the war, and the decline of orders, Colt's purchased a small company producing Autosan industrial dishwashers. Boosted by the Colt name and professionalism, the Colt Autosan was soon installed in the kitchens of many well-known institutions including Hartford Hospital and the University of Connecticut.

The purchase of the Johns-Pratt Company in the early 1920s led to creation of the Colt Noark Electrical Equipment Division. The wide range of industrial electrical products meant a variety of new specimens of Colt's productivity. A small plastics company was purchased during this same period of diversification, and was expanded by Colt's into a pioneer in production of moulded plastics, sold under the tradename Coltrock. Buttons and buckles were made for the garment industry, brake linings and product packaging were also produced, as well as a general line of everyday objects: toothpaste caps, roller skate wheels, cosmetic travel kits, thermos tops, costume jewelry ("Coltstones") and powder containers. Smoking accessories (from the early Colt plastics line) are the most popular item among Colt collectors.

The creation and accelerated growth of Colt Industries in the early 1960s has spawned a whole new series of "Colt Memorabilia" or "Coltiana". These bear the newly designed Colt gear trademark, and only the Firearms Division uses both the gear and the rampant colt. With nearly 30 divisions at this writing, and having a wide range of individual products, the collector would be hard pressed to put together even a representative grouping of contemporary Colt Industries memorabilia. The Firearms Division, however, manages to continue in the tradition of prolific advertising and promotion established originally by Samuel Colt. Colt Memorabilia has a continuing role in the makeup of the modern firm as exemplified by a belt buckle series, silk ties, deluxe edition of books (e.g., the leather bound *The Colt Heritage*) and sundry promotional aids for jobbers and dealers.

This writing is an outgrowth of research in preparation for an exhibition at The Museum of Connecticut History in Hartford. A great deal of newly-located material has resulted, in addition to a synthesis of discoveries from recent years. This chapter holds a sampling of these findings, as well as a presentation to readers of the numerous historically significant Colt artifacts that are available. This is an on-going search for new aspects of Colt Memorabilia and the collection at the Museum of Connecticut History is a permanent depository for any Colt findings.

Cari Peretzman
Museum of Connecticut History
June 1981

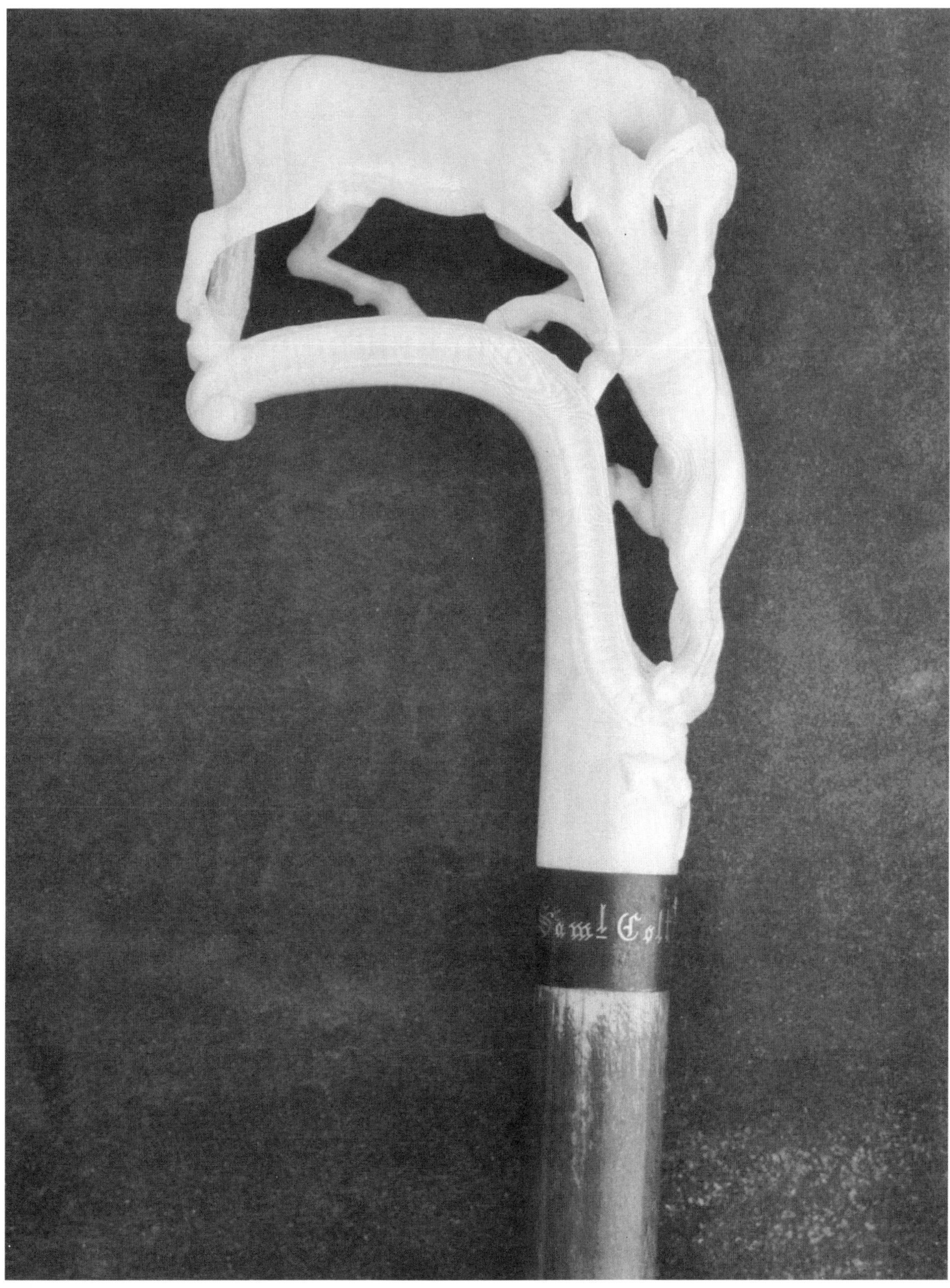

This ivory-handled cane is the only known item to hold such a rare personal link to Samuel Colt. The steel ferrule is inlaid in gold with Saml Colt in old English letters. The definite mastery of this work has been attributed to the skillful hands of Gustave Young, as well as the fine work of ivory carving. This carving depicts a colt battling the wolf. The wolf is seen as "the wolves" or the many competitors, trying to infringe on Colt's patents, and the colt — Samuel and his firm protecting what is rightfully his. In addition to the gold inscription, there is a significant detail below the hind legs of the wolf — a relief carved crossed Model 1851 Navy revolvers design. (Photo by Sid Latham; courtesy of R.L. Wilson)

COLT'S PEOPLE

Colt Bicycle Club Tournament Badge, 1890-97. The Colt Bicycle Club adopted an encircled rampant colt for its letterhead. Each tournament badge also displayed the popular motif as shown here.

(Opposite and Above) Colt employees during the Gay Nineties. Detail of photograph shown on page 69.

Device from Colt's Armory Band letterhead.

COLT'S ARMORY BAND

Detail from photograph shown on page 110.

From the 1850s throughout the war periods to 1945, the Colt's Armory Band performed at a great many of Hartford functions — from holiday and military parades to funerals to concerts in the park. In the 1880s, they became the official band of the First Regiment, and voted as a group, 23 strong, to be on call as a volunteer regiment.

1923 photograph of band at Undercliff Tuberculosis Sanitarium, Meriden, Connecticut.

1907 concert at the State Capitol. Scott Snow is bandmaster.

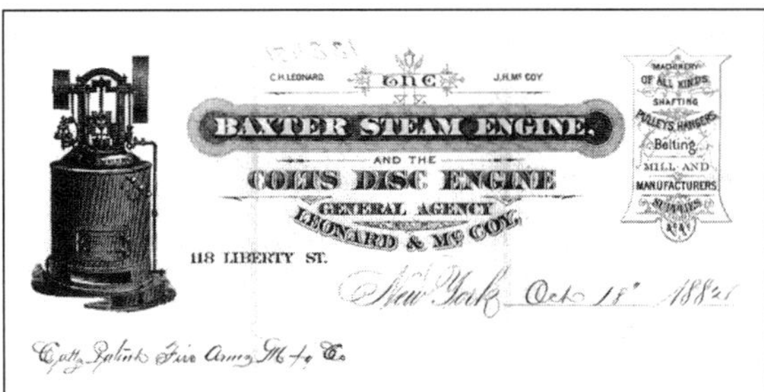

Before the advent of the gasoline engine, the Baxter Portable Steam Engine and Colt's Disc Engine were quite popular and won many awards and medals at international expositions and scientific fairs. Both were manufactured by Colt's in the 1870s, and the Baxter was produced as late as 1894.

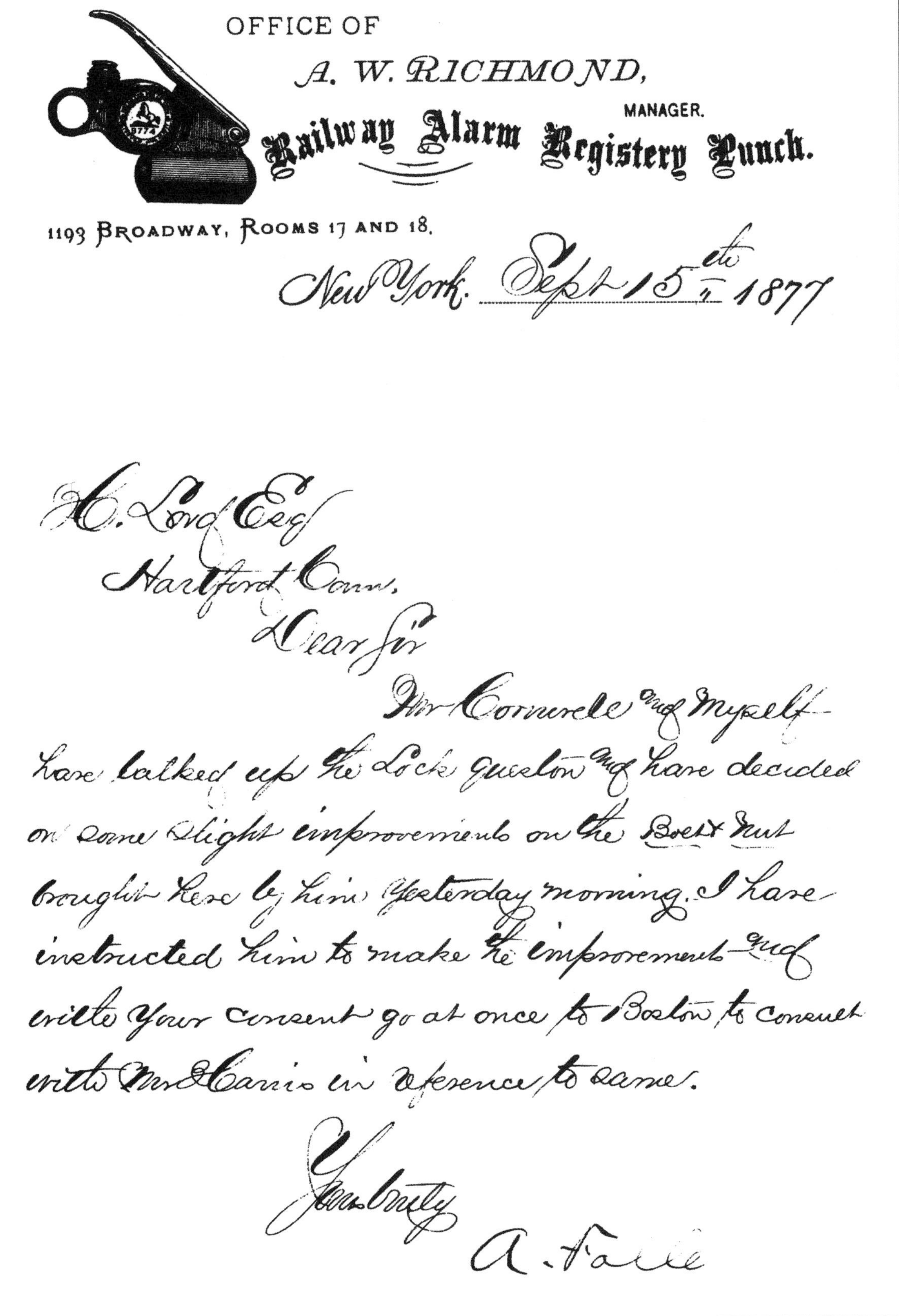

OFFICE OF

A. W. RICHMOND,

MANAGER.

Railway Alarm Registery Punch.

1193 BROADWAY, ROOMS 17 AND 18.

New York. Sept 15th 1877

H. Lord Esq

Hartford Conn.

Dear Sir

Mr Cornell and Myself have talked up the Lock question and have decided on some slight improvements on the Bolt & Nut brought here by him Yesterday morning. I have instructed him to make the improvements and with Your consent go at once to Boston to consult with Mr Harris in reference to same.

Yours truly

A. Falle

Railway Alarm Registering Punches were made at Colt's in the 1870s for a New York firm. Notice the rampant colt trademark. Colt's also manufactured fare-recording devices for streetcars for this company.

COLT AND THE GRAPHIC ARTS

Colt's Armory was also the manufacturer of printing presses in the late 1870s for the John Thomson Press Company of New York City. Pictured is the 1901 catalogue cover. The name "Colt's Armory Press" was adopted for their machine, as well as the Colt trademark, evident in all advertisements and catalogues.

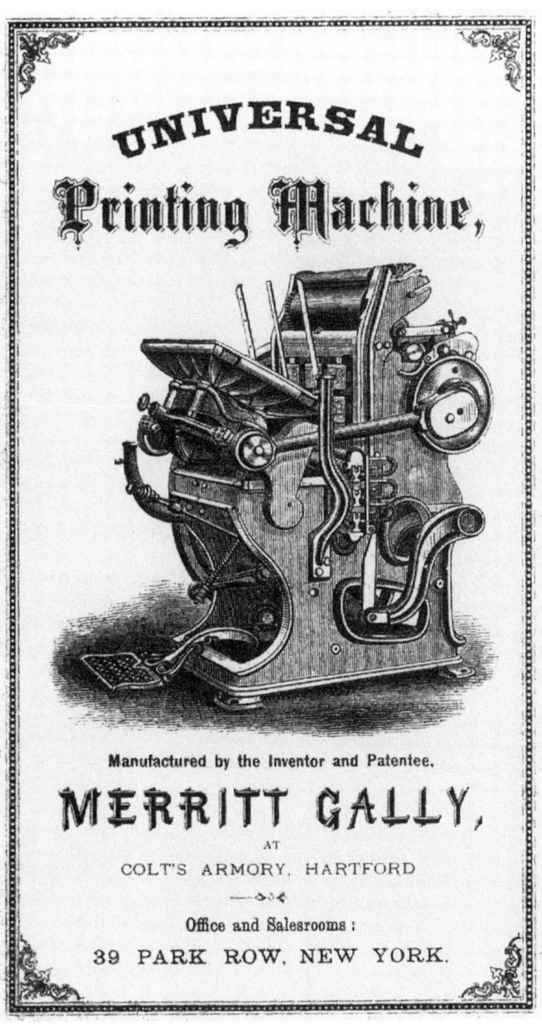

(Above) Practical operation of the Thorne Cylindrical Typesetting Machine, manufactured in the 1880s by Colt's Armory, was popular in many well-known institutions including Hartford's *Daily Post*. *(Right)* The Universal Press, manufactured by the inventor, Merritt Gally, at Colt's Armory was awarded numerous exposition medals and was shown at the U.S. Centennial Exhibition.

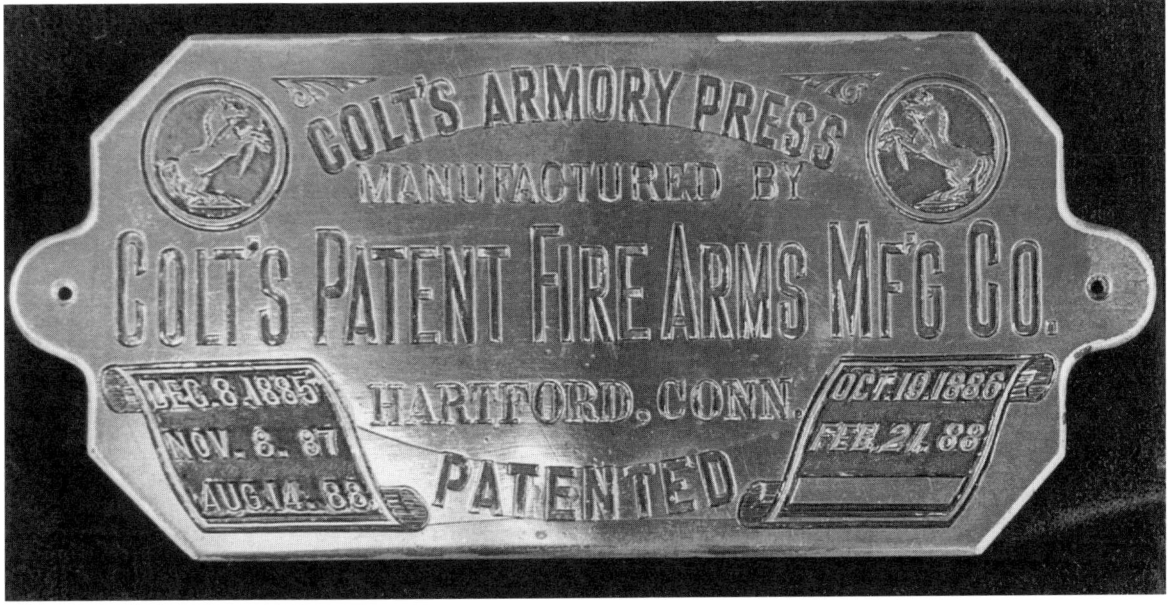

The Universal Press brass nameplate beautifully engraved with the characteristic rampant colt trademark.

SEWING MACHINES.—MACHINISTS.—LIME, CEMENT, ETC. 237

UNDER VIEW
THE MOST SIMPLE.

THE MORRISON PATENT SEWING MACHINE

AND TABLE,

MORRISON & CO., Manufacturers,

CLOSED

THE MOST COMPACT.

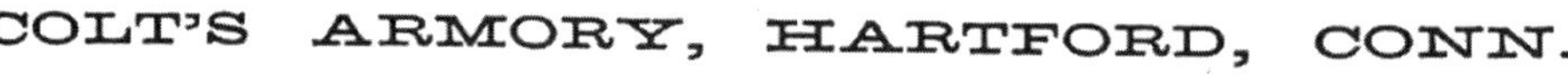

The Most Simple, Most Silent, Most Light and Swift Running, the Best Constructed and Finished, and Most Novel, Useful and Strictly FIRST-CLASS **SEWING MACHINE** *in the Market.*

OPEN

THE MOST CAPACIOUS.

Circulars Mailed on Application. Correspondence with Responsible Dealers for Territory Solicited.

1881-82 advertisement featured in Geer's Hartford Directory for Morrison's sewing machine.

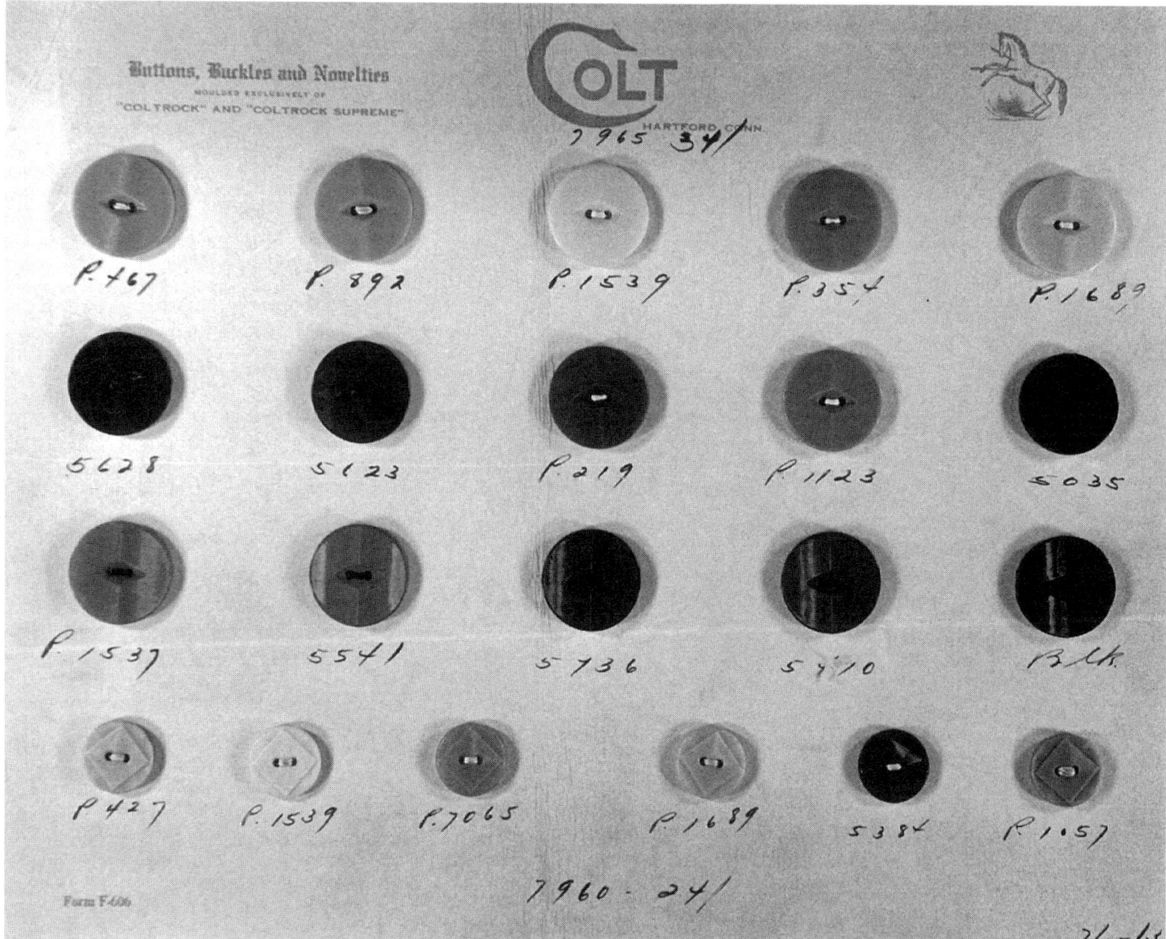

The Plastics Division began in the 1920s and expanded over the years to become one of the top three manufacturers of moulded plastics. In answer to the heavy demand by the garment industry, one of the departments of this division began producing buttons and buckles in a large variety of colors.

Federal "A" Adding Machines

New $250 Machines

$42.50

Crated F. O. B. Cleveland, Ohio

WHILE THEY LAST!

This is a heavy duty machine, built for service and continuous use as required in banks and offices of all types. We guarantee every machine shipped to be in perfect order and will replace *free* any defective parts returned to us within one year. Special discounts allowed on orders of five or more.

Federal "A" Features

Manufactured by Colt's Pat. Fire-arms Mfg. Co., Hartford, Conn.

Adding and listing cap 9,999,999.99

Carriage takes 13-inch paper, prints 7 or more columns.

All figures instantly visible.

Send check or $10 deposit today. No consigned shipments.

RALPH ROSEN, Inc.

Auctioneer and Liquidator

1119 Genesee Bldg., Buffalo, N. Y.

The Federal Adding Machine Company contracted Colt's to produce their Federal "A" Adding Machines from 1919-1922. Pictured is an advertisement believed to date from April 1937.

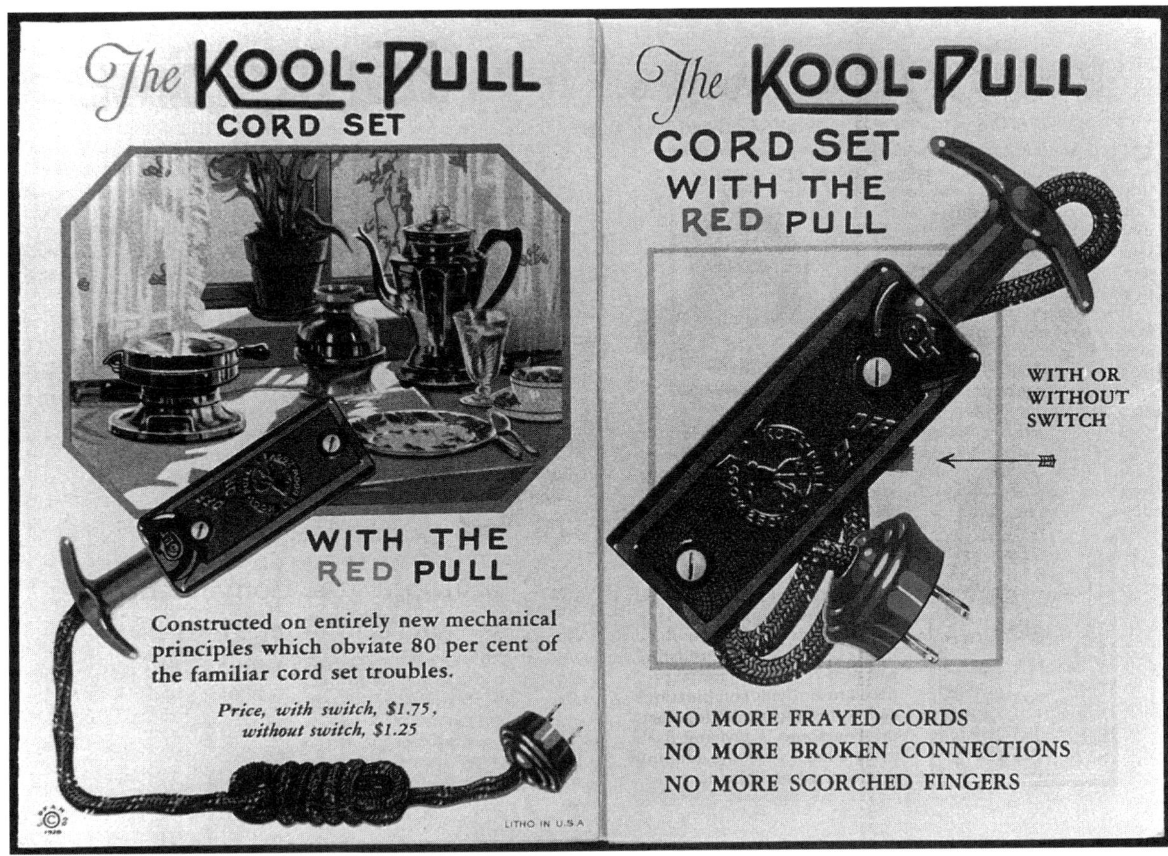

The Kool-Pull set was a product of the combined efforts of the Electrical and Plastics Divisions. It was designed to alleviate household problems with electrical cords by using the T-shaped pull for easier and safer removal from the socket.

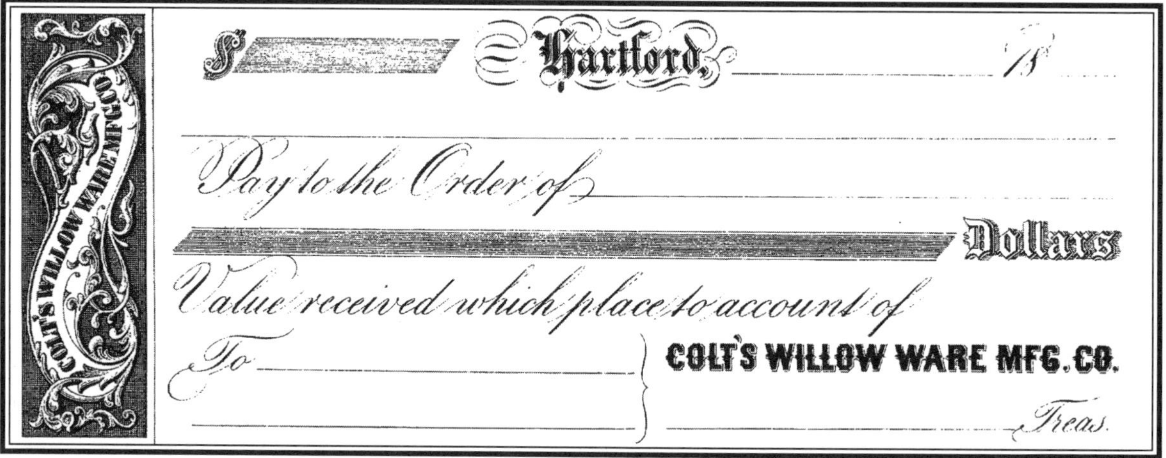

(Above) Willow Ware Manufacturing Company check — one of the first Colt company sidelines. Established in the mid-1850s, this company was on its way to successful manufacture of willow ware products, but was destroyed by a fire in 1873 and never rebuilt. Factory building and willow workers' homes still stand at South Meadows. *(Below left)* Colt's catalogues and brochures were distributed internationally, with various countries deserving a special appeal. Here we have a Colt circular specifically directed at its prospective Chinese buyers. *(Below right)* Present-day advertising for the renovated homes in South Meadows which have been converted into condominiums.

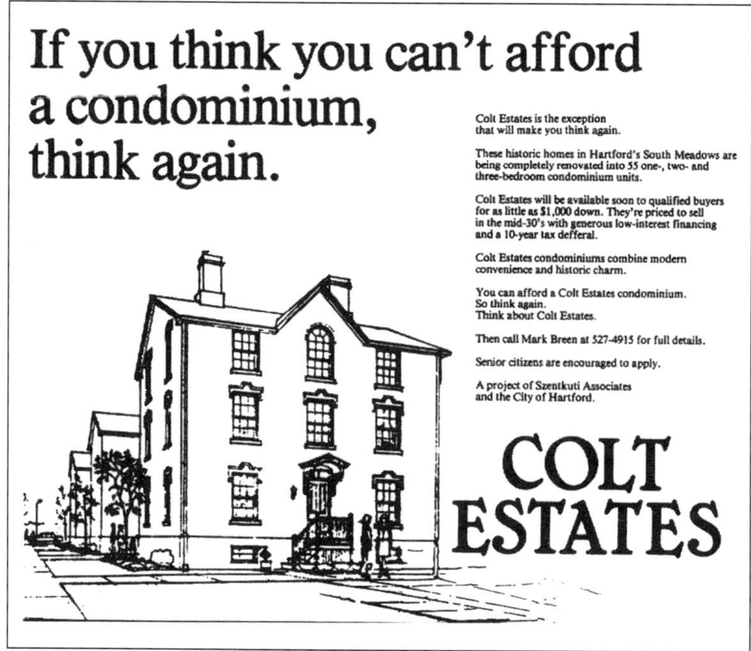

Accessory Sales Items

A Brochure of 1968

COLT SCREW DRIVERS
A handy combination key chain and multiple screw driver, good for a thousand uses —

COLT TIE CLASP
.45 CAL. AUTOMATIC
Gold Plate

COLT GUN OIL
Finest Quality Gun Lubricating Oil. 101 uses For Home or Range

.45 CAL. AUTOMATIC TIE TAC
Gold or Silver Oxide

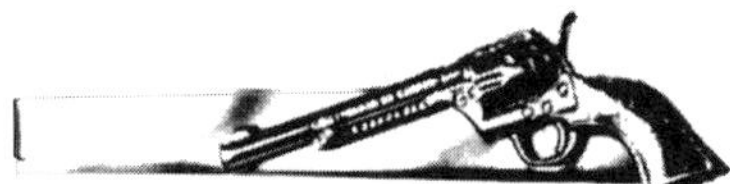

COLT TIE CLASP
Single Action Army, Gold Plate

PYTHON TIE TAC
Gold or Silver Oxide

A variety of objects for the Colt enthusiast. Single Action Army, Automatic, Python or rifle pins and tie-bars in various materials including gold-plated, gold-filled, and rare 1930s Sterling Silver. Most significant here is the flat screwdriver, an innovative accessory with the rampant colt on reverse, c. 1951-present.

Company brassard from the 1930s.

1856. 

SECOND EDITION.

 1890.

PATENT FIRE-ARMS MANUFACTURING CO.,

——MANUFACTURERS OF——

MILITARY, SPORTING, AND DEFENSIVE ARMS,

——ALSO——

BAXTER STEAM ENGINES

COLT'S ARMORY AND UNIVERSAL PRINTING PRESSES.

ALL OF OUR WORK IS GUARANTEED, HIGHEST STANDARD ATTAINED.

HARTFORD, CONN., U. S. A.

10 FRONT ST., San Francisco, Cal. } ••DEPOTS•• { 14 PALL MALL, London, S. W.

JANUARY, 1890.

Title page of Colt catalogue of 1890 with two rampant colts depicted at the top corners of each page throughout.

COLT AND THE WARS

Appendix II

PRESIDENTS OF COLT'S

Samuel Colt	1855-1862
Elisha K. Root	1862-1865
Richard Jarvis	1865-1901
John Hall	1901-1902
Lewis C. Grover	1902-1909
William C. Skinner	1909-1911
Col. Charles L.F. Robinson	1911-1916
William C. Skinner	1916-1921
Samuel M. Stone	1921-1944
Graham H. Anthony	1944-1949
B. Franklin Conner	1949-1955
Chester Bland	1955-1958
Fred A. Roff, Jr.	1958-1962
David C. Scott	1962-1963
Paul A. Benke	1963-1969
William H. Goldbach	1969-1972
David C. Eaton	1972-1976
C. Edward Warner	1976-1981
Gary W. French	1981-1990
Richard F. Gamble	1990-1990
Ronald E. Stilwell	1990-1992
Ronald C. Whitaker	1992-

COLT'S SALES, EARNINGS & EMPLOYMENT 1909-1954

Year	Average Employment	Sales	Net Earnings
1909		$1,164,000	
1910		1,300,000	
1911		1,418,000	$ 400,000
1912		1,903,000	641,237
1913	1,000	n.a.	766,000
1914	1,056	2,284,000	965,589
1915	1,285	5,000,000	2,471,000
1916	2,400	10,000,000	6,346,000
1917	3,874	16,215,417	5,445,000
1918	10,000	32,693,000	6,318,000
1919	3,160	Surplus declined	not
1921	1,185	from $5.5 mill.	available
1922	965	to $3.5 mill.	
1923	1,605		
1925	1,334		
1926		Sales not	662,109
1927		available	
1928			
1929	1,559	Surplus declined	291,000
1930	1,476	to $2.9 mill. in	103,000
1931	1,471	1932, and then	64,203
1932	1,389	rose steadily to	20,795
1933	1,554	$8.3 mill. in Jan.	675,132
1934	1,675	1943	577,823
1935	1,948		562,285
1936	2,000		825,652
1937	2,100		1,161,946
1938	1,925		1,143,620
1939	2,600		1,367,755
1940	3,000+		1,906,000
1941	7,000+		2,560,867
1942	to		1,222,230
1943	16,000		1,010,196
	at peak	$4.9 mill. surplus	
1944			loss
1945	below		loss
1946	1,000		- 753,895
1947			149,196
1948			100,000
1949		(sales)	
1950	2,000	9,533,205	944,117
1951		11,478,262	655,982
1952		16,164,997	677,527
1953	1,500	21,306,111	703,770
1954	750	16,649,241	246,670

CHRONOLOGY

1847 - Sam Colt returns to Hartford to make his revolver.
1854 - Fales & Gray boiler explosion.
1855 - Colt Armory opens.
1860 - Hartford's population doubles to 29,000.
1862 - Colonel Colt dies in January; Root becomes president.
1864 - Fire destroys original Colt building.
1865 - Richard Jarvis succeeds Root as president.
1867 - New Armory completed; Gatling machine gun unveiled.
1868 - Mark Twain visits Armory.
1869 - Woman's suffrage movement in Connecticut founded by Isabella Hooker.
1888 - Great Blizzard.
1889 - Park Central Hotel fire.
1890 - Pope Manufacturing Company formed.
1891 - John Browning, inventor, pays first visit to Colt's.
1894 - Caldwell Colt dies mysteriously.
1895 - Browning develops his machine gun and automatic pistol; first Pope electric vehicle runs.
1900 - Hartford now has 80,000 residents.
1901 - Mrs. Colt sells Armory; John Hall stays on as president for a year.
1905 - Mrs. Colt dies.
1911 - Colt .45 pistol developed by Browning.
1914 - Automobile industry in Hartford ceases; Colt's and other plants are booming; heavy immigration of workers.
1917 - United States enters World War I; Browning's automatic rifle and heavy machine gun approved by government.
1918 - Armistice signed in November. Colt's makes huge profits during war period.
1919 - Colt's reconverts to peacetime and begins to diversify.
1920 - Women get the vote after a 50-year struggle.
1921 - Browning's last invention: the .37mm anti-aircraft cannon; Colt's profits depressed; Samuel M. Stone elected president.
1926 - Colt's recovers; Browning dies.
1935 - First Armory-wide strike; Cheney Brothers in Manchester go into bankruptcy.
1936 - Great Flood and Hartford's Tercentenary.
1938 - The Great Hurricane.
1941 - Colt's is unionized and World War II begins.
1942 - Colt's wins coveted Army-Navy "E"
1944 - Circus fire. Colt's suffers from low production and internal union dissension; losses mount; Stone retires.
1945 - V-E and V-J Days mark end of World War II.
1947 - 1861 Colt building torn down.
1948 - Speculators raid the treasury.
1949 - Colt's in financial trouble.
1950 - Hartford's population reaches peak of 177,000.
1955 - Penn-Texas takes over.

1957 - Colt collection of guns given to State Library.
1959 - Contract for M-16 automatic rifle.
1960 - Manufacturing supremacy in Hartford ends.
1963 - Colt's receives large contract for M-16 rifles.
1964 - The parent company changes its name to Colt Industries.
1969 - Colt delivers its millionth M-16 rifle.
1976 - Custom Gun Shop established.
1981 - Colt's moves its offices to a new building in West Hartford, vacating the old East Armory.
1982 - Three-year contract with union averts strike and keeps 1,500 on job in Hartford and West Hartford; Colt's receives $13 million contract to equip new Bradley infantry vehicle.
1984 - Colt's withdraws from competition to sell Pentagon 9mm handgun.
1986 - 1,050 members of Local #376, U.A.W., strike on January 24th after failing to get a new contract.
1988 - Colt loses government contract for M-16 rifles.
1989 - In April, Colt Industries, Inc. announces its decision to sell the Firearms Division; in September, NLRB orders Colt's to rehire striking workers.
1990 - The Division's sale and formation of a new company ends the four-year strike.
1990 - Colt's receives large order for M-16 rifles from Kuwait.
1991 - Army contract of $9.53 million for M-16 rifles.
1992 - Colt Manufacturing files for Chapter 11 Protection in March; Autorino resigns as chairman.
1993 - Plan to buy Colt's collapses in December.
1994 - New group of investors takes over company in September and Colt emerges from bankruptcy; Introduction of M4 A1 carbine; Colt abandons old Armory and consolidates all operations in West Hartford.

SELECTED REFERENCES

A Century of Achievement, 100th Anniversary of Colt's Patent Fire Arms Mfg., 1937

Andrews, Kenneth R. — *Nook Farm, Mark Twain's Hartford Circle*, Cambridge, Mass: Harvard University Press, 1950

Barker, Corinne M. — "Connecticut's Share in Furnishing Munitions for the World War", unpublished MA thesis, Columbia University, 1925

Brown, Walter — "Hartford in the Gay Nineties", Hartford *Courant*, June 10, 1928

Browning, John & Gentry, Curt — *John M. Browning, American Gunmaker*, New York: Doubleday & Company Inc., 1964

Chapman, Helen Post — *My Hartford of the Nineteenth Century*, Hartford: Edwin V. Mitchell, 1928

Countryman, William A. — "Connecticut's Position in the Manufacturing World", *Connecticut Magazine*, Vol. 7, No. 1, March-April 1901

Cross, Wilbur L. — *Connecticut Yankee*, New Haven: Yale University Press, 1943

Cuntz, Herman F. — "Hartford, the Birthplace of Automobile Industry", Hartford *Times*, Sept. 16-18, 1947

Grant, Ellsworth S. — *Yankee Dreamers & Doers*, Chester: Pequot Press, 1974

Hartford Board of Trade — *Hartford Conn. as a Manufacturing, Business & Commercial Center*, Hartford, 1889

Hatch, Alden — *Remington Arms in American History,* New York, Rinehart & Co., 1956

Kihn, Phyllis — "Colt in Hartford", Connecticut Historical Society *Bulletin*, Vol. 24, No. 3, July, 1959

Malcolm-Smith, George — "The Flood of 1936", *The Travelers Beacon*, April, 1936

Parker, T.H. — "The Great Flood of 1936", Hartford *Courant*, April 5, 1936

Pawlowski, Robert E. — *How the Other Half Lived*, West Hartford, Northwest Catholic High School, 1973

Phelps, William Lyon — *Autobiography With Letters*, New York: Oxford University Press, 1939

Saunders, Dero A. — "Belligerent Penn-Texas", *Fortune*, March, 1957, Vol. LV, No. 3.

Silverman, Rabbi Morris — *Hartford Jews 1659-1970*, Hartford: Connecticut Historical Society, 1970

Spencer, Christopher M.	Letter to Horace B. Cheney dated June 8, 1908, on letterhead of Universal Machine Screw Company, Hartford
Van Duesn, Albert E.	*Connecticut*, New York: Random House, 1961
Weaver, Glenn	*Hartford Steam Boiler Inspection & Insurance Company 1866-1966*, Hartford: 1966, Chapter I
Williamson, Harold F.	*Winchester, the Gun That Won the West*, New York: A.S. Barnes & Co. 1952

Also:

The Colt Collection and the Record of the Connecticut Woman Suffrage Association 1869-1921 in the Archives of the Connecticut State Library; biographical material in the Connecticut Historical Society; newspaper clippings filed in the Hartford and West Hartford Public Libraries under various headings; the Colt File in the Hartford *Courant* library; articles on Penn-Texas in *Newsweek* and *Time* magazines; and the daily pages of the Hartford *Courant* and Hartford *Times* from 1864-1955.

Appendix III

THE VALUE OF COLT STOCK RESEARCHED IN 1990

To: Julius Levinson, Vice-President, Taxes, Colt Industries
Re: Selling Price of Colt's Patent Firearms in 1901

To determine the value of Colt's at the time of its sale by Mrs. Samuel Colt in 1901, it is necessary to review the company's financial history beginning with the death of its founder on January 14, 1862.

1862

The Armory was originally capitalized at $1.2 million. Working backward from the subsequent distribution, it appears that 10,000 shares were outstanding. According to his biographer, William B. Edwards, 88½ percent of the shares were held by Colt at the time of his death.

That year the Armory earned $1,344,568, and in 1860 the average monthly wage was $41.64, according to Joseph W. Roe.

Colt's entire estate, including stock, land and personal property, was appraised at $3.2 million. A quarter of his estate was in land, mainly the South Meadows of Hartford and his residence Armsmear. Subtracting this amount leaves a value for his 88½ percent interest in the Armory of approximately $2.4 million.

The acknowledged historian of Colt guns, R.L. Wilson, maintains that Mrs. Colt "inherited nearly all of the Colonel's stock, real estate and other holdings." Actually, the total was somewhere between two-thirds and 78 percent after the final settlement. The distribution of Colt stock under Colonel Colt's last will, dated February 1859, was complicated by the claims of relatives, chiefly the James and Christopher Colt families, and by the fact that a substantial portion of his estate was intestate.

In his first will, made in 1856, Colt had set aside 2,500 shares for the establishment of a "practical school for instruction in the mechanics and engineering" for the benefit of Hartford and Connecticut students, but his bitter disputes with the City of Hartford resulted in his revoking this provision in the codicil of 1859. In his last will, Mrs. Colt was the direct beneficiary of 1,500 shares, 500 more than specified in the 1856 will.

1866

The first administration account in 1866 stated that Mrs. Colt received "the whole amount of real and personal estate...being in value equal to 12/18 of the value of all the testate estate." It did not give the number of Colt shares. The remaining 6/18ths were divided among Colt's nephews and nieces. This distribution, in each case, included land as well as stock.

Also, the intestate portion of the estate was distributed as follows:

	Shares	**Value**	**Cash (To equalize shares)**
Mrs. Samuel Colt	717	$143,535	$105,196
Caldwell Colt	716	143,200	105,532
Richard Jarvis	716	143,200	105,532
(as administrator for Henrietta Colt, deceased)			
Total	**2,149**		

The shares of Caldwell Colt, her son, and Richard Jarvis, her brother, a total of 1,432, eventually reverted to Mrs. Colt. Each share was then valued at $200.19.

1873

The third administration account in 1873 stated that the following number of shares had been distributed in 1866:

To Mrs. Colt	2,149
To James Colt	575
To children of Christopher Colt	500
To LeBaron & Pomeroy Colt	430
Total	**3,654**

1884

The fourth administration account in 1884 distributed 575 more shares to Mrs. Colt as the result of the successful court case against the estate of James Colt. At the same time, additional shares were distributed as follows:

Mrs. Colt	2,149	
Mrs. Colt	138.5	(from intestate portion)
Caldwell Colt	69	
Richard Jarvis	69	(as administrator)
Relatives	158	

Again, the Caldwell Colt and Jarvis shares, totaling 138, reverted to Mrs. Colt in 1894.

1894

A final accounting of the Colt estate was not made until November 12, 1894 following the death of his son Caldwell Colt, who died on January 21st. His total estate came to $785,496. The inventory valued his shares of Colt stock at $500,000, which reverted to his mother. (However, the number of shares, 4,794 or $104.30 per share, seems to have been in error, because the figure bears no relationship to the other transactions.)

Altogether, it is apparent that Mrs. Colt ended up owning the following number of shares:

1866	2,149	(testate portion)
	717	(intestate portion)
1884	575	(from James Colt estate)
	138.5	(adjustment)
	2,149	
1894	785	(from Caldwell Colt estate)
	785	(from Henrietta Colt's estate)
Total	**7,298.5**	

Samuel C. Colt, her nephew, the children of Christopher Colt and various Colt executives received 2,007 shares, making a grand total of 9,305. The rest had been given by Colonel Colt to his associates during his lifetime.

1901

On June 19, 1901 this article appeared on the front page of the *Hartford Times*:

NEW OWNERS OF COLT'S
Mrs. Colt Sells Her Shares
John H. Hall To Be President of the Company With A Large Interest in the Works

At present, the capital stock is $1 million. It is to be increased to between $1.5 and $2.0 million, though the exact amount is not known, as none of the officials — brokers or attorneys — seen would state...$1.25 million of bonds are to be issued, and the amount increased to $1.5 million if necessary. Subscription for these new bonds have already been offered to parties in Hartford, Boston, New York, and Springfield, and it is said that the entire amount has been taken.

"At the present capital of $1 million, Mrs. Colt owns more than 75 percent. It is said on good authority that for this stock she will receive $500,000 in cash and the balance in bonds of the new company."

The *Hartford Courant* on the same date ran a very short article with no details. How much in bonds Mrs. Colt got was never revealed. Mrs. Colt was represented in the sale by the Hartford law firm of Gross, Hyde & Williams. Unfortunately, the Colt files were destroyed long ago.

The buyer was Armstrong, Schirmer & Company of New York, a private investment firm apparently affiliated with the George R. Armstrong Company of Boston. There is no listing of either company after 1930 in Moody's. The new owners, as reported, retained the Colt management headed by John Hall, who lived only another year. When he died on June 25, 1902, his family held a substantial interest in Colt's through various trusts administered by his daughter, Grace Hall Wilson, until the early 1940s.

1905

Mrs. Samuel Colt died on August 22, 1905. At this time, Colt common stock was quoted on the local market at $75-77 a share and its 5 percent bonds at $104½.

Her inventory:	Bonds & stocks	$2,357,631
	Real estate	191,180
	Jewelry, etc.	162,971
	Misc. assets	36,601
	Total	**2,748,382**

Included among her stocks were 500 shares of Colt valued at $37,500 or $75 a share. Her major bequests were $800,000 in trust for the maintenance of the Church of the Good Shepherd and the Caldwell Colt Memorial. $200,000 to her sister, $200,000 to her niece, and $50,000 to the Wadsworth Atheneum, which also received $108,445 in furniture and art works.

Summary

How much did Mrs. Colt receive for the sale of the majority interest in Colt Patent Firearms in 1901? There are two ways of computing the amount. First, assuming she held 7,298.5 shares in 1894 and the stock was worth $75 a share as it was in 1905, then her proceeds must have been $509,887.50 (allowing for her retention of 500 shares). In addition, as reported, she must have received at least $500,000 and up to a million more in bonds. Note that her holdings represented 78.4 percent of the total, which percentage jibes with that reported in the newspaper in June 1901. Also, this valuation is supported by the strong financial condition of the company at the turn of the century.

Second, based on the inventory value of her stocks and bonds, the figure increases to $2,357,671. There is no evidence of her making gifts of stock or expending large sums between 1901 and 1905, though she was well-known as a benefactress to many local institutions. It is possible that her portfolio suffered losses during these four years.

There remains the necessity of converting 1901 dollars into 1988 dollars in order to determine the real value today. The Bureau of Labor Statistics began keeping records of the Consumer Price Index and the Purchasing Power of the Consumer Dollar in 1913. There is no indication of material change between 1901 and 1913. Table #113 of the Handbook of Labor Statistics, Department of Labor, 1989, reveals the following changes since 1913:

Year	**CPI (for urban wage earners)**	**Purchasing Power of $ (1982-84 = $1.00)**
1913	10.0	10.023
1988	117.0	.855
Increase	11.7 times	11.7 times

Thus, in 1988 dollars, the evaluation would be:

(1) Based on Colt stock only owned in 1901	$ 5,965,684
(2) Based on stocks & bonds held in 1905	$27,584,750

Index

U

V

W

Z

About the Author

ELLSWORTH S. GRANT was born in Wethersfield, Connecticut and has lived in West Hartford since 1922. A graduate of Harvard College, he has successively been a journalist, personnel director, manufacturer, museum president, mayor, writer, and educational film producer. He is the author of *Yankee Dreamers & Doers* (Pequot Press, 1974) and *The Miracle of Connecticut* (Connecticut Historical Society, 1992) and ten other histories of Connecticut corporations. He is also a contributor to various magazines including *American Heritage*, *Northeast*, *Connecticut*, and *Cruising World.*